Be Thou My Vision

Be Thou My Vision:

The Story of
Trinity Episcopal Church,
Indianapolis

By

John B. Bridge

International Standard Book Number: 987-0-692-03700-3

Library of Congress Catalog Card Number: Available upon request.

Printed in the United States of America.
This book is printed on acid-free paper.

Photography and Other Credits:

Photograph of Trinity Episcopal Church, Indianapolis, on the cover © Gary Potts. Used with permission.

Photograph of the Rt. Rev. Jennifer Baskerville-Burrows in her foreword © Casey Cronin. Used with permission.

Photograph of the Rev. Julia E. Whitworth in her foreword © Trinity Episcopal Church, Indianapolis. Used with permission.

Other figures from Trinity Episcopal Church, Indianapolis, are used with permission.

Figures from the Indiana Historical Society and its collections are used with permission.

Photograph of the Rt. Rev. John Hazen White in Chapter 3 © Episcopal Diocese of Northern Indiana. Used with permission.

Photograph of the Rt. Rev. Joseph Marshall Francis in Chapter 3 © National Portrait Gallery, London. Used with permission.

Photograph of Gary Cooper in Chapter 5 © Auburn Cord Duesenberg Museum. Used with permission.

Photograph of George B. Kessler in Chapter 6 © Landmarks Association of St. Louis, Inc. Used with permission.

Photograph of Eli Lilly in Chapter 7 © Lilly Endowment, Inc. Used with permission.

Map of proposed interstate highways in Chapter 10 used courtesy of the Trustees of Purdue University.

Photograph of the Rt. Rev. John Pares Craine and Jacqueline "Jackie" Means in Chapter 13 used courtesy of Jacqueline Means.

Photograph of the Rt. Rev. Catherine Maples Waynick in Chapter 14 © Lindsay Haake. Used with permission.

First photograph of Monument Circle in Chapter 15 © Harold Lee Miller. Used with permission.

Selected photographs in Chapter 15 © John Lavengood. Used with permission.

Photograph of the MacPherson Stolen family in Chapter 15 © Towne Post Network, Inc. Used with permission.

Selected photographs in Chapters 17 and 18 © Casey Cronin. Used with permission.

Selected photographs in Chapters 18 and 19 © Kyung-Won On. Used with permission.

Photograph of the Rt. Rev. Jennifer Baskerville-Burrows and the Rt. Rev. Barbara Harris in Chapter 19 © Chris Denny. Used with permission.

Photograph of the Rev. Julia E. Whitworth, the Rev. Dr. Benjamin J. Anthony, and the Rev. Erin Hougland in Chapter 19 © Kelly Kennedy Bentley. Used with permission.

Miracles, Major and Minor, by Edith W.H. Clowes, from the Clowes Family Collection of the Indiana Historical Society. Used with permission.

For Cathy

Be Thou My Vision

Be Thou my Vision, O Lord of my heart;
Naught be all else to me, save that Thou art.
Thou my best Thought, by day or by night,
Waking or sleeping, Thy presence my light.

Be Thou my Wisdom, and Thou my true Word;
I ever with Thee and Thou with me, Lord;
Thou my great Father, I Thy true son;
Thou in me dwelling, and I with Thee one.

Be Thou my battle Shield, Sword for the fight;
Be Thou my Dignity, Thou my Delight;
Thou my soul's Shelter, Thou my high Tow'r:
Raise Thou me heav'nward, O Pow'r of my pow'r.

Riches I heed not, nor man's empty praise,
Thou mine Inheritance, now and always:
Thou and Thou only, first in my heart,
High King of Heaven, my Treasure Thou art.

High King of Heaven, my victory won,
May I reach Heaven's joys, O bright Heav'n's Sun!
Heart of my own heart, whatever befall,
Still be my Vision, O Ruler of all.

Old Irish hymn, *Rop tú mo Baile*,
attributed to Saint Dallán Forgaill, *circa* sixth century.
Original English translation by Eleanor H. Hull, 1912.
Usually sung to the tune of the Irish folk ballad, *Slane*.
The version used by The Episcopal Church is
Hymn 488 in *The Hymnal 1982*.

Contents

Foreword

by the Rt. Rev. Jennifer Baskerville-Burrows, Bishop of Indianapolis

B y the time this volume is initially in print, it will be four years since I first visited Trinity Episcopal Church. I was a nominee to be the eleventh bishop of Indianapolis, and I remember how, on that seasonable October day, sunlight streamed through a clerestory window as if ushering the Holy Spirit into our midst. I knew then that I was on sacred ground.

Today Trinity's soaring beauty is part of my daily life, and I know that its walls and arches of Indiana limestone were crafted in the mid-twentieth century, through the vision and generosity of many parishioners, to create a nearly authentic English Gothic church. In its vast and holy space, many strands of our long history as Episcopalians and as Hoosiers are woven together. So it is fitting that in *Be Thou My Vision*, longtime Trinity member John Bridge takes us on a sweeping historical journey that begins more than a century before the founding of the parish he chronicles and encompasses the history of our region, our diocese, and the faithful Episcopalians whose legacy we now steward.

John, a gifted writer, chronicles our church and our state with both a firm command of historical narrative and a fondness for the foibles of our beloved church. In these pages, you will learn about the strong stand against the Ku Klux Klan mounted by both our diocese and Trinity's earliest leaders, about the part we played in the long struggle for women's ordination, and about the parish's essential role in the extraordinary generosity of Eli Lilly that makes so much ministry possible. But you will also discover that in its early days, the parish now known as Trinity went through four rectors in eight years, struggled to pay its bills, and adopted an unforgettable Depression-era slogan: "Religion costs money—Irreligion costs more!"

Thankfully, religion won the day, and God has been at work on the corner of 33rd and Meridian Streets for more than a century now. Our common life in the Diocese of Indiana has been shaped by the witness of Trinity and its people, and so where this masterful history leaves off, our part begins. May our ministry make us worthy of those blessed saints who have gone before us and whose story is now ours.

The Rt. Rev. Jennifer Baskerville-Burrows
Bishop of Indianapolis
The Feast of Saint Philip and Saint James
2020
Casey Cronin

Foreword

by the Rev. Julia E. Whitworth, Rector of Trinity Episcopal Church, Indianapolis

At the writing of this foreword, Trinity Episcopal Church, as all parishes in the Diocese of Indianapolis, has just completed 12 weeks of socially distanced life as a community of faith. Constrained to our homes in an attempt to suppress a novel coronavirus pandemic, we have learned new modes for gathering virtually unimagined by our founders in 1919. Whether in worship on the website, forums on Facebook, vestry via Zoom, Sunday school by snail mail, and pastoral care via email and text . . . for the time being, we have traded our spaces of regal stone and polychromed wood for data-bytes and broadband. To practice our call to love of neighbor, we are learning to be the Church away from the church.

In the four years since I became rector at Trinity, I have discerned that Trinity's history has been a faithful journey of leadership, vocation, and vision. John Bridge's *Be Thou My Vision* traces that 100-year journey with precision and scope, using an archivist's eye and a historian's sense of narrative and context. Though our name and buildings have changed, along with our neighborhood and our city, what has remained constant is the work of leaders—lay and ordained—listening for the call of God for this worshipping community. Time and again that call has yielded courageous vision which has ultimately transformed the church from a modest neighborhood parish to the center for urban ministry Trinity finds itself to be today. Even in this time of uncertainty, I know that the skill, faithfulness, and vision of this parish's leaders will see us through these anxious days.

Last week Trinity celebrated our Feast of Title. It was a Trinity Sunday unlike any in the parish history. Ordinarily, our sanctuary would be packed, with swirling white streamers in procession and an overflowing choir filling our space and our souls with a joyful noise. We would have tumbled onto the St. Richard's soccer field for a parish picnic to celebrate a year of common life together. Instead, the church was nearly empty as I celebrated the Eucharist for the first time at our altar in months. During the livestream last Sunday, however, we included a montage of photographs from a year of life at Trinity. Over the majestic strains of the hymn *St. Patrick's Breastplate*, faces of young and old, black and white, long-timers and newcomers flashed on parishioners' screens at home, while the refrain rang out: "I bind unto myself today, the strong name of the Trinity . . . ."

Trinity's parishioners may be distanced from one another at this moment, but we are indeed bound: by a common faith in the Trinity and by membership in Christ exercised through this extraordinary church bearing its name. With 100 years of leadership, faith, and vocation anchoring us, I feel confident we will emerge from this time of trial with fresh vision for the next century and beyond.

I hope you enjoy this inspiring telling of Trinity's visionary past as we prepare for our future ahead.

The Rev. Julia E. Whitworth
Rector of Trinity Episcopal Church, Indianapolis
Feast of St. Barnabas, Apostle
2020
Trinity Episcopal Church

Introduction

A church can be many things and, as a result, is often complicated. It can be a stately and inspirational structure, and it can be a group of congregants seeking spiritual nourishment. It can be a place to worship God, and it can be a place to put God's love into action by serving humanity. It can be a place of quiet contemplation, and it can be a place of vigorous activity. It can be a place to celebrate joyful events, and a place to comfort loss. The Episcopal parish church now known as Trinity, Indianapolis, has been all of those things, and it certainly has been complicated.

Trinity came into being 100 years ago. The church originally had a different name—the Church of the Advent—but is still in the same location where it was founded. Starting as an under-funded, struggling mission parish for affluent suburbanites on the northern edge of the city, Trinity has transformed itself into a well-funded, diverse, dynamic, inner city church. During the past 100 years, Trinity not only has been a place of worship connecting generations of parishioners to God, but has played an important role in the Episcopal Diocese of Indianapolis and The Episcopal Church, has created an impressive record of work within its community, and has developed great potential to make even more contributions in the future.

The process that led to *Be Thou My Vision* began in 1999 when I wrote a brief history of Trinity for the parish profile prepared during the search for the eleventh rector of Trinity. I offered to turn that short piece into a longer work for the parish's centennial 20 years later because I wanted to share what I had learned about this amazing church. Once into it, I decided to call this version a *story* rather than a *history* for two reasons. First, I did not want to make it a scholarly work meriting the title of *history* but instead wanted to write something that people would enjoy reading, a popular history, if you will. Second, it was the stories I found in my research that struck me and that I wanted to retell.

A number of things stood out for me as I worked on this book, and a theme began to emerge: in story after story, it was clear that someone had a vision, and time after time the vision became a reality. This book's title, *Be Thou My Vision*, from the ancient Irish hymn of the same name, is telling. Visions abound in the stories here. The vision of early state leaders to locate a new capital in the unexplored and inaccessible wilderness . . . of a missionary bishop from the civilized East to bring the Gospel to the far frontier . . . of a rector and vestry to defy a bishop to preserve a church that later would become a cathedral . . . of a young business leader to create a foundation for the good of humanity . . . of a parishioner to build an English Gothic church on a street corner in an American city . . . of the parish and diocese to oppose injustice in many forms . . . of priests and parishioners to expand outreach missions throughout the community.

It is striking how young are the state of Indiana, the city of Indianapolis, and Trinity parish. The state was organized slightly more than 200 years ago, the city a few years after that, and Trinity just 100 years ago. My wife, Cathy, and I have been parishioners of Trinity for more than one-third of its entire existence. Other living parishioners have worshipped and served at Trinity much longer than that. When I was born, my life expectancy was 65 years. If you think of a typical human lifetime as 65 years, the stories of Indiana and Indianapolis have lasted only slightly more than three lifetimes, and the story of Trinity has taken not even two.

Something else that is noteworthy is that in the short time that Indiana, Indianapolis, and Trinity have been in existence, each has had to meet and overcome numerous significant crises. As I write these words, the world is in the grip of the COVID-19 pandemic, an event outside the timeframe covered in this book. The strength and resilience evident in the stories told here are relevant, though. Indiana and Indianapolis were formed just after a major war pitting the young United States against what was then the greatest power in the world. A short time later, the city and state endured the bloodiest war the country has ever known. Trinity parish was formed just after another major war, at that time called the Great War, and the greatest pandemic of modern times up to now, the Spanish flu, but then had to survive the Great Depression and the even greater Second World War. In later years, Trinity had to keep things together during the Lost Decade and the Great Recession but would emerge with worship, music, youth, and outreach programs that are the envy of any church anywhere.

To put the story of Trinity into context, I have tried to weave the stories of the state, the city, and the church together. Part One of this book tells how the state of Indiana and the city of Indianapolis came to be and how The Episcopal Church arose there in those early years. Part Two deals with

Trinity in its original incarnation as the Church of the Advent and with Indianapolis during that time. Parts Three through Five tell the story of Trinity from the time of the creation of its existing English Gothic church building to its hundredth year.

I have added some appendices that I hope will be informative. These include a glossary of Episcopal terms to aid better understanding of some of the terms used by the denomination. In addition, included is a piece written by Edith Whitehill Clowes about her involvement in the concept, design, and construction in the existing church building that was predicted to stand for 2,000 years. Finally, a list of the bishops of Indiana and Indianapolis and the rectors and senior wardens of Trinity Episcopal Church, Indianapolis, and a list of maps and illustrations are provided.

I hope that you will enjoy reading this story as much as I have enjoyed telling it.

John B. Bridge
Indianapolis, 2020

Part One

An Interesting and Inviting Place: 1816–1918

Monument Circle, Indianapolis
Library of Congress

Chapter 1

People of Faith in a New City: 1816–1860

The state of Indiana—the Hoosier State—was created by the U.S. Congress as the nineteenth state in 1816, shortly after the end of the War of 1812 with Great Britain. At that time, rivers not only were an important mode of transportation, they were natural barriers which created boundaries for distinct economic, political, and cultural regions. Indiana, therefore, was wedged between the already existing state of Ohio to the east, the Ohio River and the already existing state of Kentucky to the south, and the Wabash River to the west. The non-indigenous population of the new state, however, was settled almost entirely in the south along the north shore of the Ohio River, one of the most important routes for American settlers migrating westward.

The state, situated on the edge of the western frontier of the United States, was carved out of what had been known as the Northwest Territory and at the time was known as the Indiana Territory. The region had been claimed and ruled by France from the sixteenth century until the British victory in the French and Indian War in 1763. After that, it was claimed and ruled briefly by Great Britain as part of the colony of Virginia.

During the Revolutionary War, the American colonists laid claim to this land after a tough band of Virginia militia and French-speaking frontiersmen under 26-year-old Lieutenant Colonel George Rogers Clark defeated British redcoat regulars at the Battle of Vincennes in 1779. This American victory in what would become southern Indiana was decisive in the United States acquiring the Northwest Territory from Great Britain under the terms of the 1783 Treaty of Paris, which ended the Revolutionary War.

The Northwest Ordinance of 1787 guaranteed religious freedom and prohibited slavery within the territory's boundaries. The Northwest Territory increased the size of the new country by more than half and triggered

3

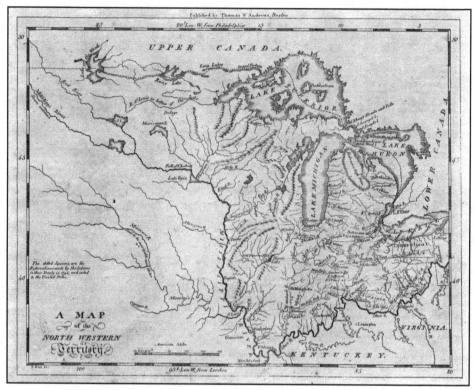

A map of the North Western [sic] *Territory, circa 1790s.*
Indiana Historical Society

its expansion westward. Eventually, not only the state of Indiana but the states of Ohio, Illinois, Michigan, Wisconsin, and Minnesota were created out of the territory.

At the time of the state's formation, the landscape of Indiana was not as it is today with farmhouses, barns, grazing livestock, and fields of soybeans and corn. In 1816, the land was covered almost entirely with dense virgin forests of towering hardwoods as well as vast swampy wetlands that could be traversed only by canoe. The great prairies of the continent's central plains did not begin in Indiana but commenced just west in what would become the state of Illinois. Abraham Lincoln, who moved with his family from Kentucky to Indiana in 1816 when he was seven years old and grew up there until he was 21, described Indiana at the time as "a wild region, with many bears and other wild animals, still in the woods."

The meaning of Indiana's name—Land of the Indians—was apropos. In 1816, numerous Native American tribes populated the entire area, including the Lenape/Delaware, Piankashaw, Kickapoo, Wea, Shawnee, Wyandot, Potawatomi, and Miami tribes. Relations between the new settlers and the indigenous population were tense and often hostile and violent. The last significant armed conflict fought by U.S. forces and Native Americans east of the Mississippi River was in 1811 at the Battle of Tippecanoe, near the confluence of the Wabash and Tippecanoe Rivers and what is now the town of Battleground, Indiana. It was considered such a significant victory for the U.S. forces that their commander, Indiana Territory Governor William Henry Harrison, was elected president of the United States in 1840 with the campaign slogan, "Tippecanoe and Tyler Too!" Tragically, Harrison died after only a month in office. The leader of the Shawnee forces, the great Chief Tecumseh (who was not present at the battle), became a brigadier general in the British Army during the War of 1812 and was killed by U.S. forces in 1813 at the Battle of the Thames in Canada.

Pursuant to treaties, the U.S. government as early as 1795 began to relocate the Native American population from what would become the state of Indiana. The largest single relocation occurred in 1818 in an area in central Indiana from the Wabash River nearly to the Ohio River called the New Purchase. The Treaty of St. Mary's (signed in St. Mary's, Ohio) creating the New Purchase was really six treaties with the Wyandot, Potawatomi, Wea, Delaware, Miami, and other tribes. Such relocations of Native Americans accelerated after 1830 until treaties covered the entire state by 1846.

On January 11, 1820, the Indiana General Assembly, then located in the original state capital of Corydon on the Ohio River, authorized a selection commission

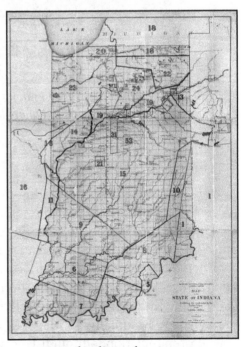

Map of Indiana showing treaty boundaries of lands ceded by Native American tribes to the United States.
Indiana Historical Society

to choose a permanent, centralized site for a new state capital and sent the commission north into the heart of the New Purchase. On June 7, 1820, the commissioners selected land along the east bank of the west fork of the White River, two miles northwest of Indiana's geographic center.

Commissioners appointed by the Indiana General Assembly selecting the site for Indianapolis, 1820.
Indiana Historical Society (image cropped)

The farsighted members of that early General Assembly could envision that the population of the state would expand northward, as well as from the north and east, and that a state capital at the extreme south of the state eventually would become a drawback. In a manner similar to what the founders of the United States had done with Washington, D.C., the early leaders of Indiana determined to create a new, centrally located capital city from the ground up. In essence, therefore, it was an artificial city—like the nation's capital—created as a result of a top-down decision by movers and shakers rather than by economic, historic, strategic, or geographic forces.

On January 6, 1821, the General Assembly ratified the site selection on the White River for the new state capital of Indiana. The state's early leaders considered Native-American-derived names for the city, including Tecumseh, but eventually chose a Greek-derived name—*Indianapolis* (City of the Land of the Indians)—the pronunciation of which would be the subject of some debate. Eventually, IN-dia-NA-po-lis became the generally accepted official pronunciation, although Hoosiers have managed to pronounce the name in many different ways to this day. In December 1821, the General Assembly created Marion County and made Indianapolis the county's seat of government.

In that same year, the General Assembly also hired Alexander Ralston and Elias Pym Fordham to survey, plat, and develop a city plan for the new capital city. The English-born Fordham lived in Illinois at the time, and little more is known about him other than that he eventually returned to England. Much is known about the Scottish-born Ralston, though. At the time, he conveniently lived in Salem, Indiana, but also had important relevant experience. In 1791, he had been an assistant to the French-American architect Pierre L'Enfant in developing the city plan for Washington, D.C. Ralston, however, also was a controversial character. He had left the East in 1815 and relocated in the frontier of Indiana, in part because of his involvement with former U.S. Vice President Aaron Burr's alleged conspiracy to create a second independent nation in North America out of parts of the United States and Mexico.

Ralston and Fordham were directed by the General Assembly to plat a city of four square miles. When they arrived in the area approved by the legislature, however, they found it to be—like a large part of Indiana at the time—a huge wetlands or, as it would have been referred to in those days, a swamp. The only river in the area, the White River, had been assumed to be navigable but proved not to be. Few non-indigenous people lived in the area. Initially, as it would turn out, few more non-indigenous people would want to live there.

Ralston took the initiative and concluded that the new city would never exceed one square mile in size. He, therefore, platted the "Town of Indianapolis" on the basis of a Mile Square bounded by North Street, East Street, West Street, and South Street and bisected east and west by Washington Street and north and south by Meridian Street. At the intersection of Market and Meridian streets in the very center of the city plan was what would become known as Governor's Circle, on which was to be constructed the Indiana governor's house. (A governor's house was erected on Governor's Circle in 1827, but due to its exposed location and poor construction, no governor's family ever consented to live in it. The house eventually was sold and demolished in 1857.)

The plan also showed locations for the Indiana Statehouse and the city's courthouse. Unusual for American city planning and unique in the Midwest, four streets (later renamed avenues)—Indiana, Massachusetts, Virginia, and Kentucky Streets—radiated diagonally from the corners of the Mile Square. This concept of a circle with radiating avenues had been used in the city plan for Washington, D.C., and Ralston clearly borrowed heavily from that

*The site selected by the Indiana General Assembly for
Indianapolis as Ralston and Fordham found it.*
Bass Photo Co. Collection, Indiana Historical Society (image cropped)

plan for his new capital city design. While Indianapolis grew far beyond his original concept, the center of downtown Indianapolis remained largely as Ralston designed it.

In 1824, Indianapolis officially was made the capital of Indiana, and the state legislature moved there in 1825. At that time, the city's population consisted of about 500 hardy souls. Politically, the location selected for the capital city was a good one. The white settlers of Indiana did indeed come from both south of the Ohio River and westward from New England and Europe, and the two waves met in the center around Indianapolis. This mixture of northern and southern peoples and cultures resulted in a blend of the two that eventually would become thought of as the Midwestern culture and personality. Hoosiers would become identified with the best of hospitality and openness, and the people who settled in Indiana would become known as honest and hardworking.

Indiana's leaders were not as farsighted financially as they were politically, however. In the 1830s, the General Assembly embarked on what would turn into an economic catastrophe. Intending to build a transportation network through the state's wild terrain, the legislature passed the Mammoth Internal Improvement Act in 1836, raised $10 million of debt in London

($235 million in 2019 dollars—a staggering figure given that the state's entire population was less than 700,000), and proceeded to build canals as a primary mode of transit. The unfeasibility of the idea and the financial panic of 1837 brought the state to the brink of bankruptcy, which it avoided only by turning all of its transportation projects over to its London creditors. The Central Canal that runs from the Broad Ripple neighborhood to downtown Indianapolis is a vestige from that time. Another more impactful result was the new Indiana Constitution adopted in 1851, which put severe restrictions on the state's ability to incur debt.

A second economic disaster was the absence of a navigable river for Indiana's new capital city. In 1831, the first and only steamboat ever to make it up the White River to Indianapolis arrived; it promptly ran aground in shallow water, though, when it attempted to

Plat of the Town of Indianapolis,
by Alexander Ralston, 1821.
Bass Photo Co. Collection, Indiana Historical Society

leave. As a result of being effectively land-locked, until the 1850s Indianapolis failed to grow as rapidly as the nearby river cities of Cincinnati, Louisville, and St. Louis. This stunted growth of the capital city certainly slowed the state's development, as well. As a result, Indiana would remain a state of small towns for much of its history, and Indianapolis would grow to be a mid-sized city with a small-town feel.

Organized religion arrived in Indianapolis quickly, however. A plaque in the Indiana Statehouse rotunda indicates that the first formal religious service in the area was held in 1819 before the city even was platted. A Methodist circuit-riding minister named Resin Hammond led that surely emotional gathering under a walnut tree on what are now the grounds of the Indiana Statehouse. The plaque also indicates that the first church in the city, Wesley Chapel, was organized in 1821 in Isaac Wilson's log cabin on the same grounds by another Methodist circuit-riding minister, William Cravens. What became Meridian Street United Methodist Church at 5550 North Meridian Street has claimed descent from this early church.

In the following year, 1822, First Baptist Church was formed in Indianapolis—and also claimed to be the first congregation in the city. First Baptist remained in existence and eventually would be located at 8600 North College Avenue. Then in 1823, the Presbyterian Church of Indianapolis was formed. This church did not become First Presbyterian Church until a congregation that became known as Second Presbyterian Church split off in 1838 over theological issues affecting the entire Presbyterian denomination: succinctly, all Presbyterians agreed that people were sinful, but they could not agree whether it was because of Original Sin (Old School) or their own actions (New School). Oddly, perhaps, both Presbyterian churches for a time were located on Governor's Circle. Although Redeemer Presbyterian Church occupied the last site of First Presbyterian Church at 1505 North Delaware Street in 1998, Redeemer has not claimed affiliation with the original church, which appears simply to have faded from existence. Second Presbyterian Church, therefore, eventually located at 7700 North Meridian Street, appears to be the oldest Presbyterian congregation in the city.

It should be mentioned that the first pastor of Second Presbyterian who led the split from the Presbyterian Church of Indianapolis was Henry Ward Beecher, whose anti-slavery sermons later during the 1840s brought him national prominence. In 1847, Beecher moved from Indianapolis to serve as pastor at Plymouth Congregationalist Church in Brooklyn, New York, where he would become one of the century's most famous orators and advocates for social reform.

Thus, during the early 1820s, three mainstream Protestant denominations—Methodists, Baptists, and Presbyterians—arrived in the Hoosier capital at about the same time, and all three created churches there. By the end of the decade, the population of Indianapolis had creeped up to an estimated 1,900.

Itinerant Episcopal clergy occasionally appeared in Indianapolis in the 1820s to perform marriages and baptisms. It was not until September 25, 1835, however, that The Episcopal Church consecrated the Rt. Rev. Jackson Kemper as its first missionary bishop with responsibility for establishing churches in the relatively new states of Indiana and Missouri. Bishop Kemper's consecration was held in the East at St. Peter's, Philadelphia, but his interest in what was then the West was long-standing. In fact, he had been the first Episcopal priest to preach west of the Allegheny Mountains in rugged areas of Pennsylvania, Virginia, and Ohio. The following November, he arrived on horseback in Indiana, the farthest west he had yet traveled, and recorded in his diary, "Indiana looked woody, interesting, and inviting." The highly civilized Bishop Kemper proceeded to take the word of God to settlers in their frontier cabins, trading posts, and taverns along the Wabash, Mississippi, and Missouri Rivers and became a revered and beloved figure to those tough and roughhewn people.

The Rt. Rev. Jackson Kemper, first missionary bishop to Indiana, in his later years, circa 1860s.
Library of Congress

Shortly after the consecration of Bishop Kemper, The Episcopal Church arrived in Indianapolis in a permanent sense with the establishment of a congregation in 1837, which will be described later in this chapter. At approximately the same time, a Lutheran church arrived, and the first Roman Catholic church in the city was established by Irish and German immigrants. From the 1830s to the 1850s, religion in Indianapolis started settling into what would become the standard U.S. religious configuration until the last part of the twentieth century: a Protestant mainstream majority, a strong Roman Catholic minority, a Jewish congregation, and a scattering of other denominations including European Reformed Churches, African-American Baptists and Methodists, Unitarians, Universalists, Quakers, and Mormons.

The appearance of The Episcopal Church in Indianapolis was tardy but well-timed. In its first decades, Indianapolis suffered from its remoteness and difficult access and, as a result, slow growth in its population. The city's unfortunate location on a non-navigable body of water eventually was compensated for with the arrival of new effective modes of transportation.

Two roads into Indianapolis, circa *1830s:*
South Meridian Street crossing Pleasant Run (top);
East Washington Street (the National Road)
crossing the White River (bottom).

Bass Photo Co. Collection, Indiana Historical Society (top);
General photograph collection, Rare Books and Manuscripts,
Indiana State Library (bottom)

First to arrive were roads. In the 1820s, the east-west National Road was built (consisting of Washington Street in downtown Indianapolis), which was the first direct route between Washington, D.C., and the Mississippi River. In the 1830s, the north-south Michigan Road was constructed through Indiana, which was the first direct route between the Ohio River and Lake Michigan. The southern terminus of the Michigan Road was

Madison, Indiana, then the largest city in the state. Madison had boomed as a result of its position on the north shore of the Ohio River where resolute settlers traveling down the river in flatboats and keelboats could disembark, buy provisions, and continue overland to the north and west.

The second and greater boost to Indianapolis, however, came with the arrival in 1847 of the first railroad line to the Hoosier capital built by the Madison & Indianapolis Railroad Company. Like the Michigan Road, this rail line connected Indianapolis to the city of Madison and the Ohio River. At that time, Indianapolis had fewer than 8,000 residents. Within five years, however, seven different railroad lines converged on the city. Steel rails would deliver to Indianapolis the hoped-for development and prosperity that the White River had not.

Until the 1850s, most railroad companies built their own stations in cities they served, resulting in many stations in a single city and confusion for travelers and shippers. In 1853, four of the railroad companies serving Indi-

anapolis built in the city what is claimed to be the world's first Union Terminal. This new station put into practice the radical idea of one train station in a city for all railroad lines coming into it and, thereby, providing the convenience of a centralized transportation facility. By 1860—only 13 years after the arrival of the first railroad line from the Ohio River boom town of Madison—Indianapolis's population had grown to more than 18,000, and Indianapolis surpassed Madison as the largest city in the state.

Under the eye of Bishop Kemper, the first Episcopal congregation in Indianapolis was born, consisting of families who initially worshipped in private homes and a rented

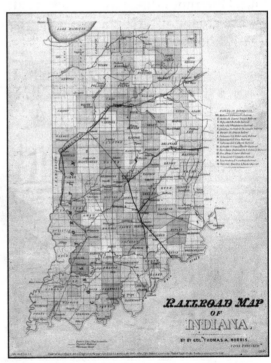

Railroad Map of Indiana, *showing 15 rail lines, 1850; a few years before, there had been none.*
Library of Congress

room on Washington Street. On July 13, 1837, 30 individuals—11 women and 19 men—organized the parish of Christ Church. The first vestry of five men was elected on August 21, 1837. The first rector was the Rev. James B. Britton, who came from Ohio.

The congregation purchased a site on Meridian Street on the northeast quadrant of Governor's Circle. There, the foundation of the first Christ Church building was consecrated by Bishop Kemper on December 16, 1837. The cornerstone was laid by the rector on May 7, 1838, and work progressed rapidly on the wood-frame building. The church was open for services on November 18, 1838, and was consecrated by Bishop Kemper a month later on December 16.

An article written by a certain W.R. Holloway in 1870 stated, "This church was a plain, but neatly finished and strongly built Gothic edifice, of wood, which, while it made no pretensions to architectural beauty, was very far superior to any house of worship then erected in [Indianapolis] . . . ." At the time, Governor's Circle was a muddy, rutted road, and Christ Church built a fence around its grounds because, according to the church's present-day website, "it was the only way to keep pigs out of the churchyard."

The first, wood-frame Christ Church
on Governor's Circle, circa 1850s.
Bass Photo Co. Collection, Indiana Historical Society

*The Indiana governor's house and Christ Church
on Governor's Circle, circa 1850s.*
Bass Photo Co. Collection, Indiana Historical Society

In 1842, Bishop Kemper was elected to serve as the true, not missionary, bishop of Indiana, but he reluctantly refused the position due to what he felt were his responsibilities to the larger Church as a missionary bishop. Indeed, Bishop Kemper had served and continued to serve The Episcopal Church far beyond the borders of Indiana. Over his life as a missionary bishop, Bishop Kemper organized six new Episcopal dioceses in addition to Indiana: Wisconsin, Missouri, Iowa, Minnesota, Kansas, and Nebraska. Finding that the priests he recruited from the East did not adapt well to conditions on the frontier, Bishop Kemper founded Racine College and Nashotah House in Wisconsin to educate Midwesterners for the priesthood. He also promoted mission work among Native Americans from the Potawatomi, Seneca, Oneida, and Huron tribes. He ended his career as the first bishop of Wisconsin.

Finding another bishop willing to serve in the hinterlands of Indiana, however, turned out to be difficult. It was not until 1849—seven years later—that the first full-time bishop of Indiana, the Rt. Rev. George Upfold, was consecrated at Christ Church. At the time, Christ Church's physical grounds were quite small. When a cathedral for the Diocese of Indiana was established in 1849, it was located at St. John's, Lafayette, Indiana, because St. John's was the only parish in the diocese that had adequate housing for the bishop. Bishop Upfold, however, served as the priest at both St. John's, Lafayette, and Christ Church, Indianapolis. At the time, it was a common practice for an Episcopal bishop also to serve as a parish priest.

In 1857, the parish of Christ Church sold its original wood-frame building to Indiana Station, an African-American Methodist Episcopal church founded in 1836 and the first African-American congregation in the city. (In the late 1860s, Indiana Station adopted the name Bethel African Methodist Episcopal Church, the name by which this historic congregation became best known.) Indiana Station moved the wooden structure to the congregation's location on Georgia Street between Senate Avenue and the Central Canal to replace the structure its members had built there in 1841. The building later would meet an unfortunate fate while owned and occupied by Indiana Station, as will be described in Chapter 2.

After the sale of its first structure, the parish of Christ Church started construction of a new stone church building on its property at Meridian Street and Governor's Circle. Designed by Irish-born architect William Tinsley in an English Gothic Revival style, its cornerstone was laid on June 24, 1857. During construction of the new church, Episcopal services were held in the Indiana Statehouse, separation of church and state being secondary to the demands of a rapidly growing city.

*The second, and last, Christ Church
building on Governor's Circle.*
Bass Photo Co. Collection, Indiana Historical Society

The new stone Christ Church building was completed in 1859, in the same location where it remained into the twenty-first century. The first worship service was held on May 22, 1859. A spire was added to the church's tower in 1869, an Episcopal residence was constructed in 1871, and a Sunday school building was built in 1876.

Notably, there were four other Protestant churches on Governor's Circle at that time: two Presbyterian churches, a Methodist church, and a Congregationalist church. Eventually, The Episcopal Church was the only denomination still to have a church on the Circle. As we will see in Chapter 3, the survival of Christ Church on the Circle was not a certainty late in the nineteenth century.

By 1850, Episcopalians made up only about one percent of the people affiliated with some religious denomination in Marion County, where Indianapolis is located. On a percentage basis, Episcopalians would never make up more than two percent of the churchgoing population of Marion County. Indeed, by 1990, the percentage of Episcopalians among religiously affiliated persons in Marion County dropped below one percent. Nevertheless, The Episcopal Church's important role in the history of Indianapolis would surpass out of all proportion the small number of its members.

Chapter 2

A House Divided: 1861–1865

Indiana before and during the Civil War—like Ohio and Illinois, its neighbors north of the Ohio River—was divided in its feelings about the North and the South, the Union and the Confederacy. Indiana was a free state in which slavery was illegal, but not an insignificant number of Hoosiers were Copperheads, i.e., Southern sympathizers who supported or at least did not oppose institutionalized and legal slavery in the South. (The derogatory term, Copperhead, came from the common name for *Agkistrodon contortrix*, a species of poisonous snake most commonly found in the southern part of the United States.)

The possibilities of aid to Confederate states from the Midwest, of disruption by Midwestern states of Northern efforts to preserve the Union, and even of efforts of Midwestern states to secede from the Union were not far-fetched. Much of Indiana's white population had come from the slave states of Kentucky and Tennessee, and much of Indiana's economic trade was with those and other slave states farther down the Ohio and Mississippi Rivers. (Not only was Indiana's trade with the South facilitated by those rivers, trade elsewhere was hindered by the vast wetlands that existed north of the Wabash River.)

In March 1861, the month before the first shots of the Civil War were fired at Fort Sumter in South Carolina, members of the Democratic Party in Indiana met in Indianapolis and determined to support the South in the event war broke out. Local lawyer, Democratic politician, and future U.S. Vice President Thomas A. Hendricks (whose statute stands on the grounds of the Indiana Statehouse) publicly advocated a union of the Midwest with the South.

In 1862, the original Christ Church building owned and occupied by Indiana Station, the African-American Methodist Episcopal congregation, was burned to the ground. The congregation had openly and actively supported abolitionism and the Underground Railroad that ran through Indianapolis and provided protection to escaped slaves fleeing the South on their way to freedom in Canada. The members of Indiana Station firmly believed that the fire was arson committed by Hoosier Copperheads who supported the Confederacy.

Despite these pro-Southern sympathies, however, Indiana overall supported the Union financially, industrially, and agriculturally. The state, which had the fifth highest population of the states remaining in the Union, ranked second among Union states in terms of the percentage of its men of military age who served in the Union's armed forces. Indiana contributed 210,000 men, roughly 15 percent of the state's total population, to serve in the Union Army, Navy, and Marine Corps. Those Hoosiers fought in more than 300 engagements during the war.

A key figure for the state during the Civil War, and a major reason for Indiana's active support for the Union, was 37-year-old Governor Oliver P. Morton, President Abraham Lincoln's professed favorite governor. Morton, whose fierce visage over a black goatee gave him a slightly diabolical look, held that, "If it is worth a bloody struggle to establish this nation, it is worth one to preserve it." During the war years 1861–1865, he ignored the limits of his constitutional authority and was seen to have ruled Indiana and parts of Kentucky as a dictator, but he was instrumental in keeping both states in the Union. Morton used aggressive measures, as did Lincoln in Washington, D.C., including persuading Republican representatives in the Indiana General Assembly to boycott the Democratic (i.e., pro-Southern) majority legislature, thereby effectively disbanding

Indiana's Oliver P. Morton is given pride of place at the top of the center circle of Union governors, 1865.

Indiana Historical Society, P0455

it, in order to prevent Copperhead legislators from frustrating Indiana's war efforts. Because a disbanded legislature could not authorize a budget, Morton funded Indiana's war effort privately.

It should be said that Abraham Lincoln, who grew up in Indiana, always had a fondness for the state. On February 12, 1961, he made a stop and spent the night in Indianapolis on his way to Washington, D.C., to be sworn in as the sixteenth president of the United States. He was greeted on his arrival in the city by Governor Morton and 20,000 supporters. Tragically, Lincoln's next visit to Indianapolis was on April 30, 1865, when Governor Morton and members of the Indiana General Assembly and the Indianapolis City Council met the train carrying the president's body from Washington on its way to its final resting place in Springfield, Illinois. While Lincoln's body laid in state under the dome of the Indiana Statehouse, an estimated 50,000 Hoosiers passed by his coffin.

Major (later Colonel) Eli Lilly of the Union Army, circa 1863.
Library of Congress

Mention also should be made of one particular Hoosier who served the Union. Eli Lilly was commissioned as an officer in the Union Army in 1861 at age 23. Lilly led the 18th Indiana Battery of Light Artillery and later served with the 21st Indiana Infantry and the 9th Indiana Cavalry. He fought in several battles in Kentucky and Tennessee before he was captured by Confederate forces in Alabama in 1864. Lilly was held as a prisoner of war in Mississippi until he was released pursuant to a prisoner swap in 1865. He then was promoted to colonel and served the rest of the war with the Union Army at Vicksburg, Mississippi. After he was mustered out of the army at the end of the war, he always was known as Colonel Eli Lilly. The succeeding decades would prove that it was most fortunate for the history of Indianapolis and The Episcopal Church that Colonel Lilly survived his time as a combatant and prisoner during the Civil War.

After the Civil War, Oliver P. Morton served in the U.S. Senate as a Radical Reconstructionist who advocated greater rights for African-Americans and harsh policies for the defeated South. On July 1, 1869, Senator Morton from Indiana was the featured orator at the dedication of the Soldiers' National Monument, the centerpiece of the National Cemetery in Gettysburg, Pennsylvania, built to honor the more than 3,500 Union soldiers laid to rest there who gave their lives in the great battle during July 1–3, 1863. (President Lincoln had delivered his Gettysburg Address at the the dedication of the National Cemetery itself on November 19, 1863.) In his speech, Morton did not hold back his feelings: "The Rebellion was madness. It was the insanity of States, the delirium of millions brought on by the pernicious influence of human slavery. The people of the South were drunk with the spoils of the labor of four millions of slaves."

Morton's importance to the state of Indiana and to the preservation of the United States was such that one statue of him stands in front of the Indiana Statehouse and a second stands by the Soldiers and Sailors Monument, constructed in Indianapolis at the turn of the nineteenth into the twentieth century. Moreover, a statue of Morton is one of the two from Indiana in Statuary Hall in the United States Capitol Building.

Churches, of course, were not immune to tensions caused by the Civil War. In fact, the parish of Christ Church eventually would split as a result of

Camp Morton with Confederate prisoners of war
standing on both sides of the "Potomac," circa 1864–1865.
Indiana Historical Society, P0388

them. Part of the cause of this split was the parish's controversial rector and his work at Camp Morton in Indianapolis. Located on the former grounds of the Indiana State Fair, 36 acres bordered by present-day Central Avenue and 19th, 22nd, and Talbot Streets, Camp Morton initially was a military training base. Between 1862 and 1865, however, it was transformed into a Confederate prisoner of war camp. By 1864, the camp held up to 5,000 prisoners. Water for drinking and washing in the camp came from a ditch in the middle, ironically called by prisoners the "Potomac," which flooded in rainy seasons and disappeared but for some stagnant fetid pools in hot weather. More than 1,700 prisoners died in the camp. Conditions, as one can imagine, were ghastly.

At the beginning of the Civil War, the rector of Christ Church was the Rev. Horace Stringfellow, Jr., a native of Virginia. Although Rev. Stringfellow professed loyalty to the Union, he was frequently but without evidence accused of disloyalty. He even was rumored to be a Confederate spy. The most serious written accusation was contained in an 1862 article in an Indianapolis newspaper, the *Daily Journal*, which arose from Rev. Stringfellow helping the sick and wounded in the prisoners' hospital at Camp Morton. Rev. Stringfellow wrote a retort to that newspaper, stating, "My only object in what I have voluntarily done has been to relieve suffering humanity by . . . attending to the personal wants of the sick. Beyond this I have had no motive . . . ."

As a result of this controversy, Rev. Stringfellow tendered his resignation as rector to the vestry of Christ Church. The vestry, in a strongly worded written show of support, requested him to withdraw his resignation, which Rev. Stringfellow did. Accusations against the rector continued, however. A short time after his first attempt to resign, Rev. Stringfellow again tendered his resignation. Again, the vestry refused to accept it.

But finally, Rev. Stringfellow's involvement in what might have been a simple misunderstanding proved to be his undoing. Governor Morton asked the churches of Indianapolis to peal their bells to announce a meeting in the Indiana Statehouse for the purpose of raising funds for the families of Union volunteers. Rev. Stringfellow consented, but only to the use of Christ Church's largest bell. Then, when the people tasked with ringing that one bell instead sounded all of the church's bells, Rev. Stringfellow reportedly rushed to them and angrily halted the entire peal.

The rector's motives were unclear, but the worst was suspected. For the third time, Rev. Stringfellow submitted his resignation, and this time it was accepted. Upon leaving Christ Church, Rev. Stringfellow sent his family to Canada for safety, returned to Virginia, and joined General Robert E. Lee's Army of Northern Virginia as a captain of ambulances. Toward the end of the war, he fled the South and rejoined his family in Canada.

After the conclusion of the bloody and traumatic Civil War in 1865, three amendments to the U.S. Constitution accomplished the most radical and rapid social and political change in American history: the abolition of slavery (Thirteenth Amendment) and the grant to former slaves of equal citizenship (Fourteenth Amendment) and voting rights (Fifteenth Amendment). Four million slaves, thus, were transformed into voting citizens of the United States.

For a 12-year period of Reconstruction after the Civil War, the promise of equal rights for African-Americans was fulfilled for a brief time; afterwards, that promise was largely abandoned for many decades. The wounds suffered by the United States as a result of the Civil War, the legacy of slavery, and the failure of Reconstruction have never healed. Indeed, the damage from those wounds would remain embedded in American politics, economics, and society well into the twenty-first century.

Chapter 3

Expansion and Division:
1866–1899

In 1866 after the Civil War had ended, a group of mostly Democratic Southern sympathizers split off from Christ Church and organized a new parish, which they named St. Paul's. The group selected as their rector none other than Rev. Horace Stringfellow, the former rector of Christ Church, who accepted their call and returned to Indianapolis from Canada. Critics of St. Paul's then disparaged it as "the Church of the Holy Copperheads" and "St. Butternut's." (Butternut was a derogatory term for Confederate soldiers derived from their homespun grey uniforms which, as they weathered and faded, took on a light brownish, or butternut, appearance.) Nevertheless, Rev. Stringfellow preached at Christ Church shortly after he arrived in Indianapolis, and his return was regarded with good will by most. The hostilities between the parishes of Christ Church and St. Paul's that marked their separation, of course, in time would fade away.

St. Paul's new, large, cathedral-like church building was dedicated in 1869 in downtown Indianapolis at the corner of New York and Illinois Streets, three blocks away from Christ Church. The church in 1875 indeed did become the cathedral of the Diocese of Indianapolis for a short period of time.

From the end of the Civil War through the remainder of the nineteenth century, The Episcopal Church in Indianapolis formed a number of other new parishes, including Grace Church on the north side of the city, St. George's on the south side, and St. Phillip's on West Street for an African-American congregation.

Grace Church's wooden building, constructed in 1866, was located at the southeast corner of Pennsylvania and St. Joseph Streets. In 1886, St. Paul's abrogated its position as cathedral of the diocese, and Grace Church became the pro-cathedral of Indianapolis in the absence of another true cathedral

The first, downtown St. Paul's, Indianapolis, circa *1900.*
Bass Photo Co. Collection, Indiana Historical Society

building. In 1889, the members of Grace Church physically moved their building further north to the southeast corner of 16th Street and Central Avenue at what was then the northern extent of the growing city. As will be discussed in Chapter 4, All Saints Cathedral absorbed and replaced the parish of Grace Church in 1911 when Grace's wooden structure was demolished and the new cathedral building was built on the same location.

During this time in the late nineteenth century, The Episcopal Church was grappling in America with the Oxford Movement that was rocking the Church of England and the rest of the Anglican Communion. The movement, which started at the University of Oxford in England, was led by prominent Anglicans in that country, foremost among them John Henry Newman, Edward Pusey, and John Keble.

The origins of the Oxford Movement were complex and involved political as well as religious causes, but generally the movement reasserted the apostolic and catholic heritage of Anglicanism and called for the Church of England to return to the ways of the ancient and undivided church in matters of doctrine, liturgy, and devotion. In the United States, the Oxford Movement had its greatest influence in the Midwest, and The Episcopal Church in Indianapolis swerved from its Low Church, Protestant leanings to a more High Church, Roman Catholic-like ritual and practice, complete with vestments, processions, genuflection, incense, signing the cross, greater pastoral care, and frequent communion.

Another development that The Episcopal Church in Indiana experienced in the late nineteenth century came about due to the discovery of natural gas deposits and the resulting gas boom in the state. The natural gas belt found underground in Indiana was the largest such deposit discovered anywhere up to that time. Immigrants from Great Britain swarmed to Indiana to work in its gas fields, causing a significant increase in congregants in Episcopal parishes in the state. Of course, many of these people settled in rural areas rather than the urban areas where The Episcopal Church was strong, so the potential for even more growth was seen to be considerable. (This view, unfortunately, would turn out to be overoptimistic.)

Into these heady times for The Episcopal Church in Indiana came the Rt. Rev. John Hazen White, the fifth bishop of the Diocese of Indiana. Born and bred in Ohio, Bishop White had risen to prominence at churches in Illinois and Minnesota and as warden of Seabury Divinity School in Minnesota. Upon his election as bishop of Indiana at Grace Church on February 6, 1895, a local newspaper in Minnesota described Bishop White as "a man of energy and progress" and "a ripe scholar, an indefatigable worker, and a man of great force of character and pleasant address." Judging from photographs, one could say that he also never lost the demeanor of a strict schoolmaster. Bishop White was consecrated on May 1, 1895, at St. Paul's, Indianapolis.

The Rt. Rev. John Hazen White, fifth bishop of Indiana and first bishop of Michigan City (later Northern Indiana).
Diocese of Northern Indiana

Bishop White began his tenure in a highly energetic and aggressive manner, proposing a new cathedral for Indianapolis to replace the wood-frame pro-cathedral, Grace Church. The cost of this plan, however, called for the sale of Christ Church's building on Governor's Circle as well as Grace Church's structure. By 1884, Christ Church was the last church remaining on Governor's Circle: the First Presbyterians had left in 1866, the Second Presbyterians in 1867, the Methodists in 1869, and the Congregationalists in 1884. Beginning in 1888, the parish of Christ Church had suffered through repeated efforts to have it leave the Circle and merge with Grace Church or St. Paul's or move to a new north side location.

Bishop White's plan for a new cathedral had the support of the rector of Christ Church, the Rev. J. Hilliard Ranger, who agreed with the bishop that the church was too small and had no realistic future. But when Rev. Ranger died suddenly from pneumonia contracted on a trip to Minnesota, Bishop White lost his primary supporter. The bishop immediately took personal control of the situation and put Christ Church's building up for sale in 1896. His action, however, was not decisive. In the following year, Christ Church's vestry and new rector, the Rev. Andrew J. Graham, announced that they firmly opposed the sale, in direct opposition to Bishop White's wishes. A group from Grace Church soon joined this position, and the bishop's plan for a new cathedral was quickly squelched. Christ Church on the Circle was saved, but Bishop White was greatly displeased.

The relationship between Bishop White and the parishioners of Christ Church and Grace Church soon deteriorated rapidly. The members of those parishes proposed the construction of a new church, St. David's, in the then far-northern reaches of Indianapolis at 21st and Talbot Streets. St. David's would gain distinction in the diocese by cultivating even more of a High Church, Anglo-Catholic ritualistic worship style than the other parishes in the diocese.

Still seething from the rebuke of his cathedral plans, Bishop White gave his informal consent but declined to grant his official approval for the new St. David's. In a caustic speech, he denounced the actions of the groups from Christ Church and Grace Church, claiming that their conflict with him existed "because [they] have chosen to withdraw from the church as the bishop is administering it and force my hand to make martyrs of them or force them to commit suicide. I prefer that they should commit suicide if they are determined upon that course."

Another of Bishop White's goals was to have the Diocese of Indiana divided into smaller, more manageable components to deal with increasing numbers of congregants. Membership in The Episcopal Church in Indiana was growing in urban areas, and there still was seen to be potential for more growth in rural parts of the state. Bishop White proposed that three new dioceses—northern, central, and southern Indiana—be created out of the Diocese of Indiana. The General Convention of The Episcopal Church held in Washington, D.C., in October 1898, though, approved the creation of only a new diocese in northern Indiana, splitting the old diocese into two dioceses instead of the bishop's proposed three.

The newly truncated Diocese of Indiana encompassed roughly the lower two-thirds of the state and retained approximately 75 percent of the former statewide diocese's assets. The new diocese created in northern Indiana, originally called the Diocese of Michigan City, covered roughly the upper one-third of the state but had only about 25 percent of the old diocese's assets. Under the canon law of The Episcopal Church, the serving bishop of a divided diocese could choose which new diocese he would continue to serve. In part because of the bad feelings toward him in Indianapolis, and in part because he was the person who had initiated the split, Bishop White chose to lead the much smaller and poorer Diocese of Michigan City. He was consecrated the bishop of Michigan City on April 25, 1899.

Bishop White's relationship with the churches in northern Indiana proved to be similar to his turbulent relationship with the churches in Indianapolis and had a lasting effect on his new diocese. In 1911, Bishop White severed his ties to Trinity, Michigan City, which up to then had served as the pro-cathedral of the diocese, and the vestry of that church voted to end its cathedral status. By 1912, Bishop White was spending more time in South Bend, Indiana. Eventually, St. Paul's in neighboring Mishawaka, Indiana, became the pro-cathedral of the Diocese of Michigan City. The diocese voted to be renamed the Diocese of Northern Indiana in 1919, and the new name took effect in 1921.

Of course, the division of the Diocese of Indiana and the departure of Bishop White from Indianapolis to Michigan City made it necessary to elect and consecrate a new bishop for the Diocese of Indiana. The diocese held a convention during June 6–8, 1899, for that purpose. Seven names were placed into nomination for bishop. Balloting began in the evening on June

The Rt. Rev. Joseph Marshall Francis,
sixth bishop of Indiana (later Indianapolis).
National Portrait Gallery, London

7, continued until 1 a.m. on June 8, then resumed for three more hours later that morning. The Rev. Joseph Marshall Francis, the rector of St. Paul's, Evansville, Indiana, finally was elected the sixth bishop of Indiana after 26 ballots by the clergy and 23 ballots by the laity.

On September 21, 1899, at his church in Evansville, Bishop-elect Francis was consecrated bishop of Indiana and became, at age 37, the youngest Episcopal bishop in the United States. A man of patrician looks and bearing, Bishop Francis happened to be a graduate of Racine College and Nashotah House in Wisconsin, two educational institutions founded by Indiana's original missionary bishop, the Rt. Rev. Jackson Kemper. His coming to Indianapolis from Evansville was something of a miraculous happenstance, however. Earlier, he had been rector of a church in Wisconsin and also had served at the Episcopal cathedral in Tokyo. He had been called as the rector of a church in Evansville only two years before his election as bishop of Indiana largely because he had greatly impressed Bishop White, then the bishop of Indiana, when the two chanced to meet in Europe while the young Rev. Francis and his wife were returning to the United States from Japan.

The Diocese of Indiana voted to change its name to the Diocese of Indianapolis on September 1, 1902, primarily to avoid the impression that it was the only diocese in the state. This, in effect, also changed Bishop Francis's title to bishop of Indianapolis. Bishop Francis would remain bishop of Indianapolis for 40 years until he died in 1939, by then the second-oldest member of the House of Bishops of The Episcopal Church. An ardent baseball fan throughout his life, he also enjoyed raising purebred Airedale dogs, which he trained to bow during prayer. Bishop Francis also would become a key figure in the story of Trinity Episcopal Church, Indianapolis.

Bishop Francis (back row, center) with other Episcopal,
Roman Catholic, and Russian Orthodox bishops, 1900.
The Church of the Advent, Boston, Massachusetts

Chapter 4

Advances During Peace and War: 1866–1918

Throughout the period between the Civil War and World War I, Indianapolis was a dynamic city fully participating in the frenzied modernization of America then taking place. Indiana and the other states of the Midwest were transforming from the frontier to the industrial and agricultural heartland of the nation. During 1860–1910, the population of Indianapolis grew more than 10 times from 18,611 to 233,650. In the 1890s, the city and state became linked by a 2,400-mile network of interurban railroads. By then, Indianapolis had become a national railroad center, in the Midwest second only to Chicago, as well as a major meat packer, behind only Chicago and Cincinnati in the region. The sights, sounds, and smells of a rapidly expanding downtown, complete with clangorous factories belching smoke, a rail yard loading and unloading several hundred trains per day, and acres of stockyards teeming with hogs and cattle, must have been overwhelming.

In 1872, Lyman S. Ayres acquired the controlling interest in a dry goods company and renamed it L.S. Ayres and Company in 1874. The company's original building and flagship store at the southwest corner of Meridian and Washington Streets—designed by Vonnegut & Bohn, author Kurt Vonnegut's grandfather's architectural firm—would remain at that location well into the twentieth century and be enlarged several times. L.S. Ayres eventually would grow to become the dominant retailer in the state. The descendants of Lyman S. Ayres would become parishioners of the Church of the Advent and Trinity Episcopal Church, Indianapolis.

Two years later in 1876, Colonel Eli Lilly, the Civil War veteran, opened his pharmaceutical laboratory on Pearl Street in downtown Indianapolis. Eli Lilly and Company was incorporated in 1881 and grew to 100 employees by the late 1880s. By this time, the population of Indianapolis had increased to more than 100,000.

In 1890, Colonel Lilly and other civic leaders in Indianapolis founded the Commercial Club, and Colonel Lilly was elected as its first president. The club, renamed the Indianapolis Chamber of Commerce in 1912, was the main vehicle for Colonel Lilly's city development goals. The Commercial Club was instrumental in making numerous advances for the city, including citywide paved streets, elevated railroads so vehicles and people could pass underneath, and a city sewage system.

The descendants of Colonel Lilly—particularly his grandson and namesake, Eli Lilly—would become vitally important not only to Trinity but to many other churches, the Diocese of Indianapolis, and The Episcopal Church.

In 1888, local attorney Benjamin Harrison was elected president of the United States. Harrison, a native of Ohio—and the grandson of U.S. president and victor at the Battle of Tippecanoe, William Henry Harrison—had moved to Indianapolis in 1854 to start his law practice. At the beginning of the Civil War, he joined the 70th Indiana Infantry. With the 70th Indiana, he fought in several battles and rose to the rank of brigadier general.

Also during this period, four other Hoosiers—Schuyler Colfax, Thomas A. Hendricks, Charles W. Fairbanks, and Thomas Riley Marshall—were elected as U.S. vice presidents. Fairbanks was honored by having the city

Christ Church on Governor's Circle, circa 1880s;
Plymouth Congregationalist Church
can be seen opposite on Meridian Street.
Bass Photo Co. Collection, Indiana Historical Society

of Fairbanks, Alaska, named after him while he was the senior U.S. senator from Indiana. His descendants became parishioners of the Church of the Advent and Trinity.

In 1888, the year Harrison was elected president, the new Union Station (which replaced Union Terminal) and the new Indiana Statehouse were completed. The historic Union Station remained in downtown Indianapolis into the twenty-first century, eventually housing a hotel and venues for special events. Its majestic red brick and granite head house has been recognized as one of the finest Romanesque Revival-styled structures in America.

The centerpiece of Indianapolis, the Soldiers and Sailors Monument, was constructed between 1888 and 1901 on the site of Alex-

Illustration of Union Station from the pamphlet, The Industries of the City of Indianapolis, *1889.*
Indiana Historical Society

ander Ralston's Governor's Circle, renamed Monument Circle in 1893. Originally intended to commemorate Hoosier veterans of the Civil War, the monument's design was expanded to incorporate tributes and statuary honoring the common soldiers and sailors from Indiana who had served in all of the wars of the United States up to that time. Also included were statues of Lieutenant Colonel George Rogers Clark, commander at the Battle of Vincennes, General William Henry Harrison, commander at the Battle of Tippecanoe, and Civil War Governor Oliver P. Morton. The laying of the cornerstone in 1889 was such an important event that President—and Civil War veteran from Indianapolis—Benjamin Harrison himself came to the ceremony to deliver a speech.

At the dedication ceremonies for the monument 13 years later on May 15, 1902, thousands of people attended a parade of veterans of the Mexican-American, Civil, and Spanish-American Wars; dignitaries made several speeches; Indianapolis poet James Whitcomb Riley gave a reading

The Soldiers and Sailors Monument
under construction, circa *1890; in the distance is*
the Indiana Statehouse, completed in 1888.
Bass Photo Co. Collection, Indiana Historical Society

of his poem written for the occasion, *The Soldier*; and John Philip Sousa, the famous composer and bandleader known as the March King, conducted a performance of a work he composed for the ceremony, *The Messiah of the Nations.* The Episcopal contribution to the event was an evening vesper service at Christ Church across the street, after which the church's bells pealed and its choir sang the patriotic anthem, *My Country, 'Tis of Thee.*

During this same time, the city expanded its educational and cultural offerings as well. In 1883, the Art Association of Indianapolis was formed largely through the efforts of women's rights activist and suffragette Mary Wright Sewall. In 1895, Indianapolis businessman John Herron bequeathed $225,000 ($6.8 million in 2019 dollars) to the Art Association of Indianapolis, stipulating that the money be used to build a museum and art school in his name. With Herron's gift, the John Herron Art Institute was formed in 1902. Its new buildings were completed at the corner of 16th and Pennsylvania Streets in 1906 and were designed, again, by the Vonnegut & Bohn architectural firm. The Art Association of Indianapolis opened its first permanent museum in 1906 at the Herron Institute.

*Dedication ceremonies for the
Soldiers and Sailors Monument, 1902.*
Bass Photo Co. Collection, Indiana Historical Society

In addition to fine arts, the economy also was thriving. The city soon became the center for the booming auto industry in the state. Eventually, more than 250 car and truck manufacturers would be founded and based in Indiana, 60 of them in Indianapolis. It would not take long for this new means of transportation to serve as the catalyst for the creation of the venue and event for which the city would become best known throughout the world.

In 1909, local businessmen Carl G. Fisher, James A. Allison, Frank H. Wheeler, and Arthur Newby purchased land west of the city for $72,000 ($2 million in 2019 dollars), invested an additional $250,000 of capital ($7 million in 2019 dollars), and built the Indianapolis Motor Speedway. With the huge number of car makers and suppliers in the city, Fisher proclaimed, "Indianapolis is going to be the world's greatest center of horseless carriage manufacturers. What could be more logical than building the world's greatest racetrack right here?" The 2.5-mile Speedway was completed as a test site for automobiles in September 1909. In its first two years of operation in 1909 and 1910, the Speedway also was the scene of a hot-air balloon race, motorcycle races, and more than 60 automobile races.

The construction of the Speedway had taken 500 laborers, 300 mules, and a fleet of steam-powered machinery. The track surface originally consisted of graded and packed soil covered by gravel, limestone covered with tar and oil, crushed stone chips covered with more tar and oil, and a final topping of crushed stone. Tests on the track caused concerns about the relatively soft surface, however. After a fatal accident during a 250-mile auto race believed to be caused by the surface, the entire track was paved with 3.2 million hand-laid bricks; hence, the Speedway's nickname, the Brickyard.

Poster for the opening of the Indianapolis Motor Speedway, Greatest Race Course in the World, *1909.*
Library of Congress

The first Indianapolis 500 was run on Memorial Day, May 30, 1911, with 40 cars entered and an estimated 80,000 spectators in attendance. The inaugural race was won by Ray Harroun at an average speed of nearly 75 miles per hour. His race car, the *Marmon Wasp*, had been built by the Indianapolis automobile manufacturer, the Marmon Motor Company. Every other car in the race carried not only the driver, naturally, but a riding mechanic as well. One of the jobs of the mechanic was to look back to see what was going on behind the car. Harroun decided to skip the mechanic to save weight and, in order to see behind him, installed on the *Wasp* the first rearview mirror in automotive history.

What Harroun's *Wasp* and all other cars in the race lacked, though, was any protection for the occupants. Drivers and mechanics wore no crash helmets, seat belts, or flameproof clothing. Death or serious injury in a wreck was almost a certainty. The courage it took to drive one of the early cars at the Speedway at top speeds close to 100 miles per hour is hard to imagine.

Other Indianapolis landmarks also came about at this time. The city's first skyscraper, the 17-story Merchants Bank Building on the southeast corner of Meridian Street and Washington Street, one block south of Monument

*Cars entering the first turn of the inaugural
Indianapolis 500, 1911; winner
Ray Harroun in the* Marmon Wasp.

Bass Photo Co. Collection, Indiana Historical Society

The Circle Theater with its original sign and clock, 1916.
Indiana Historical Society, P0174

Circle, was completed in 1913. (The Merchants Bank Building later was named the Barnes and Thornburg Building and housed the head office of the law firm, Barnes & Thornburg LLP.)

In 1916, the Circle Theatre, the first theater built in Indianapolis for the purpose of showing moving pictures, was completed. (The Circle Theatre later was named the Hilbert Circle Theatre and became the home of the Indianapolis Symphony Orchestra.) And in 1917, the Indianapolis Public Library's Central Library was constructed along St. Clair Street, where it continued to stand and serve the city into the twenty-first century.

In 1910, the Madam C.J. Walker Manufacturing Company, which made cosmetics and haircare products for African-American women, was incorporated in Indiana and its headquarters established in Indianapolis. The company's founder, Madam C.J. Walker, was born Sarah Breedlove in 1867 to freed slaves on a plantation in Mississippi. After her first husband died, she began her career selling cosmetics door-to-door. Madam Walker used her married name professionally after her second marriage to Charles Joseph Walker in 1906.

By the time Madam Walker moved to Indianapolis, she and her husband had divorced, and she had become not only the wealthiest African-American woman but the wealthiest self-made woman of any background in the country. She was a noted philanthropist, activist, and patron of the arts. Before her death in 1919, she started the development of the Madam C.J. Walker Theatre at 617 Indiana Avenue. The building (later renamed the Madam Walker Legacy Center) was completed in 1927 in an African–Art Deco style and continued to stand as a tribute to the barrier-breaking Madam Walker.

As the city grew, so did the Episcopal diocese. The wood-frame Grace Church on 16th Street built in 1866 had been the pro-cathedral of the Diocese of Indiana since 1886. Bishop John Hazen White's efforts to build a new cathedral in the late 1890s had ended in failure. By the end of the first decade of the twentieth century, however, the Diocese of Indianapolis determined that a proper cathedral was truly necessary. Construction of the new All Saints Cathedral began on the site of Grace Church in 1910, and the building was dedicated on All Saints Day, November 1, 1911. The 1912 Annual Convention of the Diocese of Indianapolis designated the new cathedral as "a House of Prayer, where all persons, of whatever race or nation, may have opportunity to worship God."

Madam C.J. Walker,
early twentieth-century America's most
successful self-made businesswoman.
Madam C.J. Walker Collection,
Indiana Historical Society

During the 1890s, 20 percent of the population of Indianapolis had been born in Germany, there were five daily German-language newspapers, and every city ordinance was published in both English and German. Proud German-Americans gathered at clubs like the iconic *Das Deutsche Haus* (The German House) on East Michigan Street, designed by Vonnegut & Bohn in the architectural style of the old country.

In 1914, Europe and parts of the rest of the world plunged into what first became known as the Great War and only later as World War I. When America entered the war in 1917, Indiana Governor James P. Goodrich set the tone for the state when he declared, "There can be no middle course in this war. There are just two kinds of people in America—patriots and

Das Deutsche Haus *with the flags of the United States
and the German Empire flying over its entrance,* circa *1905.*
Indiana Historical Society, P0411

traitors." The population of Indianapolis quickly turned from being isolationist and antiwar—and outwardly very German—to patriotically American and enthusiastically supportive of the U.S. war effort. In short order, German instruction was banned in many schools, German-language newspapers ceased publication, and German names of institutions were changed. By way of example, *Das Deutsche Haus* was renamed the Athenaeum.

After the United States entered the war in 1917, Bishop Joseph Marshall Francis announced at the Annual Convention of the Diocese of Indianapolis, "I ought to inform you that, acting under a compelling sense of duty, I have offered myself to the President of the United States for any service that the Government may think me capable of rendering." The government accepted his offer, and the 55-year-old bishop was sent to serve as a U.S. Army chaplain at Base Hospital No. 21 at Contrexeville, France.

The hospital, located in the foothills of the Vosges Mountains, 220 miles east of Paris and 50 miles behind the front lines, was created and funded by J.K. Lilly Sr., son of Colonel Eli Lilly and at that time president of Eli Lilly and Company, with the assistance of William Fortune, president of the Indianapolis Red Cross. (The family of William Fortune would later become parishioners at the Church of the Advent and Trinity.) In his eight and one-half months at the hospital, Bishop Francis witnessed unbelievable carnage but also great heroism. The doctors and nurses of the hospital treated 9,698 soldiers during the war while suffering only 118 deaths among its patients. Bishop Francis was awarded the Order of the Crown (French: *Ordre de la Couronne*; Flemish: *Kroonorde*) by the Kingdom of Belgium for his service at the hospital, being recognized "for personal generosity far beyond the call of duty."

One of Indianapolis's most notable connections to America's efforts in the Great War was Captain Edward V. "Eddie" Rickenbacker. Rickenbacker, a native of Columbus, Ohio, drove in several automobile races at the Indianapolis Motor Speedway, including the inaugural Indianapolis 500 in 1911 and each subsequent 500 mile race until the country's entry into the war. As a pursuit pilot in the 94th Aero Squadron of the U.S. Army Air Services—one of the only such pilots without a college degree—he was able to convert his car racing abilities into deadly aerial combat skills. Ultimately, Rickenbacker became the greatest American flying ace of World War I, shooting down 26 enemy aircraft in a little over six months. Awarded the Congressional Medal of Honor, the Distinguished Service Cross eight times, and the French *Légion d'honneur* and *Croix de Guerre*, Rickenbacker also was one of the most highly decorated Americans of World War I. (After the war, Rickenbacker was involved in many businesses and owned the Indianapolis Motor Speedway from 1927 until 1945, when he sold it to Tony Hulman.)

While World War I was still raging, the most severe pandemic since the Middle Ages broke out in waves in 1918, the waves continuing into 1919 and possibly 1920. The pandemic was caused by the H1N1 virus with genes showing it originated in birds. There was no consensus about the place where it originated, however. The most common theories were northern China, a British Army base in France, or a U.S. Army base in Kansas. The pandemic was commonly called the Spanish flu, although it

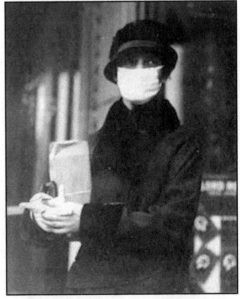

Indianapolis woman wearing a mask during the Spanish flu pandemic, 1918.
Indiana Historical Society, P0173 (image cropped).

undoubtedly did not start in Spain. It gained that name because, while censorship in warring nations blocked mention of the pandemic, the newspapers in neutral Spain had no such censorship and were free to report on it extensively, giving the false impression that Spain was particularly hard hit.

In the United States, the Spanish flu was first identified on military bases. The virus also was common among military personnel in Europe, whose immune systems were worn down by stress, malnutrition, exposure, filth, and vermin. The close quarters and massive troop movements common to wartime probably also increased the lethality of the virus. It struck hardest at young, healthy people between 15 and 45 years of age, people who commonly do not die from influenza, because a feature of the virus was that it caused the victim's immune system to work against itself. The Centers for Disease Control and Prevention (CDC) estimated that approximately 500 million people, or one-third of the world's population, became infected with the H1N1 virus. Estimates of deaths caused by the virus range from 17 million to 50 million worldwide and from 500,000 to 675,000 in the United States. What makes these staggering numbers even more horrifying is that the world's population in 1918 was less than a quarter of what it would be in 2019 and the nation's was less than a third.

In Indianapolis, the Spanish flu made its appearance at Fort Benjamin Harrison in September 1918. Fort Ben, as it was familiarly known, had been constructed a decade before just nine miles northeast of downtown Indianapolis for the purpose of stationing one infantry regiment. When America entered the Great War, the fort became an important training site for soldiers and served as a mobilization center for both Army and National Guard units. By September 1918, a major part of the fort was converted into a hospital for wounded soldiers from Indiana, Kentucky, and Illinois returning from the war, but the returning wounded soon became ill from the H1N1 virus. In only a few weeks, Indianapolis would be infected with more than 6,000 cases with Fort Benjamin Harrison caring for over 3,000 patients in a 300-bed facility. Hard work by the fort's medical staff and brave men and women volunteering as nurses converted a hospital designed for a few hundred injured men into a giant one caring for thousands.

In response to the pandemic, Dr. John Hurty, secretary of the Indiana Board of Health, advised Hoosiers to avoid crowds, avoid spitting on the sidewalks, stay in "splendid condition," "tone up our physical health," cover mouths when coughing, sleep in well-ventilated bedrooms, eat plain foods, and avoid meat and alcohol. Indianapolis Mayor Charles W. Jewett directed

Dr. Herman G. Morgan, secretary of the city's Board of Health, to order that all public places be cleaned and fumigated. People were discouraged from gathering in crowds and people with coughs were told to stay home. By October 1918, Dr. Morgan announced a sweeping order prohibiting gatherings of five or more persons, including at churches, schools, theaters, and funerals. Only gatherings connected to the war effort were exempt. Indianapolis streets became deserted, and the city took on the appearance of a ghost town.

By November 1918, the pandemic had run its course in Indianapolis. Schools reopened on November 4, and people with no symptoms were allowed to ride street cars and attend theaters. On November 11, the Armistice was signed ending the Great War. About 1,420 Hoosiers, 350 from Indianapolis, died in the war. The state's loss from the Spanish flu was much greater—3,266 Hoosiers according to the *Indianapolis Star*. Because many of those who died were young parents, 3,020 children were orphaned. Indianapolis, however, benefited from the leadership of the city and the state as well as cooperative citizens. The University of Michigan Center for the History of Medicine reported, "In the end, Indianapolis had an epidemic death rate of 280 per 100,000 people, one of the lowest in the nation" and attributed that to "how well Indianapolis as well as state officials worked together to implement community mitigation measures against influenza." Indianapolis leaders had presented a united front, commercial establishments had complied with restrictions despite the financial losses they endured, and brave men and women had volunteered their services to nurse victims of the Spanish flu at great risk to their own lives.

On May 7, 1919, some 15,000 to 20,000 Hoosier service members returning from Europe and carrying their regimental colors were led by the Purdue marching band for five miles to Monument Circle, past a crowd of 175,000 flag-waving and cheering spectators, past buildings festooned with red, white, and blue bunting, and through a replica of Paris's *Arc de Triomphe* constructed of plywood, chicken wire, and plaster. Many of those marching and spectating had survived the H1N1 virus, had nursed the sick, or lost a friend in the pandemic. Not a single newspaper article covering the parade mentioned the Spanish flu, however.

In the aftermath of the unimaginable horrors of World War I, monarchs and empires were toppled, colonies changed hands, new countries and borders were created, and economies and governments were set on the path to economic depression and dictatorship. Millions of combatants

*Returning soldiers marching past
Christ Church and around Monument Circle, 1919.*
Bass Photo Co. Collection, Indiana Historical Society

and non-combatants—primarily in Europe and the Middle East but also in Africa and Asia—had perished or were permanently injured. Although Indianapolis suffered few combat deaths from the war compared to those in the Civil War or later in World War II, the effects of World War I on the city also would be profound.

By this time, the state of Indiana had been in existence for barely more than 100 years, and in even less time Indianapolis had transformed from a swampy woodsy wilderness to the state's thriving political, cultural, and economic capital. The Episcopal Church, arriving late, had become firmly established as a small but mighty presence in the Hoosier heartland. The next 100 years would see wide swings in growth and progress for both the city and the Church. Those years also would witness the establishment of a new, farthest-north Episcopal parish that would struggle but become a stable boon of an ever-changing neighborhood.

Part Two

The Mission to the North: 1919–1949

The Church of the Advent
Trinity Episcopal Church

Chapter 5

A Time of Good and Evil:
1919–1929

After World War I, Indianapolis emerged as an even stronger economic power than it had been before. Its population had nearly doubled in 20 years, growing from 169,164 in 1900, to 233,650 in 1910, and to 314,194 in 1920.

Auto production in the state of Indiana and Indianapolis grew exponentially. By the 1920s, the value of automobiles manufactured in Indianapolis—nearly all of them ultra-high-end luxury vehicles—exceeded the value of those made in Detroit and would continue to do so until the Great Depression. Some of the major automakers headquartered in Indianapolis during this time included Marmon, Waverly, Premier, National, Overland, Cole, Pathfinder, Stutz, and Duesenberg.

*Hollywood icon Gary Cooper proudly posing
with his Indianapolis-built Duesenberg convertible.*
Auburn Cord Duesenberg Automobile Museum

49

During the 1920s, Indianapolis was still a major railroad hub, but in 1929 the city bought nearly 1,000 acres on the west side for the purpose of building Indianapolis Municipal Airport. Airline traffic first operated from the airport two years later in 1931. The airport was renamed Weir Cook Airport in 1944 in honor of Colonel H. Weir Cook, a Hoosier World War I flying ace who helped select the site and who was killed in a plane crash during World War II. (The airport again would be renamed Indianapolis International Airport in 1976.)

The 1920s saw the creation of two establishments that would benefit Hoosier children for many decades: Riley Hospital for Children was completed in 1924, and the Indianapolis Children's Museum was founded by Mary Stewart Carey in 1925.

Even though the Midwest's culture of the early twentieth century would be criticized and satirized by many native Midwestern authors, Indianapolis had become something of a cultural center. Indianapolis was the home base for a well-respected group of visual artists, the Hoosier Group, whose members T.C. Steele, William Forsyth, J. Ottis Adams, Otto Stark, and Richard Gruelle created an indigenous school of impressionism. Indianapolis boasted several famous authors, as well, led by poet James Whitcomb Riley and novelist Booth Tarkington, a Pulitzer Prize winner in 1919 and 1922.

The 1920s, however, also left a permanent scar on the reputation of the Hoosier capital and state. Shortly after World War I, the Ku Klux Klan began its ominous and ignominious rise to become the dominant state and city political power for a number of years. Indeed, the Indiana Klan in the 1920s was the largest, most powerful Klan organization in America.

The Ku Klux Klan organized its first office in Indianapolis in 1921. Within a short time, the official membership of the Klan may have included as many as 40 percent of white Protestant men in Indianapolis, including Methodists, Presbyterians, Baptists, and Disciples of Christ. Women were not innocent of Klan involvement: an organization known as Women of the Ku Klux Klan also existed and may have been as large. In the state and national elections of 1924, a Klansman, Edward L. Jackson, was elected governor of Indiana, full Klan-endorsed slates of state officials and legislators were elected, and all but a few congressional representatives from Indiana were Klan-supported.

One target of the Ku Klux Klan, of course, was the city's African-American population. This community was in the process of doubling in size, from about 22,000 in 1910 to 44,000 by 1930, making it one of the largest African-American populations in any northern U.S. city at that time. Although

Ku Klux Klan cross burning in Indianapolis, 1924.
Bass Photo Co. Collection, Indiana Historical Society

the Indianapolis public schools were racially integrated before the Klan's rise to power, the Klan's influence caused the schools to become racially segregated in 1927. The newly created and completely segregated Crispus Attucks High School became the only high school available in Indianapolis for African-American students.

But the Klan's efforts to discriminate, intimidate, and terrorize were not limited just to African-Americans. The 1920s version of the Klan also was anti-immigrant, anti-Semitic, and anti-Catholic. Catholics, who by the 1920s numbered about 60,000 in the city, were primarily from northern Europe, particularly Germany and Ireland, and so were no different racially than the members of the Klan. Nevertheless, many Protestants in Indianapolis were hostile to Catholics due to paranoid fear of them being controlled by an authoritarian and inquisitorial Pope. In general, the Klan and its members were actively hostile to anyone who was not white, native-born, English-speaking, and Protestant.

Through all of this, Episcopalians in Indianapolis behaved more admirably than did other Protestants. For one, Episcopal churches in the city had a lower percentage of members involved in the Klan than any other mainline

Protestant denomination. Moreover, and more importantly, the Episcopal Diocese of Indianapolis was the only mainline Protestant organization in the entire state that took a strong stand against the Ku Klux Klan.

In the fall of 1922, the Federal Council of Churches, representing 30 denominations and 20,000,000 members, passed a resolution condemning masked and secret bodies without referring to the Ku Klux Klan by name. Just a few months later, on January 26, 1923, at the close of its annual two-day business session, the diocesan council of the Diocese of Indianapolis adopted a resolution calling out by name and strongly condemning the Klan. The resolution, which was reported in the local media, read:

> *As representatives of the Protestant Episcopal church of the diocese of Indianapolis in annual council assembled, we feel that we should be false to our Christian profession if we failed to record our strong disapproval and condemnation of the Ku Klux Klan, and all other secret political societies as un-American, and as a menace to peace and order, and to social security and well-being. The so-called enforcement of law and the attempted regulation of community morals by bands of masked and hooded men can accomplish no good, but, on the contrary, are bound to work great harm. Under such cover there is afforded abundant opportunity to wreak private vengeance and to satisfy private grudges.*
>
> *We further deplore and denounce the appeal to religious and racial prejudice and hatred as political motives. Nothing could be more un-Christian. Our religion, as we understand it, is not Protestant nor Roman Catholic, but Christian. The apostolic principle has never been repealed. It is as follows: "Lie not to one another, seeing that ye have put off the old man with his deeds; and have put on the new man, which is renewed in knowledge after the image of him that created him; where there is neither Greek nor Jew, circumcision nor uncircumcision, Barbarian, Scythian, bond nor free; but Christ is all, and in all." The rule for all Christians, of whatever variety, is: "Let every one [sic] that nameth the name of Christ depart from iniquity." This church has a well-earned reputation for broadness and toleration, and also for proud Americanism, which it must maintain. By the very law of its life, therefore, it is bound to condemn the Ku Klux*

Klan, its narrow intolerance and un-Americanism and the class spirit which it fosters, and which is a menace to liberty and to free and democratic institutions.

No other mainline Protestant denomination in Indiana did anything like this in opposition to the Klan. Indeed, other such denominations at best did nothing and at worst provided membership, supported the Klan's principles, and took positions that were consistent with the Klan's view of a besieged white Protestant America.

Fortunately, the Klan's power in Indiana and the nation began to decline in the middle of the decade. In 1925, the head of Indiana's Ku Klux Klan, Grand Dragon D.C. Stephenson, was convicted of the kidnapping, rape, and second-degree murder of a young Indianapolis woman, Madge Oberholtzer, and sentenced to life in prison. Stephenson's trial, conviction, and sentence did much to disrepute the Klan's leadership. While in prison, Stephenson naturally expected a pardon from Indiana Governor Ed Jackson, whose nomination and election had been backed by the Klan. When that pardon did not occur, the outraged and vengeful Stephenson readily provided damning information to the newspapers about his involvement in Indiana politics. The resulting news coverage brought an abrupt end to the political careers of Governor Jackson and Indianapolis Mayor John L. Duvall, both of whom resigned in disgrace.

Indeed, Indianapolis's newspapers were crucial to the demise of the Klan as a state power. Numerous local city publications reported diligently on the corruption, political influence, and bigotry of the Klan. The leader in this was the *Indianapolis Times*, which in 1928 won a Pulitzer Prize for its four years of investigative reporting on the Klan. By that year, the Klan had ceased to be an effective political force in Indiana and throughout most of the rest of the nation. Nevertheless, racial and ethnic discrimination would continue to stain the state's culture in the years to come.

Chapter 6

Advent at 33rd and Meridian: 1919–1929

It was into this time of good and evil that Trinity Episcopal Church, Indianapolis, came into being under its original name, the Church of the Advent. By the end of World War I, less than 100 years after being platted, Indianapolis had grown northward past 38th Street, more than three miles beyond the original vision of Alexander Ralston. Mapleton, a village formed *circa* 1871 in the vicinity of the intersection of 38th and Meridian Streets, was annexed by Indianapolis in 1902.

In 1908, the city of Indianapolis hired the German-born, American-raised, and German-trained city planner and landscape architect George E. Kessler to improve its new park system. Kessler was a prodigious talent: in his 41-year career, he completed more than 200 projects and prepared plans for 26 communities, 26 park and boulevard systems, 49 parks, 46 estates and residences, and 26 schools. His projects are located in 23 states and 100 cities.

After a year studying Indianapolis's transportation system, waterways, and existing parks, Kessler submitted his Indianapolis Park and Boulevard Plan in 1909. The waterways of Indianapolis—the White River, the Central Canal, Fall Creek, Pogue's Run, Pleasant Run, and Eagle Creek—were the key components of the plan, and landscaped boulevards and attractive bridges linked the parks together. Twelve city parks—including Garfield Park, Brookside Park, Riverside Park, Military Park, and University Park—were part of Kessler's original plan. Other smaller parks were added later.

The city adopted Kessler's Park and Boulevard Plan, and Kessler led the Indianapolis Parks Commission from 1909–1915 while the plan was executed. Several wide, beautiful bridges were built across Fall Creek. Two of his major thoroughfares north were Fall Creek Parkway and Meridian Street.

In time, the neighborhood bordered by Meridian Street on the west, 38th Street on the north, and Fall Creek Parkway on the south became known as Mapleton-Fall Creek in homage to the small village that once had been at the northern end of the neighborhood and to the waterway that flowed along the southern edge.

The new thoroughfares designed by Kessler allowed residents of the northern extremities of Indianapolis to travel easily by automobile over bridges across Fall Creek. The combination of cars and bridges contributed to the rapid growth of the area north of the city, far from the stench, soot, and noise of the factories, railroads, and stockyards downtown. Commercial nodes consisting of restaurants and shops developed along major roadways, including 38th and Meridian Streets. Attracted to the tree-lined streets in the former village of Mapleton, affluent residents of Indianapolis—industrialists, professionals, and merchants, in general the foremost financially-successful *belle monde* in the community—located and built stately homes in the area in a variety of styles, including Tudor Revival, Colonial Revival, and Arts and Crafts.

George B. Kessler, circa *1910s.*
Landmarks Association of St. Louis, Inc.

At this time, no officially sanctioned Episcopal parish existed farther north in Indianapolis than All Saints Cathedral at 16th Street. St. David's, formed through the initiative of members of Grace Church and Christ Church and attended by High Anglican Episcopalians, had struggled to survive for about 10 years at 21st and Talbot Streets but eventually had closed its doors due to financial difficulties.

Kessler's decorative Meridian Street Bridge
over Fall Creek, completed in 1917.
Bass Photo Co. Collection, Indiana Historical Society

Bishop Joseph Marshall Francis returned to Indianapolis after his service in World War I and considered what to do about the northward migration of Episcopalians he encountered. In 1904, having previously foreseen this movement, he had initiated a purchase by the diocese of a lot at the corner of 30th and Pennsylvania Streets for the purpose of building a new church there, but the diocese sold the property a few years later due to a lack of support for that idea. In 1918, Bishop Francis approached the diocesan council and again suggested starting a new parish in what by that time had become the northern suburbs of the city.

Aquilla Q. Jones, a prominent Indianapolis attorney, the chancellor and a trustee of the diocese, a member of the diocesan Finance Committee, and a resident of the northern suburbs, volunteered to lead the Mission to the North project. A veteran of more than 40 years of legal practice, Mr. Jones was the senior partner of the Indianapolis law firm, Jones, Hammond, Buschmann & Boyd, and concentrated his practice in business and probate law. He also served as president of the Indianapolis Bar Association in 1918.

On January 16, 1919, Mr. Jones took the first step in the Mission to the North project by purchasing land from the Indiana Baptist Convention at the southeast corner of 33rd and Meridian Streets, the address of which

was 3261 North Meridian Street, Indianapolis, Indiana. The land contained 100 feet of frontage on Meridian Street and 189 feet of frontage east on 33rd Street. The cost of the land and improvements was $13,000 ($192,000 in 2019 dollars), payable in installments.

On the property stood an abandoned Baptist church made of brick and timber with a seating capacity of about 250. The church had been founded in 1898 as University Place Baptist Church by Rev. Cincinnatus Hamilton McDowell, who became its pastor. The church went out of existence in late 1918 for reasons that are not clear. The vacant church building included pews, chairs, and carpeting, but no organ.

Aquilla Q. Jones,
leader of the Mission to the North and
Advent's first senior warden, circa 1920s.
Indiana Historical Society

Furnishings for the new Episcopal church on the site, including the altar, altar appointments, and a pipe organ, were donated by parishioners of the failed High Anglican St. David's. The layout of the church building required the altar to be on the south side of the sanctuary, which was wider than it was long, an unusual arrangement for an Episcopal church. But the availability of an existing building and used furnishings speeded the readying of the church for its new congregation.

On March 23, 1919, over 60 students began Sunday school classes in the yet-to-be-named church at 33rd and Meridian. One week later, William W. Hammond, secretary of the diocese, treasurer of the Mission to the North project, and law partner of Aquilla Q. Jones, suggested naming the church the Church of the Advent because, as he said, "this is a coming church."

The Church of the Advent, circa *1920s.*
Trinity Episcopal Church

On Palm Sunday, April 6, 1919, the first worship service was held in the new Church of the Advent, using a former High Anglican altar in a former Baptist building. In attendance was a total of more than 250 congregants, including the 27 founding members of Advent—men and women—who had come from Christ Church, All Saints Cathedral, and St. David's. Eighty students filled the Sunday school.

At that first service, the Rev. Charles E. Bishop from Sturgis, Michigan, was installed as rector of Advent by Bishop Francis. At the same time, Charles H. Abbett, the young son of Advent parishioners, became the first person baptized in the new church. The new rector's first sermon was on the daunting subject, "The Lord, Thy God, is a Jealous God." As we will see, Rev. Bishop's tenure at Advent would be brief.

On April 22, 1919, the Altar Guild was organized. On April 28, the first nine-man vestry was elected. (Women were not permitted to serve on the vestry until 1962.) Two of the new vestry members were Aquilla Q. Jones, who also served as the first senior warden, and William W. Hammond, who also served as the first junior warden. A point of pride for Advent—and, by extension, Trinity—was that the church's first two wardens, Mr. Jones and

Mr. Hammond, both were officers of the diocesan council that adopted the resolution condemning the Ku Klux Klan in 1923 described in Chapter 5.

On April 29, 1919, the day after the vestry was elected, the women of the parish formed the first Women's Guild, which would be devoted to money-making and service projects. Many other guilds and organizations organized and run by women at the church would follow. Indeed, the women of the parish would be of paramount importance in holding things together during the entire precarious history of the Church of the Advent.

The 1919 parish report showed a congregation of 148 communicants, 235 baptized persons, and a Sunday school of 175 pupils. The Episcopal parish at 33rd and Meridian Streets was launched.

Beginning in the 1920s and through the 1940s, the neighborhood surrounding the Church of the Advent would become home to the wealthy and socially elite of Indianapolis. As it turned out, other Protestant denominations also saw the need to expand to the new northern suburbs. Our Redeemer Lutheran Church was founded in 1920 on Park Avenue. Tabernacle Presbyterian Church, founded as Third Presbyterian Church in downtown Indianapolis in 1851 and renamed in 1883, moved in 1921 to 34th Street and Central Avenue. Broadway Methodist Church (later renamed Broadway United Methodist Church) was founded in 1925 on East 29th Street.

The beginnings of the Church of the Advent in this posh neighborhood, however, were anything but encouraging. For one thing, the parish suffered a constantly revolving door with its rectors, going through four rectors in eight years: the first rector, Rev. Bishop, who lasted less than 12 months; the Rev. George H. Richardson, who lasted a little over two years; the Rev. Albert L. Longley, who lasted not quite seven months; and the Rev. Clarence W. Bispham, who served for three years before resigning in 1927 because of ill health. Rev. Bispham apparently was much loved by the congregation, however, and the parish stayed in contact with and continued to honor him until his death in 1929.

Whether the parish cared to admit it or not, it struggled financially despite being located in an affluent area. To be a parish in the Diocese of Indianapolis under the Constitution and Canons of the diocese adopted in 1918, a congregation had to be self-supporting. On April 8, 1919, two days after the first service in the church, the members of the new congregation at the Church of the Advent resolved to be a self-supporting parish. While, strictly speaking, the parish did stay self-supporting, it was forced to resort to a number of, it could be said, creative ways of doing so. These included not paying diocesan assessments and regularly cutting (or simply postponing) the pay of the rector on an as-needed basis. The parish also used more standard ways of staying self-supporting, such as borrowing money from lending institutions and requesting special pledges.

In March 1923, the Women's Guild contributed $3,000 ($45,000 in 2019 dollars) as a down payment for the purchase of the house immediately south of the church building on Meridian Street. A proposal that the house be used as a residence for the rector was protested by the Women's Guild, whose members urged that it be used as a parish house for all members of the church. The Guild's wishes were followed. Upon the closing of the purchase of the parish house, the Women's Guild took charge of paying for the house's maintenance and repairs and continued to do so until the 1940s.

In 1926, the principal founder of the parish and the first senior warden, Aquilla Q. Jones, died at age 73. William W. Hammond, Mr. Jones's law partner in Jones, Hammond, Buschmann & Boyd and the person who had suggested the name of the parish, became the new senior warden, a position he would hold until 1953—an astonishingly long period of 27 years.

In 1928, the parish finally called a rector with staying power. The Very Rev. George S. Southworth, dean of St. Paul's Cathedral, Marquette, Michigan, accepted the call by the vestry of the Church of the Advent. He would remain the rector for 14 years.

Despite the upheavals in clergy and scarcity of funds experienced by the Church of the Advent in the 1920s, the church adequately served its function as a neighborhood church for the northern suburbanites of Indianapolis. In addition to the Women's Guild, the parish organized a Men's Club and a full men and boys choir and, in addition, took over the sponsorship of Boy Scout Troop 80.

Nevertheless, just as the parish was beginning to experience some financial stability, in March 1929 the vestry appointed a committee to confer with Bishop Francis and a committee from St. Paul's on the proposition that the parishes of Advent and St. Paul's be merged. Negotiations concerning the merger continued throughout the following months. No acceptable basis for a merger was ever agreed upon, however. Some wags joked that the reason was that Advent approved of baseball on Sundays while St. Paul's did not. The real reason, however, seems to have been the onslaught of the Great Depression.

Advent's men and boys choir, 1922;
the Rev. George H. Richardson,
second rector of Advent, stands on the left.
Trinity Episcopal Church

Chapter 7

The City and Advent in Crisis:
1930–1939

Indianapolis suffered much during the Great Depression. The city's economy had been exceptionally strong throughout the decade of the 1920s, and there was close to full employment in 1929. The city's population had grown slightly to 364,161 by 1930. In that Depression year, though, employment in the city had dropped to 17 percent below the peak 1929 employment level, slightly worse than the national average of 15 percent. In 1931, most workers still employed were working part time, and employment had fallen to 25 percent below 1929 levels.

The hardest years in Indianapolis during this time were 1932–1933. By 1932, the rate of employment had shrunk to 30 percent below that of 1929, and by 1933 it was 37 percent below. In early 1933, the Indiana General Assembly created the Governor's Commission on Unemployment Relief. By the fall of that year, early New Deal programs were beginning to have a positive impact on the local economy. By July 1934, employment had climbed back to just 20 percent below the 1929 peak.

In many respects, Indianapolis suffered less than other Midwest cities thanks to its diversified economic base. Nevertheless, a catastrophic loss to Indianapolis during the Depression was the collapse of its great automobile manufacturing industry. In 1986, *American Heritage* magazine listed the 10 greatest cars ever made in America. Three of these were made in Indianapolis during the Depression: the 1931 Marmon V-16, the 1932 Duesenberg Model SJ, and the 1932 Stutz DV-32.

Unfortunately for Indianapolis, its auto industry concentrated largely on handcrafted luxury cars for the high-end market. In 1935, the Stutz Motor Car Company of Indianapolis was building some of the finest luxury automobiles in the world, yet the company could sell a total of only six cars in that Depression-ravaged year. Detroit, on the other hand, focused on mass-produced cars for the middle- and low-end markets. As a result, Detroit's auto industry survived the Depression, and Indianapolis's did not. The Indianapolis Motor Speedway and the Indianapolis 500 remained after the Depression as testaments to the force that the auto industry had been in the city's development, but manufacturers such as Marmon, Stutz, and Duesenberg were gone forever, and their names would fade into legend.

Compared to the rest of the country, however, Indianapolis's eventual recovery from the Depression was very slow. The leadership of Indianapolis was staunchly conservative and anti-New Deal and, with long-term disastrous effects for the city, was determined to oppose federal funding for Indianapolis for the next 30 years.

Miraculously, a critically important organization for the good of the city and state emerged during this time of total dependence on the private sector. In 1936 while on holiday at the family's cottage on Lake Wawasee in northern Indiana, Eli Lilly—the bespectacled 51-year-old grandson of Colonel Eli Lilly—suggested to his 74-year-old father, J.K. Lilly Sr., and his 42-year-old younger brother, J.K. Lilly Jr., that they start a charitable foundation to continue the family tradition of being generous in public affairs. In 1937, the three men founded Lilly Endowment, Inc., with a gift of Eli Lilly and Company stock valued at $262,500 ($4.7 million in 2019 dollars). Over time, Lilly family members would contribute to the Endowment additional stock

Eli Lilly, grandson of Colonel Eli Lilly and elder son of J.K. Lilly Sr., circa 1930s.
Lilly Endowment, Inc.

worth hundreds of millions of dollars. Since its inception, the Endowment has granted nearly $10 billion to close to 10,000 organizations—a very large number of them in the state of Indiana and the city of Indianapolis.

At the time he proposed the idea for the Lilly Endowment, Eli Lilly was president of Eli Lilly and Company and later would become chairman of the company. He also was a life-long Episcopalian and devoted member of Christ Church parish. Eventually, he would play a monumental role in the history of Trinity Episcopal Church, Indianapolis, and The Episcopal Church locally and nationally.

As the Depression raged, another organization also emerged and quickly became one of the crown jewels of the city's cultural life. The Indianapolis Symphony Orchestra (ISO) was founded in 1930 by Ferdinand Schaefer, a local violin professor, with the help of Leonard A. Strauss, who became the first president of the ISO. In 1937, the ISO hired Fabien Sevitzky as the orchestra's first music director. Sevitzky was born in Russia into the Koussevitzky family. His uncle was the longtime and world-famous Boston Symphony Orchestra conductor, Serge Koussevitzky. When Uncle Serge learned that his nephew Fabien had landed his own conducting position, the uncle made the nephew shorten his name to Sevitzky to "avoid confusion." Under Maestro Sevitzky, the ISO quickly ascended to national prominence and issued a series of phonograph recordings on RCA Victor and Capitol Records in the 1940s and early 1950s.

Meanwhile, the situation at the Church of the Advent was growing dire. To the extent the church had financial difficulties during the prosperous

Indianapolis Symphony Orchestra
syndicated radio broadcast advertisement, 1938.
Indiana Historical Society, M0614

1920s, the difficulties became desperate in the depressed early 1930s. One of the ideas proposed in 1932 by Advent's rector, Rev. George Southworth, gives an idea of the challenging times that the parish experienced. The proposal, called a Mile of Pennies, consisted of collecting penny cards holding enough pennies to stretch a mile. The rector's thinking was that a mile of such cards would hold $844.80 of pennies, enough to pay either the diocesan assessment or the interest on the mortgage for the summer. Unfortunately, the penny cards cost 3¢ each and held only 16¢. The idea was, in the words of eminent Trinity leader and historian Bill Ehrich, "a complete bomb [that] produced nothing for the dismal finances of the parish."

The written records indicate that the real leadership of the Church of the Advent at this time came not from the rector, Rev. Southworth, but from laity within the parish. Some of the key providers of this leadership were the senior and junior wardens, William W. Hammond and Henry W. Bliss, and, in the summer of 1933, a new parishioner, Dr. Walter A. Jamieson, chair of the church's Finance Committee.

When Dr. Jamieson took charge of the parish finances, Advent was in arrears $3,400 ($67,000 in 2019 dollars), including money owed to the rector, two years of diocesan assessments, and interest on the mortgage. Foreclosure of the parish's mortgage appeared to be imminent. Under Dr. Jamieson's leadership, the Finance Committee drew up a plan that included arranging for about 30 people to make special pledges, convincing the other parishioners to continue their pledges, and persuading the parish's mortgagee to reduce interest on the mortgage by a full point.

The Church of the Advent's slogan during this time was, "Religion costs money—Irreligion costs more!" The Finance Committee's proactive measures resulted in the parish averting foreclosure in 1933 and meeting its financial obligations within two years thereafter. From that point on, Advent's financial health continued to improve steadily.

Despite the financial difficulties faced by the parish, in other ways the 1930s were relatively good times for the Church of the Advent. Members of the parish suffered less unemployment than other congregations—undoubtedly due to the affluence of the parish as a whole. The Bible class taught by Senior Warden Hammond continued to thrive. The Sunday school grew to have the second largest enrollment in the diocese. In November 1934, Advent's rector, Rev. Southworth, praised the parish: "Your church has continued every phase of church activity during the last five years of financial depression."

*Advent's junior choir, 1935; the Rev. George S. Southworth,
fifth rector of Advent, stands on the left.*
Trinity Episcopal Church

The Women's Guild, the Mothers' Guild, and the Women's Auxiliary devoted many hours of service to helping the community during the Great Depression. In 1933 and 1934, the Women's Auxiliary contributed great numbers of garments to the Red Cross, raised funds in various ways including making and selling hundreds of pounds of mincemeat at Christmas, and supported families with donations of clothing, food, and toys during the holidays. By 1939, when the Church of the Advent celebrated its twentieth anniversary, 19 different parish organizations were functioning.

In 1937, the Church of the Advent began plans for a comprehensive remodeling of the interior of the church building with the help of architect Ernest R. Steeg. The altar was moved from the south side to the east side of the church, pews were rearranged to face east, and a simple rood screen was created with choir pews on either side of the chancel, the part of the church nearest the altar. The remodeling was completed in late 1937. At last, the church looked more traditionally Episcopal. On December 26, 1937, Bishop Joseph Marshall Francis blessed the remodeled and refurbished Church of the Advent.

By 1938, Bishop Francis was becoming seriously ill. Because Episcopal affiliation in rural parts of the state had never gained traction, there were appeals in some places to recombine the Diocese of Indianapolis and the Diocese of Northern Indiana. Bishop Francis, however, worked to keep the two dioceses separate, mainly for the reason that he and other clergy in the

Interior of the Church of the Advent after remodeling, 1937.
Trinity Episcopal Church

southern diocese objected to what they regarded as the excessively High Church style of their counterparts in northern Indiana.

On February 8, 1939, with Bishop Francis in failing health and at his urging, the Diocese of Indianapolis elected a new bishop coadjutor, the Rev. Richard Ainslie Kirchhoffer, rector of Christ Church, Mobile, Alabama. Based on the new bishop coadjutor's last name, most Hoosiers would think that he was of German heritage. Bishop Coadjutor Kirchhoffer, however, was born in Canada to parents who had emigrated from Ireland. One of his grandfathers and two of his great-grandfathers had been priests in the Anglican Church of Ireland. Throughout his life, his speech carried a bit of Irish brogue that he had picked up from his parents, and those close to him called him by his Irish-derived nickname, "Mac."

On February 13, Bishop Francis died, and Bishop Coadjutor Kirchhoffer succeeded as bishop of Indianapolis, only five days after his consecration as bishop coadjutor. Bishop Francis, the prime mover in the creation of the Church of the Advent at 33rd and Meridian Streets, had been bishop of Indianapolis for 40 years, over half of his lifetime. At the time of his consecration, he was the youngest member of the House of Bishops; when he died, only the bishop of Alaska was older.

The Rt. Rev. B.F.P. Irvins, D.D., bishop of Milwaukee in 1939, wrote this about Bishop Francis:

As a Churchman and a Bishop his great love for his Lord and his devotion to the Church, and his zeal for souls made him early in his career a trusted leader and a wise counselor. . . . Somehow the Church does not seem to be producing men of his type now, and he will be sorely missed in its councils. His friends too will miss him, his genial personality, his firm hand-grasp, and his quick and ready service, his twinkling eye, and his warm heart.

Although Bishop Kirchhoffer's consecration on February 8, 1939, was held at St. Paul's in downtown Indianapolis, the bishop and his family would make the Church of the Advent their new church home.

Chapter 8

The Last Decade of Advent: 1940–1949

In the waning years of the Great Depression, the drums of war were sounding again in Europe and Asia. In 1940, the population of Indianapolis was 386,972, just slightly more than it had been 10 years before. Prior to 1941, Indianapolis was the capital of a state with fiercely isolationist politics. After Japan attacked Pearl Harbor on December 7, 1941, however, the people and leaders of Indianapolis became tremendously patriotic, just as they had when the United States entered the First World War.

Training for tank support of infantry at Fort Benjamin Harrison, 1943.

Indiana Historical Society, P0569 (image cropped)

The Second World War brought numerous changes to the city. Fort Benjamin Harrison on the northeast side again sprang into action, its Induction and Reception Center becoming the largest in the country. Fort Ben, of course, provided basic training for troops bound overseas, but it also housed the U.S. Army Finance Center, a chaplain's school, the Finance Replacement Training Center, a school for cooks and bakers, a 2,000 bed hospital, and the Midwest Branch of the U.S. Disciplinary Barracks (i.e., a military prison).

In addition, Stout Army Air Field, on the west side of the city just east of Indianapolis Municipal Airport, provided a troop carrier command and paratrooper training school, and the Heslar Naval Armory, on West 30th Street by the east bank of the White River, housed a school for radio operators. During the war, an estimated six million military personnel passed through the city.

While the war went on, food and other essential items were rationed for civilians, and various black markets developed for scarce goods. But, when patriotic feelings prevailed, there also were numerous drives to collect materials necessary for the war effort, including silk, scrap metal, kitchen fat, rubber, books, and blood. In addition, residents volunteered to perform necessary services and bought war bonds during eight war bond drives.

The city and state economies were shifted into high gear by necessary war production. Indianapolis became one of the top 10 cities, and Indiana

Hoosiers buying war bonds at Indiana National Bank, 1943.
Indiana Historical Society, P0569

became one of the top four states in America for the production of the equipment, goods, and material required by the United States to carry on the war against the Axis powers.

In addition to this economic growth, the nature of the workforce itself changed dramatically. By 1943, one third of the state's factory workers were women. Unfortunately, racial minorities were not accepted into the workforce as readily as white women. Although RCA Corporation's massive electronics plant on the east side of Indianapolis hired many African-Americans during World War II, few other Indianapolis companies followed its lead. Racial prejudice remained pronounced and, indeed, perhaps worsened.

Immediately after World War II, Indianapolis was bigger, more modern, more industrial, and somewhat more cosmopolitan than before. It also faced new problems, however, such as racial discrimination, housing shortages, and juvenile delinquency. The many accomplishments of Indianapolis during the war years of 1941–1945 would be frustrated by these and other problems inadequately dealt with by the city's leaders for the next 20 years. As a result, Indianapolis unfortunately would slide backward from its formerly prominent position in many different and important ways.

World War II also greatly affected the Church of the Advent. More than 100 Advent parishioners served in the U.S. Armed Forces during the war; seven parishioners gave their lives in the conflict. The church was the site for regular Red Cross and Civilian Defense meetings. The parish's outreach activities centered on work supporting the nation's fight in Europe and Asia.

In 1940, the Women's Guild renamed itself St. Catherine's Guild, and four years later the Women's Auxiliary and St. Catherine's Guild merged. During the war, either separately or united, the women's guilds provided food for service members away from home, knitted afghans for service members in hospitals, served dinner to service members at Christ Church on Sunday evenings, made pies and cakes for the USO, sewed

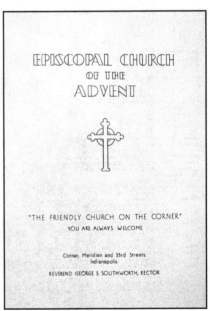

Church of the Advent bulletin cover, 1942.
Trinity Episcopal Church

garments for Russian relief efforts, and contributed funds to furnish the chapel at Camp Atterbury, a massive combat training site and prisoner of war internment compound in Johnson County, south of Indianapolis.

In May 1942, Advent's rector, Rev. George Southworth, submitted his resignation in order to devote more time to writing. This loss brought about yet another discussion regarding a merger of Advent with St. Paul's. Indianapolis had continued to grow northward. Advent was without a rector, and St. Paul's was planning to move from downtown, at the corner of New York and Illinois Streets, uptown to the corner of 61st and Meridian Streets, approximately three miles north of the Church of the Advent's location at 33rd and Meridian Streets. The proposal was for the two parishes to move to a new building to be constructed at the end of the war and for the resulting merged parish to be called St. Paul's.

At the vote on the proposal, 161 Advent parishioners voted to stay independent, 92 parishioners voted for the merger, and 67 parishioners voted to do whatever the vestry decided. At the end of 1942, the vestry determined to

The Rt. Rev. Richard Ainslie Kirchhoffer, seventh bishop of
Indianapolis; the Rev. Thomas R. Thrasher, sixth rector of
Advent; and William W. Hammond,
second senior warden of Advent, circa 1942.
Trinity Episcopal Church

remain unaffiliated with St. Paul's and called the Rev. Thomas R. Thrasher, the rector of St. Peter's, Columbia, Tennessee, to be the sixth rector of the Church of the Advent.

By 1945, the Church of the Advent was close to paying off its mortgage. With the end of its indebtedness in sight, the parish started a fund for a new church building to replace the brick and frame structure purchased in 1919. When Advent at last made its final mortgage payment in October 1945, the parishioners celebrated at a dinner at the Riviera Club on North Illinois Street during which they ceremoniously burned the mortgage agreement. By December 1945, the building fund had grown to $13,321 ($175,000 in 2019 dollars).

Another merger plan was discussed in 1945, this time between the Church of the Advent and All Saints Cathedral. Advent was on the rise, and All Saints was not. Moreover, Bishop Richard Ainslie Kirchhoffer, himself a member of Advent, saw advantages to the cathedral of the diocese moving to Advent's location on Meridian Street.

At a joint vestry meeting of the two parishes, the Advent representatives accepted the merger plan as proposed, and the All Saints representatives accepted the plan with modifications. The proposal was printed and sent to members of both parishes. At meetings of both sets of members, however, the merger proposal was defeated. Once again, the Church of the Advent remained independent; it also may have lost a chance to become the cathedral of the diocese.

After the end of the Second World War in 1946, the Church of the Advent took part with Episcopal churches across the nation in The Episcopal Church's Reconstruction and Advance Fund, which was being raised to help rebuild churches devastated during the war. Advent was given a quota of $3,200 to raise and responded by raising $3,900 ($51,000 in 2019 dollars), 22 percent more than its goal.

With the end of the war and the return home of men and women who had served in the military, parish membership grew more in 1946 than in any previous year. New committees were formed to deal with the increase, including planning, records, education, publicity, and public relations committees. As in the past, lay leadership continued to be a hallmark of Advent. Parish leaders not only served on the vestry but also chaired and served on numerous committees related to finances, including those in charge of raising money for the Reconstruction and Advance Fund, paying off Advent's mortgage, and the new building fund.

By the end of 1946, the building fund had grown to $21,113 ($277,000 in 2019 dollars). The plans drawn up for a new building, however, led to the departure of Rev. Thrasher. Although he was extremely popular and regarded as an excellent priest, Rev. Thrasher made it clear that he had no enthusiasm for being involved in a major construction project and resigned in 1947 to accept a call from the Church of the Ascension, Montgomery, Alabama.

Four key Advent lay leaders of the 1940s–early1950s: front, left to right, Willis B. Conner, Jr., and Raymond F. Crom; back, left to right, Thomas P. Jenkins and George E. Home.
Trinity Episcopal Church

The vestry thereupon began a search for a new rector for Advent. The vestry considered more than 50 candidates before calling the Rev. Laman H. Bruner, Jr., a curate at St. Bartholomew's, New York City. He accepted the call with the understanding that he would lead the parish in constructing its new church building. Rev. Bruner was installed as the seventh rector of the Church of the Advent on November 2, 1947.

At the annual parish meeting in 1948, the new rector proposed that the church remain at 33rd and Meridian and that the new church building be built there for $100,000 ($1 million in 2019 dollars). Advent had grown to more than 950 communicants, the building fund was at $35,000, and the parish had no debt. Optimistically, the members of the parish readily accepted the rector's proposals.

With a new rector, the earlier plans drawn up in 1946 were shelved. When the next plans were completed, however, the cost estimates for a new building rose to $140,000. The vestry authorized an addition to the parish hall, in part so it could be used for worship during construction of the church building. Cost estimates by then had risen to $175,000 ($1.86 million in 2019 dollars).

An early concept for the exterior of
Advent's new church building, 1949.
Trinity Episcopal Church

At the vestry meeting in December 1949, nine possible layouts of a new church building were presented. Cost estimates, however, kept rising, first to $218,000, then in 1950 to $245,000 ($2.6 million in 2019 dollars). The Lilly Endowment helped the situation by donating a large sum to the building fund, as did the family of Dr. George H.A. Clowes and Edith Whitehill Clowes, husband and wife, Advent parishioners and major philanthropists in their own right. More will be said about Dr. and Mrs. Clowes in Chapter 9.

As the first half of the twentieth century came to a close, the vestry voted to begin construction of the new church building. Amazingly, the two leaders of the vestry at this critical time for the parish continued to be Senior Warden William W. Hammond and Junior Warden Henry W. Bliss. Both men had served as leaders of the parish since its beginnings in 1919. The era of life-long lay leadership in the parish was drawing to a close, however. Rotating vestry membership would be introduced in 1950, the first year of the new half century.

In its first three decades of existence at 33rd and Meridian Streets, the Church of the Advent had weathered the Roaring Twenties, the most powerful Ku Klux Klan organization in the nation, the Great Depression, and the Second World War. Life at the Church of the Advent was anything but stable in its first 30 years. During that short time, the parish had seen a total of six rectors (average tenure, five years) come and go. But more change—and more stability—were just around the corner. During the next seven decades, the parish would be served by six effective rectors (average tenure, 11 years), it would continue to be blessed with outstanding lay leadership, and its former shaky financial footing would be made solid by the generosity of a great benefactor. This stability would enable the parish to become not only a leader in the Diocese of Indianapolis, but a leader in both its own neighborhood and The Episcopal Church.

Part Three

A Medieval Church in an Inner City: 1950–1967

Tower and Sign of
Trinity Episcopal Church
Trinity Episcopal Church

Chapter 9

Advent Transfigured:
1950–1953

The first few years of the second half of the twentieth century were eventful times for the congregants of the Church of the Advent, Indianapolis. At the top of their priorities was the most exciting project for the parish up to that time, the construction of an entirely new church building. In January 1950, the architects, McGuire and Shook, presented detailed sketches and a clay model of the proposed new church. (McGuire

Interior of the Church of the Advent
shortly before the building's demolition, 1950.
Trinity Episcopal Church

and Shook became known as Odle McGuire Shook, or OMS, and continued to do architectural work for churches in Indianapolis, including St. Paul's, Broadway United Methodist Church, and Second Presbyterian Church.) Construction started later that year with demolition of the building purchased in 1919 and remodeled in 1937. Beginning in the summer, worship services were held in the parish house.

By November 1950, the old church building was gone, and construction of the new building had begun. The Church of the Advent leaders and Rev. Laman Bruner laid the cornerstone with great ceremony on April 15, 1951. Inside the cornerstone, they placed a copper box containing a cross, a Bible, a Book of Common Prayer, records of parishioners, friends, and supporters, the ashes of the Church of the Advent's mortgage agreement, a set of U.S. currency, an American flag, a copy of the U.S. Constitution, and a letter to people of the future. The letter read:

> *(Not to be opened before 2500 A.D.) To the People of the New Planet:*
> *Greetings:*
> *We hope you will learn much from the Christian faith of which this*
> *church is a permanent and lasting symbol.*
> *As you and the people of the United States work together, the*
> *message of the cross, the Bible and the prayer book will expand far*
> *beyond the confines of the earth and reach the new lands and the new*
> *planets in God's great Universe.*

As expressed in this letter to "the People of the New Planet," the apparent belief of the author(s) in the possibility of travel "far beyond the confines of the earth" to "new lands" and "new planets" and carrying the Christian message there is quite striking. Did they also believe that the message could be carried to extraterrestrial life? That certainly could be implied but is less clear. It may be relevant, though, that the first well-known sighting of an Unidentified Flying Object (UFO) had occurred a few years earlier in 1947. In 1948, the United States Air Force began Project Sign, its first investigation of sightings of UFOs. Within a year, Project Sign was replaced by Project Grudge. In 1952, the year after the parish's letter to posterity was written, Project Grudge was replaced by Project Blue Book, thus far the longest official inquiry into UFOs.

The new building itself would be quite unique, perhaps even divinely inspired. The form of the church building literally appeared in a vision to a parishioner. While standing outside the Church of the Advent with Rev.

*Final concept for the exterior of
Advent's new church building, 1950.*
Trinity Episcopal Church

Bruner, parishioner Edith Whitehill Clowes had a vision, as she put it, of "a fine stone church with the simple lines of Early English Gothic" standing on the property. Mrs. Clowes's vision included a square tower to the west with entrance porches to the north and south, a cloister, and a knot garden. But Mrs. Clowes not only had a vision for the church, she and her husband, Dr. George H.A. Clowes, also had the means to help make the vision a reality.

Dr. Clowes was born in 1877 to a prosperous merchant family in Ipswich, Suffolk, England, a historic town 60 miles northeast of London in the area known as East Anglia. He studied chemistry at the Royal College of Science in London from 1893–1896 and at the University of Göttingen in Germany, where he received his Ph.D. in 1899. In 1901, he came to the United States to serve as co-director of the Gratwick Research Laboratory in Buffalo, New York, one of the earliest institutes to try to find a cure for cancer. While in Buffalo, Dr. Clowes met Edith Whitehill Hinkel, a native of the city, and the two were married in 1910.

In 1919, Dr. Clowes took the position of chemist at Eli Lilly and Company, and he and Mrs. Clowes moved to Indianapolis. In 1921, Dr. Clowes became director of research at Lilly. With the discovery of insulin that year, he headed up the successful efforts of Lilly to mass produce and market the drug, an effort that saved millions of lives from the scourge of diabetes and made Lilly a pharmaceutical giant. In the 25 years that Dr. Clowes headed research at Lilly, the company's sales grew 20 times. This success created a fortune for the Clowes family and, fortunately for the city, yet another group of philanthropists in Indianapolis. Dr. Clowes retired from Lilly in 1946, but his and Mrs. Clowes's active and committed service to the Church of the Advent had just begun.

Dr. George H.A. Clowes and Edith Whitehill Clowes, seated, with grandchildren and adult offspring, circa 1950s. *Younger son Allen Whitehill Clowes is standing on the right.*

Indiana Historical Society, M1028

In 1949, Dr. Clowes persuaded several Indianapolis families in addition to members of Advent parish to fund the construction of the new church building, provided that he and Mrs. Clowes could donate the money for the new tower. Within months, Dr. and Mrs. Clowes sailed to England to make an automobile tour through the counties of Norfolk and Suffolk in East Anglia, close to where Dr. Clowes grew up as a boy. During this tour, they studied thirteenth-century churches down to the details. The four churches of East Anglia that were their inspirations for the church building at 33rd and Meridian were St. Mary of the Assumption, Ufford, Suffolk; St. Peter's, Palgrave, Suffolk; St. Helen's, Ranworth, Norfolk; and St. Edmund's, South Burlingham, Norfolk.

The Clowes's ideas and research were given to the architects, McGuire and Shook, and were incorporated into their design. So dedicated was Mrs. Clowes to ensuring the authenticity of the new structure (including, it was reported, pushing into the background other parishioners with opposing opinions) that, in the words of Bill Ehrich, "she must have felt that this was her building."

In general, the construction methods for the new building were those used in England in the thirteenth century. The only steel incorporated was for the purpose of supporting the roof. The primary building material was

Indiana limestone blasted out of a cliff in Putnam County, Indiana. After the stones were cut by hand with hammers and chisels, they were laid into walls that averaged 23-inches thick. Best estimates were that the stone was three million years old. Rev. Bruner was quoted as saying the building would remain usable for 2,000 years.

One other medieval feature envisioned by Mrs. Clowes on the south side of the new church was the knot garden, or formal herb garden, designed by Dutch-born, Indianapolis-based landscape architect Frits Loosten. Loosten was nationally known and counted among his clients many well-known names in the city, including Eli Lilly, Allen Whitehill Clowes, Lyman S. Ayres, James L. Kittle, Sr., and Herman C. Krannert. He had been the official landscape architect of Indiana University since 1940. The knot garden in its own right became a favorite feature of the church for many.

One twentieth-century touch to the project was the organ built by Casavant Frères, a Canadian company based in Saint-Hyacinthe, Quebec.

Workers constructing the exterior walls of the new church building, 1952.

Trinity Episcopal Church

Arline Wagner Kirchhoffer, wife of the bishop, and Edith Whitehill Clowes (circled) stenciling the interior woodwork of the new building, 1952.

Trinity Episcopal Church

Otherwise, the new building arose as a nearly authentic thirteenth-century English Gothic church in the middle of a twentieth-century American city.

Along with the upheaval caused by the demolition of the old church building and the construction of the new, in 1951 and 1952 the members of the parish decided to deal with the collateral issue of changing the name of the church. One reason for this was that the Indiana headquarters of the Seventh Day Adventists had moved across Meridian Street from the Church of the Advent, and members of the parish feared that outsiders would mistake them for Seventh Day Adventists. But a stronger motive may have been to create a new identity.

A committee of church leaders proposed five new names for the parish in 1951: Trinity, St. Mark's, Grace, Church of the Holy Spirit, and Emmanuel. The name Trinity received a majority of parishioners' votes. In 1952, however, the subject of the name came up again, and a single vote separated two groups of parishioners: the winning side that wanted to keep the name Trinity and the other that wanted to rethink the name.

Bishop Kirchhoffer and the Rev. Laman H. Bruner, Jr., seventh rector of Trinity, knocking on the door to start the dedication ceremony, 1953.

Trinity Episcopal Church

Finally, on Christmas Eve 1952, the doors of the new Trinity Episcopal Church at 33rd and Meridian Streets opened for its first service, a 5 p.m. family carol service. The desire to have the church ready for Christmas necessitated having the first services without pews, which were yet to be installed. The official dedication of the new church, led by Bishop Kirchhoffer accompanied by Rev. Bruner, was performed on Sunday, January 11, 1953.

Having overseen Trinity's construction project to completion, however, in 1952 Rev. Bruner had accepted a call as rector of St. Peter's, a large parish in Albany, New York. Rev. Bruner submitted his resignation as rector of Trinity

Clergy from the diocese, including Bishop Kirchhoffer,
Dean John P. Craine, and Rev. Bruner,
standing in front of Trinity's parish house, 1952.
Trinity Episcopal Church

effective December 31, 1952, but stayed for the new church's dedication—and a farewell party—in January.

As a side note, Albany, as the capital of the state of New York, was the location of the New York State Assembly, and Rev. Bruner in time served as chaplain of the Assembly. Two of the vestry members of St. Peter's during Rev. Bruner's term as rector were two governors of New York who became national political figures, Thomas E. Dewey and W. Averell Harriman. For many years in summertime, Rev. Bruner also served as chaplain of St. Ann's Church, Kennebunkport, Maine, where his parishioners included the Bush family and two future U.S. presidents, George H.W. Bush and George W. Bush.

From the time of its completion to the present, the sanctuary of Trinity has impressed the people who have worshipped there as a particularly holy place. When there are no people present, the sanctuary can strike some people as cold and grey, but, when it is filled with people, it becomes vibrantly alive. Words that have been used to describe the early 8 a.m. Sunday services at Trinity include "quiet," "peaceful," "respectful," and "comfortable." Words that have been used to describe the later 10 a.m. Sunday services include "celebratory," "nourishing," "child-friendly," "family-centered," "diverse," "joyous," and "music-filled." The later service has benefited from an outstanding music program, and music has always been an integral part of life and worship at Trinity. Many people have admitted that they initially came for the music but stayed for the community.

A poignant moment at Trinity occurred on Valentine's Day, February 14, 1953, with the first wedding celebrated in the new Trinity sanctuary. The bride and groom were Miss Heberton Weiss and Mr. Peter Richardson. Miss Weiss happened to be the granddaughter of the late Rev. Clarence Bispham, the fourth rector of the Church of the Advent during the first decade of the parish in the 1920s and certainly the most beloved of its early rectors.

In June 1953, with a new building and a new name, the vestry of Trinity called the Rev. G. Ernest Lynch as the eighth rector of the parish. At the time of his call, Rev. Lynch was the rector of another Trinity Episcopal Church, a historic parish in Hannibal, Missouri. Before that, he had been a minister at Unitarian churches in Maine and Boston. Rev. Lynch would maintain his position as rector at Trinity Episcopal Church, Indianapolis, for 25 years, the longest tenure of any rector in the parish's first 100 years. Trinity, which had four rectors in its first eight years, would have only five rectors in the next 66.

Chapter 10

The City Backslides: 1950–1967

The story of Indianapolis during the 1950s and much of the 1960s can be summarized in one word: decline. By 1950, the city's population had grown impressively to 427,173, but within 10 years Indianapolis was in serious economic difficulty. The mayor of Indianapolis was limited to only one four-year term until the 1960s, and the real power in the city lay with the Chamber of Commerce. William H. Book, head of the Chamber during the 30-year period of 1934–1964, had foiled progress in the city for decades by continually blocking efforts to secure federal aid for planning and development projects.

These problems were aggravated, first, by the movement of many affluent residents to newer, greener, and—to be honest, given the racist attitudes still common in Indianapolis and elsewhere at that time—whiter suburbs and, second, by the dwindling city tax base caused by businesses and households relocating outside the city limits.

By the mid-1960s, the once dynamic city of Indianapolis, which had challenged Detroit to be the nation's automaker and Chicago to be the nation's meatpacker, was referred to pejoratively as "Naptown" (from Indianapolis) and "India-no-place" and existed in the shadows of Detroit, Chicago, St. Louis, and Cincinnati.

The Episcopal Church in Indianapolis, however, did not decline during those years, and it became more involved in social and civic issues than it had ever been before. In 1951, Christ Church vestry member Eli Lilly, by then the chairman of Eli Lilly and Company, spearheaded the effort to call the Rev. John P. Craine to be rector of Christ Church in Indianapolis. Rev. Craine was a person of great intellectual gifts, intense social consciousness, and multiple talents. A sports enthusiast, he was an avid deep-sea fisherman.

A native of Ohio, he had paid his way through Kenyon College by playing honky-tonk piano; as an alumnus in later years, he would serve as president of the board of trustees of the college.

In 1953, Mr. Lilly gave $1 million ($9.6 million in 2019 dollars) to the Diocese of Indianapolis on the condition that his church, Christ Church, be made the cathedral of the diocese. Perhaps not surprisingly, that condition was met the following year, and the seat of the bishop of Indianapolis was moved from All Saints on 16th Street to Mr. Lilly's Little Church on the Circle.

In 1956, Bishop Kirchhoffer let the diocese know of his intention to retire in 1958. Shortly after the bishop's announcement, Dean Craine of Christ Church Cathedral (now with the cathedral title of dean instead of rector), again with the backing of Mr. Lilly, was elected bishop coadjutor of the Diocese of Indianapolis and was consecrated as such in April 1957.

Bishop Richard Ainslie Kirchhoffer, who called Trinity his church home and helped dedicate Trinity's church building in 1953, did indeed retire in 1958. After that, an Indianapolis Episcopalian gave $20,000 for the construction of a dam at Waycross, the newly-created Episcopal camp in Brown County, Indiana, on the condition that the lake formed be named Lake Kirchhoffer. This prompted Bishop Kirchhoffer to quip, "They can't say that nobody gave a dam when the old bishop left." Although he and his wife, Arline, spent time in California during retirement, they requested that after their deaths their ashes be interred in Crown Hill Cemetery in Indianapolis; they felt that Indiana was where they had spent their best years.

On February 9, 1959, Bishop Coadjutor John Pares Craine was consecrated bishop of the Diocese of Indianapolis at Christ Church Cathedral. Bishop Craine, supported by Christ Church Cathedral leaders Archdeacon Frederic P. Williams, Dean Paul Moore Jr. (who had succeeded Craine as dean of the cathedral and later became a famous but, sadly, controversial bishop of New York), and Eli Lilly, became a highly respected member of the House of Bishops and a mighty force in the national Church. As a result, Bishop Craine put The Episcopal Church in Indianapolis in the forefront of social change, including actions in support of civil rights and, later, the ordination of women to the priesthood.

The year 1964 was a turning point in Indianapolis history. In that year, William H. Book, the ultra-conservative head of the Indianapolis Chamber of Commerce who had frustrated advancement in the city for so long, died, and John J. Barton was elected mayor of Indianapolis. In his single four-year term, Mayor Barton pushed for the completion of Eagle Creek Park and Eagle Creek Reservoir, a downtown convention center, and a west-side Indiana University campus. (Despite Barton's support, the west-side university campus would not come together until Barton's successor as mayor, Richard G. Lugar, was in office.) Mayor Barton's administration reactivated the Indianapolis Housing Authority, which sought federal funds for low income housing, and created the Greater Indianapolis Progress Committee, a private, not-for-profit civic improvement organization funded by foundation grants and private contributions.

Eagle Creek Park was located on the northwest side of Indianapolis. The property on which it was located originally had been owned by the younger grandson of Colonel Eli Lilly, J.K. Lilly Jr., who had attempted to sell it to the city. The city, at the time seemingly short-

The Rt. Rev. John Pares Craine,
eighth bishop of Indianapolis,
during a visit to Trinity, circa 1960s.
Trinity Episcopal Church

sightedly, refused the offer, and the property was purchased instead by Purdue University in West Lafayette, Indiana. Flooding on and around the property, however, caused the university to offer the property to the city again. In 1964, in what by then seemed a brilliant move, the city purchased the property from Purdue for the total sum of one dollar. Construction of the city's new dam and water reservoir on Eagle Creek began that year and was completed by 1968.

Eagle Creek Park became the largest park in Indianapolis and one of the largest municipal parks in the United States. It covered approximately 1,400 acres of reservoir and 3,900 acres of land, contained about 10 miles of paths, and provided facilities for boating, rowing, swimming, fishing, fitness, picnicking, and golf. It also became an important bird and wildlife sanctuary.

During this time in the 1960s, Indianapolis also was transformed by the design and construction of the interstate highway system through and around the city. The U.S. interstate highway system began as a federal initiative in 1956 during the administration of President Dwight D. Eisenhower. In 1919, Eisenhower had participated as a young officer in the U.S. Army's first transcontinental convoy of military vehicles, a trek from Washington, D.C., to San Francisco that took two months to complete. As supreme commander of the Allies' military forces in the European Theater during World War II, he had been impressed by his post-war travels on Germany's *Bundesautobahn* (Federal Motorway), built mostly under Adolph Hitler and envied by American engineers in the 1930s. Eisenhower would say, "The old convoy had started me thinking about good, two-lane highways, but Germany had made me see the wisdom of broader ribbons across the land."

The president, therefore, advocated for a national system of roads that could be used not only for private travel and commerce but for military defense in an era of growing tensions with the Soviet Union. Indiana Governor Harold W. Handley quickly committed the Hoosier state to construct 932 miles of interstate. Eventually, nearly 47,000 miles of interstate highway would be constructed in the United States, and more than 1,350 miles of interstate highway would crisscross Indiana.

President Eisenhower, however, had not foreseen interstate highways reaching cities' urban cores. Hitler's *Autobahn*, his model, had carried traffic only between and around cities, not through them. Members of Congress, however, believed that urban freeways were essential to their constituents and pressured Eisenhower to agree with plans that brought the interstates through the hearts of American cities.

State highway officials hired Chicago consultant Harry W. Lockner to recommend locations for the seven interstate highways that were to converge on Indianapolis. These highways were I-65 from Chicago in the north and from Louisville in the south; I-74 from Peoria in the west and from Cincinnati in the east; I-70 from St. Louis in the west and from Pittsburgh and Columbus, Ohio, in the east; and I-69 from Detroit in the north. Lockner proposed that two, I-65 and I-70, be constructed to continue through downtown Indianapolis. His proposals were accepted without modification by the Indiana State Highway Commission and the U.S. Bureau of Public Roads in 1959.

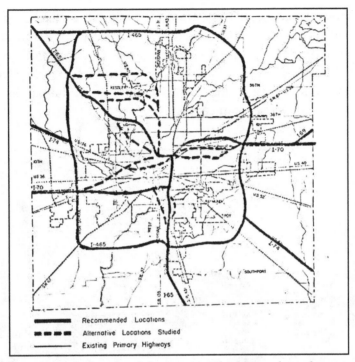

*Routes considered for interstate highways through
Indianapolis, circa 1950s. One possibility shown but not
chosen was I-65 going down Meridian Street past Trinity.*
The Trustees of Purdue University

Various individuals and entities, including U.S. Congressman Andy
Jacobs, Indianapolis City Councilman Max Brydenthal, and African-
American leader and Benedictine priest Bishop Boniface Hardin, attempted
to persuade state and local officials to reroute and redesign the downtown
interstates to minimize destruction of established inner city neighborhoods,
but such pleas were ignored by state and local officials, including Mayor
Barton. It must be said that similar efforts in other cities, such as Chicago,
San Francisco, and New Orleans, were successful in diminishing negative
impacts on downtown neighborhoods.

In Indianapolis, the African-American neighborhood surrounding Indiana Avenue radiating to the northwest, as well as neighborhoods near Foun-
tain Square on the southeast side of downtown and in the Old Northside
where President Benjamin Harrison once had lived, all paid the price of
progress. Entire blocks were erased from existence, and formerly adjoining

neighborhoods became isolated from each other. Ultimately, at great social and financial cost to neighborhoods in the inner city, 8,000 buildings were demolished and 17,000 people were relocated to accommodate the new downtown interstate highways. Eventually, easier access afforded by the interstates would aid the resurgence of downtown Indianapolis, but that benefit would be many years in coming.

The completed connector of I-65 and I-70, dubbed the Spaghetti Bowl,
on the northeast side of downtown Indianapolis where part of the
Old Northside neighborhood used to be, circa 1970s.
Bass Photo Co. Collection, Indianapolis Historical Society

Chapter 11

Trinity Shapes Its Identity:
1954–1967

The decade of the 1950s saw explosive growth in The Episcopal Church nationally and in the Diocese of Indianapolis in particular. In 1959, *LOOK* magazine cited The Episcopal Church as one of the fastest growing religious bodies in America. In that year, the Diocese of Indianapolis had 926 new confirmations, the fourth highest of any Episcopal diocese in the nation. The growth was so noteworthy that Bishop John Pares Craine joked in a speech at a diocesan Annual Convention that statistical projections indicated that eventually every person in Indiana would be an Episcopalian.

At the same time, the neighborhood in which the Church of the Advent was founded and Trinity Episcopal Church had emerged began to change. The social and economic forces discussed in Chapter 10 were causing what once had been an affluent, suburban neighborhood to become a poorer, inner-city neighborhood. Trinity's members were spreading throughout Marion County and beyond, and Trinity was ceasing to be a simple neighborhood parish whose members could walk to church from their homes. Nevertheless, the church continued to make significant advances.

It was during this time of Episcopal expansion and neighborhood change that Trinity's rector, Rev. Ernest Lynch, oversaw two important missions of the parish. The first came about in early 1955 when Atkinson and Company, a partnership engaged in real estate development owned by brothers Warren M. Atkinson and W. Linton Atkinson, made a gift to the Diocese of Indianapolis of 4.8 acres of land at 46th Street and Emerson Avenue. A nineteenth-century Lutheran church formerly had been on the site. The diocese decided that Trinity should sponsor a mission for this property, slightly north and considerably east of Trinity's location on Meridian Street.

*Sunday school classes in Trinity's
Holy Innocents Chapel,* circa 1950s.
Trinity Episcopal Church

A core of Trinity members formed a new congregation that grew rapidly while meeting at an Indiana National Bank building near the property. The congregation chose St. Alban's as its name, commemorating the first

Christian martyr in Britain, and was awarded official mission status by the diocese effective January 1, 1957. On the Feast Day of St. Alban, June 22, 1957, the mission held the groundbreaking ceremony for its new church building. Ten years later, St. Alban's would achieve the status of a parish of the Diocese of Indianapolis.

The second important mission was St. Richard's School, first proposed by Rev. Lynch in 1957. Rev. Lynch, a native of Massachusetts, had spent one year at the Huntington School for Boys in Boston and studied at Duke and Harvard Universities. A proponent of rigorous academics, he had a vision of creating a school in the image of English public (i.e., private) day schools. According to Dr. James P. Fadley's *A Brief History of St. Richard's School 1960–1995*, Rev. Lynch had a "fondness for English education with its high academic expectations and the respectful demeanor of its students."

Trinity boy choristers, 1956.
Trinity Episcopal Church

The members of Trinity solidly supported Rev. Lynch's dream, in part because a new church school building was needed in any event; the size of Sunday school classes had doubled in the previous five years. The parish conducted a successful pledge campaign, obtaining pledges totaling $100,000 ($900,000 in 2019 dollars). Unfortunately, the lowest bid for construction of the new building was $140,000, which caused the parish to obtain a mortgage loan for the building. The new wing, named St. Richard's Hall, was dedicated in November 1957.

In 1959, Rev. Lynch requested vestry member Eugene S. Pulliam—publisher of the morning *Indianapolis Star* and the evening *Indianapolis News*, the two largest newspapers in Indiana—to make a preliminary study of the feasibility of Trinity establishing a parish day school. In May of that year, Mr. Pulliam delivered to the vestry a report recommending hiring, in

*The Rev. G. Ernest Lynch, eighth rector of Trinity, and
young parishioners breaking ground for St. Richard's Hall, 1957.*
Trinity Episcopal Church

his words, one "capable" teacher for a kindergarten class only and adding one grade each year thereafter until the school had a fifth grade. Mr. Pulliam indicated that this way the school could be started with a small investment and later be made self-supporting. The vestry approved Mr. Pulliam's recommendations.

St. Richard's School opened on September 14, 1960, with 17 kindergarten students and its first teacher, Miss Helen Bevan, who had arrived in Indianapolis from Woodbridge, Suffolk, England, the previous May to visit her brother. Miss Bevan was a graduate of the Bedford Training College in England and had taught kindergarten in London and Cyprus. In that first year, the school offered only preschool and kindergarten classes as planned. Future classes were to be limited to 20 students.

Rev. Lynch determined that the only place where he could find other "capable" teachers for St. Richard's was in England. He sought teachers there by placing notices in the weekly educational supplement of the *London Times* and traveling to England in 1964 and 1966 to recruit personally for the school. In the first decade of the school's life, the overwhelming number of faculty came from England. The only exceptions were the French teacher, who came from France, and occasionally a stray American.

Young women of Trinity in their Sunday best, 1960.
Trinity Episcopal Church

The teachers from England, as it happened, were quite cost-effective as they were willing to work for low salaries in exchange for a chance to move to and work in the United States. The school also economized by supplying the teachers with furnished housing in homes owned by Trinity. The original teachers' home was a house at 3246 North Pennsylvania that was acquired by Trinity in 1961. In 1964, Trinity bought three other properties nearby and razed them all along with the teachers' home for the expansion of St. Richard's. Trinity purchased another building for teachers' housing at 35 East 33rd Street in 1966.

By the fall of 1965, St. Richard's School had grown to 140 students in kindergarten through fifth grades. In 1966, the school's board of directors decided that St. Richard's would not grow beyond a sixth grade and would be limited to 200 pupils. In the fall of that year, the school opened with 155 students and a faculty of 12. The school reached its then maximum size of 200 students in the fall of 1968, eight years after it first opened.

When he conceived his vision of a school at Trinity, Rev. Lynch was motivated not only by his desire to establish an excellent academic institution but also by his desire to anchor Trinity parish in its changing neighborhood. It is important to note that, in the early years of the school, Trinity and St. Richard's showed a combined dedication to helping the neighborhood by offering scholarships to predominantly African-American students from the school's immediate area. St. Richard's also became one of the first racially-integrated private schools in the city.

Eventually, St. Richard's would be made a Diocesan Cooperative Ministry. Important aspects of being such a ministry included support by the Diocese of Indianapolis as well as parishes in the diocese. Moreover, employees of Diocesan Cooperative Ministries benefited greatly by being eligible to participate in the diocese's generous employee benefit plans.

In 1959, the Women's Auxiliary and St. Catherine's Guild merged to become Trinity Episcopal Churchwomen. Throughout the 1960s, this organization continued to do important outreach work. The women of the parish spent time working on local projects and the then twice-yearly Women's United Thank Offering of The Episcopal Church. They also consistently contributed money to causes such as the Brazil Fund, the Presiding Bishop's Fund for World Relief, and the Henry St. George Tucker Memorial Mission to Africa.

The importance of women as leaders of Trinity was recognized in a significant way at the parish's January 1962 Annual Meeting with the election of the first woman to the vestry, Eleanor Davis Mallory. A native of New York, Mrs. Mallory's father had been a vice president of the Guaranty Trust

Trinity's knot garden in winter, circa *1960s.*
Trinity Episcopal Church

Gentlemen of the vestry, circa *1960s.*
Trinity Episcopal Church

Company of New York. At the time she joined the vestry, Mrs. Mallory was married to G. Barron Mallory, the chairman and son of the founder of P.R. Mallory & Company, Inc., a prominent Indianapolis manufacturer of electrical and electronic components and parts.

Another significant event transpired in 1962 when in October of that year the vestry formed Trinity's Memorial Fund to serve as a vehicle to receive and grow monetary gifts for Trinity's legacy. The resolution creating the fund specified that it have four separate units: a General Account, a Special Account, an Endowment Account, and a Trust Account. The resolution also included important governance policies: trustees; specific powers and duties given to the trustees and the vestry; and guidelines concerning accepting gifts, investing assets, spending, and reporting.

The story of this era would not be complete without mentioning the greatest juxtaposition of two primary characteristics of the parish in the 1950s and 1960s: a love of partying and a love of things English. The tradition of Yuletide Madrigal Feasts—based on medieval Christmas feasts, or at least on mid-twentieth century Hoosiers' sanitized concepts of what medieval Christmas feasts were like—was the creation of Georgianne Strange, who also wrote the parish's 50-year history, *Trinity Episcopal Church 1919–1969*. First started during Advent in 1963, Trinity's Madrigal Dinners (as they became known) originally featured a dinner and professional entertainment.

In time though, the Madrigal Dinners became organized, prepared for, and performed at by Trinity parishioners. With only one brief interruption, the Madrigal Dinners continued at Trinity during the season of Advent for more than 50 years.

Trinity's first Yuletide Madrigal Feast, 1963.
Trinity Episcopal Church

It can be said safely that during the 1950s and 1960s the people who filled the pews on Sundays at Trinity made up a veritable *Who's Who in Indianapolis.* The parish was filled with community leaders from the worlds of business, science, journalism, the learned professions, and even the military. According to Trinity's 1959 Annual Report, there were 933 communicants in good standing. Ten years later, there were more than 1,000 communicants in good standing. People at Trinity were justifiably proud of the numbers of awards, board memberships, and other achievements that their fellow parishioners garnered. Without a doubt, the parish was full of highly successful people who were accomplishing important things and making significant contributions throughout Indianapolis. They also were immensely fond of one another and had a great time together, both at worship and while just plain having fun.

During the 1950s and 1960s, Trinity saw much maturation and change, from the tentative beginnings of the Church of the Advent with a used building and used furnishings in an affluent neighborhood, to a self-confident parish with a striking, unique edifice in the inner city. No longer would the vestry have to pass the hat to pay the bills and the rector's salary. No longer would the leadership come only from a handful of white males. No longer would the parish be subjected to myriad possibilities of being merged out of existence as it had in the past. In ensuing years, Trinity would become more diverse and an innovator and initiator in ways that members of the Church of the Advent never could have dreamed possible.

Trinity's Easter Cross of Flowers, 1966.
Trinity Episcopal Church

Part Four

Change Is the Only Constant:
1968–1999

Knot Garden of Trinity Episcopal Church
Trinity Episcopal Church

Chapter 12

The City Redux:
1968–1999

In the late 1960s, Indianapolis was dealing with many of the same economic and social challenges as other Midwest cities, including Cleveland, Detroit, and St. Louis. While the African-American population remained in the inner city, white residents continued to move to the suburbs. Indianapolis found itself on the cusp of worsening racial tensions and economic viability.

Then, something happened in Indianapolis that would be a small ray of hope in the midst of one of the worst tragedies in American history. On April 4, 1968, the great civil rights leader Dr. Martin Luther King, Jr., was assassinated at the Lorraine Motel in Memphis, Tennessee. Later that day, U.S. Senator Robert F. Kennedy, who was running for president of the United States, arrived in Indianapolis to give a speech at 17th and Broadway Streets in a predominantly African-American neighborhood. In that time before the Internet and social media, few if any of the people gathered for the speech knew of Dr. King's murder.

Instead of the rousing campaign speech the crowd was expecting, they received an impromptu, subdued address by Senator Kennedy, who began, "I have bad news for you, for all of our fellow citizens, and people who love peace all over the world, and that is that Martin Luther King was shot and killed tonight."

People cried out and wailed in pain and disbelief, but Kennedy continued without script, delivering one of the greatest speeches ever given in America and often said to be the greatest speech he ever gave. In part, he said:

What we need in the United States is not division; what we need in the United States is not hatred; what we need in the United States is not violence or lawlessness; but love and wisdom, and compassion toward one another, and a feeling of justice toward those who still suffer within our country, whether they be white or they be black.

His words calmed those gathered and, it is thought, helped preserve peace in Indianapolis on a night that saw riots in hundreds of cities across the country.

Robert Kennedy, too, would be assassinated in California two months later. In 1995, President Bill Clinton came to the new Dr. Martin Luther King, Jr. Park at 601 East 17th Street in Indianapolis to dedicate the memorial, *Landmark for Peace*, honoring Robert Kennedy and Martin Luther King, Jr., and commemorating the site where Senator Kennedy delivered his words on the night of Dr. King's assassination.

Senator Robert F. Kennedy comforts the crowd in Indianapolis after the tragic death of Dr. Martin Luther King, Jr., 1968.
Indianapolis Recorder Collection,
Indiana Historical Society

Economically, Indianapolis had begun to come out of its 20-year post-Depression stagnation during the administration of Mayor Barton, and the trend toward prosperity continued when Richard G. Lugar became mayor of Indianapolis in 1968. Mayor Lugar continued Barton's initiatives and began new ones. Lugar's most notable achievement was the creation of Unigov, the name adopted by Indianapolis for its form of merger and consolidation of city and county government. This new structure gave the mayor control over administration within much of Marion County outside the old city limits, greatly enlarged the city's population and revenues, and enhanced the city's stature as an important American city. Lugar also broke with Republican tradition in the city and actively sought federal funding for a variety of programs.

Mayor Lugar achieved considerable national prominence while he was in office in Indianapolis. He served as the president of the National League of Cities in 1971 and gave the keynote address at the 1972 Republican National Convention. In 1976 he was elected to the U.S. Senate and became that chamber's leading expert on foreign affairs.

Indianapolis between 1968 and 1999 had a remarkable history of growth and progress. After Richard Lugar was elected to the Senate, Indianapolis continued to be blessed with two more talented mayors, William H. "Bill" Hudnut III, and Stephen "Steve" Goldsmith. And, to the great credit of Hoosier politicians at that time, these Republican mayors worked well with their Democratic governor counterparts in the Indiana Statehouse, Evan Bayh and Frank O'Bannon.

Boy Scout Troop 80's fiftieth anniversary celebration at Trinity, 1974;
Rev. Lynch and Indianapolis Mayor Richard G. Lugar
are in the back row on the left.
Trinity Episcopal Church

It seemed that every prominent government official in those days had a significant connection to Trinity. In his youth, Mayor Lugar had been an Eagle Scout with Boy Scout Troop 80, which held its meetings at Trinity. Mayor Hudnut, although himself an ordained Presbyterian minister, became a Trinity parishioner thanks to his Episcopalian wife, Beverly.

Mayor Goldsmith was a St. Richard's parent. Governor Bayh, who was in office from 1989–1997 and later was elected to the U.S. Senate, and his wife, Susan, were Trinity parishioners during their years in Indianapolis; their twin sons, Beau and Christopher, born in 1995, were baptized at the church.

During this time, Indianapolis continued to benefit from a centralized location, a diversified economic base, and a harmonious relationship among business and government leaders, including the good relationship between the city and state governments located in Indianapolis. As a result, the city began the revitalization of its downtown.

In 1969, Indiana University-Purdue University at Indianapolis (IUPUI) came to fruition as the result of the merger of the Purdue Indianapolis Extension Center and Indiana University Indianapolis. Eventually, IUPUI would offer more than 200 degree programs for an enrollment of more than 30,000 students and would host the campuses for the Indiana University School of Medicine, the Indiana University School of Dentistry, the Indiana University Robert H. McKinney School of Law, the Indiana University Graduate School of Social Work, and one of two campuses of the Indiana University Kelley School of Business.

Also in that year, the Art Association of Indianapolis, which had been located at the John Herron Art Institute at 16th and Pennsylvania Streets since its formation in 1906, changed its name to the Indianapolis Museum of Art and in 1970 moved to its new 152-acre site at 38th Street and Michigan Avenue, the former estate of J.K. Lilly Jr. Eventually, the Indianapolis Museum of Art would grow to be the eighth largest encyclopedic art museum in the United States with a permanent collection comprising more than 54,000 works including works from Africa, the Americas, Asia, and Europe. Due in part to the size and variety of its campus—which in addition to the museum hosted the Lilly House and Garden (also known as Oldfields), the Virginia B. Fairbanks Art & Nature Park:100 Acres, the Beer Garden, and more—and in part to its desire to attract more visitors, the museum and campus rebranded themselves Newfields in 2017.

In 1970, the city's interstate highway system was completed. Seven interstate routes converged on Indianapolis, more than any other city in the nation. The cost of building I-65 and I-70 borne by historic neighborhoods was high, but eventually real-estate values around the downtown interstates began to increase, reversing a decades-long decline. Moreover, Mayor Bill Hudnut credited the highways with stimulating a number of downtown projects in the 1970s, such as the $150 million expansion of Eli Lilly and Company.

The Indiana National Bank Tower under construction, 1969.
Bass Photo Co. Collection, Indiana Historical Society

Another such project credited by Mayor Hudnut with sparking the resurgence of Indianapolis was the Indiana National Bank Tower (later renamed One Indiana Square). In 1970, Indiana National Bank, one of the city's leading banks, completed the 36-story modern glass-and-steel office tower on the southern half of the block bounded by Pennsylvania, New York, Delaware, and Ohio Streets in downtown Indianapolis. For years, much of the development in Indianapolis had been along Meridian Street north of downtown. After 1970, development started happening in downtown proper.

In 1972, the Indiana Convention-Exposition Center (later renamed the Indiana Convention Center) first opened. The Convention Center continued to grow and expand, including with the addition of the Hoosier Dome in 1984 (later renamed the RCA Dome) and Lucas Oil Stadium in 2008, about which more will be said in Chapter 15.

Also in 1972, the Indiana Repertory Theatre (IRT) was founded and called the Athenaeum its first home. In 1980, the IRT moved to its present-day location at the Indiana Theatre, a former movie theater on West Washington Street that had been built in 1927 and was converted from a movie theater specifically for the IRT's use.

In 1984, the Indianapolis Symphony Orchestra (ISO) also moved downtown, leaving Clowes Hall at Butler University to take residence at the 1,700-seat Circle Theatre on Monument Circle. The theatre had been built in 1916 for the new entertainment sensation, motion pictures. In the early 1980s, it was thoroughly renovated specifically as a concert hall for the ISO. In 1996, the venue was endowed by Stephen "Steve" and Tomisue Hilbert, husband and wife, he being the founder of Conseco, Inc., and was renamed the Hilbert Circle Theatre.

In 1987, another fortuitous event lifted the prominence of the ISO. Raymond Leppard—a famous English conductor who had led groups such as the Royal Opera, the Metropolitan Opera, the New York Philharmonic, the Boston Symphony, the Philadelphia Orchestra, and the Los Angeles Philharmonic—began a transformative tenure as music director of the ISO that lasted until 2001. In that year he was made conductor laureate of the ISO, a position he held until his death in 2019. During his time as music director, Maestro Leppard enhanced the ISO's reputation for excellence and inspired the increase in its budget and endowment. He also led the orchestra in eight recordings and two European tours. The bond between Maestro Leppard and the Indianapolis community was so strong that the British native made Indianapolis his permanent home and became a U.S. citizen in 2003.

Another new skyscraper, the American United Life Building (later renamed One American Square), eventually the second-tallest building in Indianapolis, also changed the city's skyline when it opened in 1982. In 1983, the city began acquiring property in downtown for what would open in 1995 as Circle Center Mall.

The last major office tower to open during this time period was the Bank One Tower, a 49-story building located between Ohio, Pennsylvania, and Meridian Streets and Monument Circle. The building originally was conceived in the 1970s by American Fletcher National Bank (AFNB), then Indiana's leading financial institution. AFNB was acquired by Ohio's Bank One Corporation before the building was completed in 1990, resulting in the name change to the Bank One Tower. The building surpassed both the Indiana National Bank Tower and the American United Life Building and became the tallest building in Indiana. It later went through a series of name changes, first to Chase Tower and then to Salesforce Tower.

No discussion of Indianapolis during this time would be complete without including the importance of sports to the growth of the city. Indianapolis had become known as the auto racing capital of the nation with the building

Market Square Arena under construction, 1974.
Bass Photo Co. Collection, Indiana Historical Society

of the Indianapolis Motor Speedway in 1909 and the first Indianapolis 500 in 1911. For much of its existence, the Indianapolis 500 has been acknowledged to be the largest single-day sporting event in the world. Professional baseball teams, notably the AAA league Indianapolis Indians, have played in Indianapolis for more than 100 years. Nevertheless, the scale of sporting events in the city grew immensely during the 1960s through the 1980s.

The Indiana Pacers professional basketball team was first established in 1967 as a member of the American Basketball Association (ABA) and became a member of the National Basketball Association (NBA) in 1976 through the ABA–NBA merger. The Pacer's new home, Market Square Arena, was constructed in downtown Indianapolis in 1974 at a cost of $23 million ($119 million in 2019 dollars). Suddenly, people from outlying areas had a reason to venture into the city after dark: basketball!

Bill Benner, who was an *Indianapolis Star* sportswriter for 33 years, stated, "If I had to think of two things that got Indianapolis moving forward—finally—the first would be Market Square Arena, and the second would be the completion of the inner [interstate] loop, which made it much easier for people to come downtown at night." Another new basketball arena, Conseco Fieldhouse (later renamed Bankers Life Fieldhouse), would be constructed for the Pacers in 1999.

Throughout the 1980s, Indianapolis continued to make a concerted effort to become a major sports city. Public and private funding totaling $122 million ($300 million in 2019 dollars) was used to build the Indianapolis Tennis Center, the Major Taylor Velodrome, the Indiana University Natatorium, the Carroll Track and Soccer Stadium, and the aforementioned Hoosier Dome.

Results from these efforts were realized quickly. In 1982, Indianapolis hosted the largest amateur sports competition in the country, the National Sports Festival, a pre-Olympic Games event in which 2,600 American athletes vied in 33 sports. The success of the 1982 National Sports Festival led to Indianapolis hosting the 1987 Pan American Games—the world's second largest multi-sport competition after the Olympics—in which 4,300 athletes from 38 countries in the Western hemisphere competed in 30 sports.

Additionally, in 1984, the Colts of the National Football League (NFL) moved from Baltimore to Indianapolis, where the brand new Hoosier Dome awaited them. In their early days in Indianapolis, it would have to be said that the Colts were not a very good NFL team. But they would get better.

The local NBA team, the Indiana Pacers, however, were one of the professional basketball game's dominant teams in the 1990s. Led by fan favorite Reggie Miller, the Pacers were especially known for their epic battles against the New York Knicks or, as the New York City media lovingly dubbed it, "the Hicks vs. the Knicks." Hoosiers, ever Midwest-nice, of course embraced the "Hicks" sobriquet as their home team regularly defeated their rivals from the Big Apple.

Moreover, in addition to the major league Pacers and Colts, Indianapolis also was home to the minor league hockey team, the Indiana Ice, and continued to field the AAA league Indianapolis Indians baseball team.

Indianapolis's ability to host large sports competitions such as the Indianapolis 500, the National Sports Festival, and the Pan American Games, as well as NBA and NFL seasons, and the number and quality of its world-class athletic facilities would lead to more national prominence and more and more opportunities to host major athletic events in the years ahead.

In addition to its emergence as a national sports center, another trend manifested itself near the end of the twentieth century that also would have importance for Indianapolis in the twenty-first century. In 1995, new multi-millionaire Scott A. Jones returned to his hometown of Indianapolis from Boston after selling his interest in Boston Technology, where he had been instrumental in inventing a voicemail system that would be used by billions of people around the world. Jones would continue his technology entrepreneurship in Indianapolis on and off again for years. Then in 1997, IBM spent $200 million ($320 million in 2019 dollars) to acquire Software Artistry, a technology company founded and based in Indianapolis. The acquisition created a number of other new millionaires in the city, many of whom would start several other technology start-ups in Indianapolis in the years that followed.

As Indianapolis left the twentieth century, it was much better positioned than it had been 30 years before, but it also still faced numerous challenges. It was located within what once had been called the industrial heartland (i.e., central and western New York, western Pennsylvania, Ohio, Indiana, the Lower Peninsula of Michigan, northern Illinois, eastern Iowa, and southeastern Wisconsin), but starting around 1980 was being sneered at as the Rust Belt as a result of the states in the region experiencing economic decline and population loss caused by the shrinking of their once-powerful industrial sector.

Not only did Indianapolis face loss of manufacturing jobs, it also faced a dwindling base of corporate headquarters and continued flight to ever expanding suburbs, eventually outside the reach even of Unigov. The crime rate in Indianapolis, unlike the rest of the nation as a whole, continued to rise in the 1990s, in part because of drug trafficking. The combination of those problems resulted in a rending of the social fabric of the community in Indianapolis. Finding ways of mending this social fabric would continue to be probably the greatest challenge the city would face at the beginning of the twenty-first century.

Chapter 13

Momentous Events:
1968–1983

The late 1960s, the 1970s, and the early 1980s ushered in great changes to The Episcopal Church and Trinity Episcopal Church, Indianapolis. In 1976 at the General Convention of The Episcopal Church held in Minneapolis, the Church made two landmark decisions: approval of a new Book of Common Prayer and, more significantly, approval of the ordination of women to the priesthood.

The Diocese of Indianapolis, led by Bishop John Pares Craine, was instrumental in both of these changes. In 1973, The Episcopal Church's General Convention had narrowly voted down the ordination of women. Undaunted, Bishop Craine that same year began working with two women in Indianapolis, Jacqueline "Jackie" Means and Natalia "Tanya" Vonnegut Beck, to position them as possible candidates for ordination. Both women had significant experience in aiding and comforting others. Ms. Means was a licensed practical nurse with great talent as a counselor to prison inmates. Ms. Beck was the founder and executive director of The Julian Center, a refuge for battered and abused women in Indianapolis which will be referred to in Chapter 14. Bishop Craine also worked with great energy and effectiveness within the House of Bishops and the Diocese of Indianapolis to gain support for the approval of the ordination of women at the next General Convention in 1976.

But sadly, the leadership at Trinity was not in step with the efforts of the bishop and resisted welcoming women into the priesthood. Rev. Ernest Lynch, still Trinity's rector, strongly believed that endorsing women priests would create rifts with other Christian denominations, particularly the Roman Catholic Church. For Rev. Lynch, ecumenism, an important goal of The Episcopal Church, was more important than gender equality in the clergy. Moreover, Trinity's vestry backed Rev. Lynch on this issue.

*Bishop Craine conducting the diaconal
(i.e., as deacon) ordination
of Jacqueline "Jackie" Means,
the first woman to take holy orders
in the Diocese of Indianapolis.*
Jacqueline Means

Despite the delay in the ordination of female priests, the years 1973–1976 were eventful for women in The Episcopal Church. In 1973, Ms. Means, supported by Bishop Craine, announced that she would become the first woman in the Diocese of Indianapolis to be a candidate for holy orders. The vestry of the parish she was then serving, St. Matthew's, endorsed her by a single vote. In April 1974, Ms. Means was ordained by Bishop Craine as the diocese's first female deacon, a classification of clergy separate and distinct from priests.

In 1975, Deacon Means asked for an endorsement as a priest from the vestry of All Saints, Indianapolis, where she had been assigned. At first, the All Saints vestry declined to give the endorsement. The rector of All Saints, the Rev. R. Stewart Wood, in a great show of support for Deacon Means, told the vestry members that if they were going to discriminate on the basis of gender, he would consider leaving The Episcopal Church. Faced with the rector's drastic threat, the vestry then approved the endorsement, but with a caveat that it was valid only after the Church's canons, the laws of the Church, were changed to allow the ordination of women.

In 1974, the Rt. Rev. Paul Moore Jr., bishop of New York (who earlier as dean of Christ Church Cathedral, Indianapolis, had worked with Bishop Craine) came close to ordaining women as priests, albeit outside the canons of the Church, but eventually declined to do so. Three retired bishops in Philadelphia, however, that year did attempt to ordain 11 women outside applicable canon law. Afterwards, though, the House of Bishops voted 129 to nine (with seven abstentions) to invalidate the Philadelphia ordinations. One of the abstainers was Bishop Craine. He together with 66 other bishops

Trinity acolytes, circa *1970s.*
Trinity Episcopal Church

then began to co-sponsor the changes in the canon law of The Episcopal Church needed to allow the ordination of women.

By the time of The Episcopal Church's General Convention held in Minneapolis in September 1976, it was clear that the momentum for the approval of the ordination of women was irresistible, and at that convention the Church finally approved the ordination of women to the priesthood.

Bishop Craine wasted no time. In November 1976, he announced that on January 1, 1977, Deacon Jackie Means would be ordained to the priesthood at All Saints, Indianapolis, as the first female Episcopal priest in the United States, and Tanya Beck would be ordained as a priest a few days later on January 8. The services at All Saints were not uneventful. There were peaceful albeit emotional protests (e.g., cries of "Heresy!" and people walking out of the service in tears) as well as coverage by the national media, and Ms. Beck felt it necessary to wear a bullet-proof vest under her vestments. Unfortunately, Bishop Craine was too ill to perform the ordination services for which he had worked so hard, and his role in the ordinations was taken by Bishop Donald James Davis of the Diocese of Northwestern Pennsylvania, formerly the rector of St. Christopher's, Carmel, Indiana.

The groundbreaking decision to ordain women, of course, overturned nearly 2,000 years of tradition in The Episcopal Church and its forebears,

Trinity's choir, 1976; the women's
Canterbury caps later were dispensed with.
Trinity Episcopal Church

the Anglican and Roman Catholic Churches. In the years to come, women
would have a dramatic impact on The Episcopal Church throughout the
nation and in Indianapolis in particular.

Another remarkable change came out of the same General Convention
in 1976 that also affected The Episcopal Church nationally and locally. Nearly
as controversial as the approval to ordain women was the decision to replace
the 1928 Book of Common Prayer and its Low Church, Victorian influences
with a new prayer book that incorporated parts of the original Anglican
Book of Common Prayer, a more High Church liturgy, with a more modern
American style. Changes were made in the liturgy, including the passing of
the peace, the use of lay persons to pass the chalice, and a greater emphasis
on the Eucharist, i.e., communion.

Revision of the Book of Common Prayer had been commissioned at the
1964 General Convention, and at the 1967 convention a trial liturgy had
been approved. Parishes within the Diocese of Indianapolis reacted differ-
ently to the trial liturgy. In Indianapolis, both St. Paul's and the Church of
the Nativity generally were supportive. St. Christopher's in suburban Carmel
and Christ Church Cathedral were more negative. By the time the new Book
of Common Prayer arrived, the parishes that had used the trial liturgy experienced few problems with the new book.

Such was not necessarily the case with parishes that had not used the
trial liturgy, including Trinity. All during the 1970s, Trinity had battled
against revision to the Book of Common Prayer, and the vestry consistently

affirmed its dedication to the 1928 prayer book. Rev. Lynch at least managed to keep the parish abreast of the inevitable changes he saw coming, which perhaps softened the reaction at Trinity when the new Book of Common Prayer did go into effect. Nevertheless, after 1976, some conservative parishioners dropped away from Trinity over the ordination of women, the new prayer book, or both.

In 1977, two giants of The Episcopal Church in Indianapolis died: Bishop John Pares Craine and Eli Lilly. The first of these, Bishop Craine, had led the Diocese of Indianapolis through the turbulent years of the 1960s and 1970s. The Rev. Edward Witker "Ted" Jones was elected bishop coadjutor of the Diocese of Indianapolis on March 26, 1977, and was consecrated as the new bishop of Indianapolis on September 10. Bishop Craine was scheduled to retire in 1978 but, unfortunately, died on Christmas Eve 1977. It could be argued that Bishop Craine made more of an imprint on The Episcopal Church, the Diocese of Indianapolis, and the city of Indianapolis than any of his predecessors in Indiana.

The second of these giants, Eli Lilly, left a very tangible legacy. This Eli Lilly—Colonel Eli Lilly's grandson, who had persuaded his father and younger brother to found the Lilly Endowment—had become concerned that many well-established churches in Indianapolis were leaving the inner city to move to the suburbs and that the three Meridian Street Episcopal churches—Christ Church Cathedral, Trinity, and St. Paul's—might not be able to afford their inner city ministries in the future. Mr. Lilly was fond of all three churches and worshipped from time to time at both Trinity and St. Paul's in addition to Christ Church, his home parish. To ensure the continuation of the three Meridian Street churches, he provided in his will that each of Trinity and St. Paul's would receive four percent and Christ Church Cathedral would receive 10 percent of the remainder of his estate.

Upon Mr. Lilly's death in 1977, Trinity received 132,000 shares of Eli Lilly and Company common stock, valued at close to $4 million ($17 million in 2019 dollars). The gift was received by the Endowment Account of the parish's Memorial Fund. (Later, the Endowment Account of the Memorial Fund would be split off and become the Benefaction. During the 2000s, the Benefaction would become referred to more often as the Endowment and, eventually, as the Trinity Church Legacy Fund.) The gift to Trinity produced dividend income annually of approximately $250,000 ($1 million in 2019 dollars), a sum greater than the annual budget of Trinity in 1977.

The Rev. Canon James B. Lemler of Christ Church Cathedral,
Rev. Lynch, and the Rt. Rev. and Rt. Hon. Arthur Michael
Ramsey, the former archbishop of Canterbury.
Trinity Episcopal Church

Mr. Lilly also made significant bequests to The Episcopal Church and to the Diocese of Indianapolis. Because of his donations to the National Cathedral in Washington, D.C., Mr. Lilly is one of three people who have memorial plaques recognizing them in the Cathedral. The other two are John D. Rockefeller and Andrew Mellon. Mr. Lilly, through his many gifts, became one of the greatest benefactors in the history of The Episcopal Church in the United States.

It is not a stretch to say that Trinity played a significant role in ensuring that Mr. Lilly would so generously benefit the three Meridian Street churches, the diocese, and the national Church. During his later years, Mr. Lilly was tempted by friends to leave The Episcopal Church and become a member of the Congregationalist Church. It was in large part his strong bond of friendship with Rev. Lynch and members of Trinity parish that kept Mr. Lilly as an active member of The Episcopal Church.

Mr. Lilly's gifts to the three Meridian Street churches had immediate effect. The 1976 General Convention in Minneapolis—the same one that had approved the ordination of women to the priesthood and the new Book of Common Prayer—had issued a call for a Venture in Mission, providing mission development funding for the national Church. In 1978, the Most

Rev. John Maury Allin, presiding bishop of The Episcopal Church, visited the three Meridian Street churches and persuaded them to make one of the largest cooperative gifts to Venture in Mission. In 1979, Trinity and St. Paul's each pledged $1 million, and Christ Church Cathedral pledged $600,000, all payable over 10 years, none of which would have been possible without Mr. Lilly's gifts. In 2019 dollars, these amounts would total almost $10 million. The donations provided many benefits locally, such as improvements at Waycross Camp and Conference Center, but also endowed what became Volunteers in Mission, the provider of The Episcopal Church's volunteer service movement around the world.

Rev. Lynch dedicating the sundial in
the knot garden, a gift from him and his wife
upon his retirement as rector of Trinity, 1979.
Trinity Episcopal Church

The last 10 years of Rev. Lynch's tenure as rector of Trinity were noteworthy for the many changes that the parish experienced. Trinity absorbed the Lilly Benefaction, the new prayer book, new liturgies, and new lay participation in services. In December 1978, after an eventful career, Rev. Lynch retired as rector of Trinity Episcopal Church, Indianapolis.

After a year and a half search for a new rector to succeed Rev. Lynch, Trinity's vestry in April 1980 called the Rev. Roger J. White, a native of

Yorkshire, England, to be the ninth rector of the church. Father White embodied high energy, personal charisma, a fast-moving style, and a desire and ability to shake things up at Trinity. He brought a more High Church manner to worship services, licensed women to administer the chalice, organized a campaign to purchase a new pipe organ, licensed lay persons to give communion to shut-ins, and actively sought new congregants. He also was highly involved in laying the groundwork for what in 1985 would become the Consortium of Endowed Episcopal Parishes, a group of parishes that, like Trinity, were blessed with benefactions and that organized to meet and communicate about common issues.

The Rev. Roger J. White,
ninth rector of Trinity.
Trinity Episcopal Church

In July 1981, Father White made the Rev. Dr. James B. "Jim" Lemler the associate rector of Trinity. Shortly afterwards, Father White hired Scott Benhase as a deacon and, after Mr. Benhase's ordination, as a curate. With that, Trinity started making more changes.

In 1981, the Mid-North Council of Churches was organized in Indianapolis, and Trinity became a member. Also in that year, a new pipe organ was installed at Trinity by The Schantz Organ Company of Orrville, Ohio, a major national builder and restorer of pipe organs.

In January 1982, a significant event for racial diversity at Trinity was achieved when Fred Scott, an Indianapolis attorney, became the first African-American elected to the vestry. Mr. Scott, however, was only one of many people of color who would serve Trinity in a wide variety of roles and ways through the years.

Also in 1982, the Madrigal Guild proposed to the vestry that a columbarium on the east wall of the cloister walk be constructed to hold the ashes of cremated parishioners, and the Guild donated $18,000 in profits from the Madrigal Dinners for the project. The proposal was accepted, and the

Madrigal Dinner singers, circa *1980s.*
Trinity Episcopal Church

columbarium was built later in 1982. And, finally that year, The Episcopal Church's new hymnal was published and first used at Trinity's Sunday services.

The time period covered by this chapter—the late 1960s–early 1980s—was a momentous time for the nation as a whole. During these years, America went through the Vietnam War, the Watergate scandal and the resignation of President Richard M. Nixon, uncertain economic times, growing instability in the Middle East, and the beginnings of more conservative politics. The Episcopal Church, now with women priests and a new prayer book and hymnal, also experienced rapid and, for some, disconcerting change. But the changes would keep coming in the future.

Chapter 14

The End of a Millennium: 1984–1999

After four short but highly productive years as the rector of Trinity Episcopal Church, Indianapolis, Father Roger White was elected bishop coadjutor of Milwaukee in 1984. In his time at Trinity, Father White altered Trinity's course and put the parish on an exciting new trajectory. Beginning with Father White's arrival at Trinity and continuing through the rest of the twentieth century, the clergy and parishioners of Trinity would become true leaders of The Episcopal Church at both the diocesan and national levels as well as in ecumenical organizations.

The vestry of Trinity, lacking any desire to go through another protracted search for a rector and being certain that the best choice was a priest already serving at the church, immediately selected 31-year-old Father Jim Lemler as the new rector. In September 1984, Father Lemler was celebrated as the tenth rector of Trinity, and Father White was consecrated as bishop coadjutor of Milwaukee. Bishop Coadjutor White was installed as bishop of Milwaukee in 1985 and served until he retired in 2003.

More change soon was to occur for Trinity's talented group of clergy. Also in 1984, Trinity's curate, Father Scott Benhase, accepted a call to be rector of St. Paul's, East Cleveland, Ohio, an urban parish in one of the poorest communities in the country. He would later serve as rector for other inner city churches in Virginia, North Carolina, and Washington, D.C. Father Benhase, a champion for minorities in The Episcopal Church, was installed as bishop of Georgia in 2010 and served until he retired in 2019.

Father Lemler had a long and fruitful career as rector of Trinity. By way of example of Trinity's leadership at this time, Father Lemler served as president of the Church Federation of Greater Indianapolis in 1991–1992. Indianapolis's Church Federation had been founded in the nineteenth century and was the second oldest city church council in the country after Chicago's. It also was the first to include traditionally African-American churches.

During this time, Trinity also was a leader in the Indiana Office of Campus Ministry and, with St. Paul's, Indianapolis, a leader in the formation of the first Episcopal campus ministry at Butler University in Indianapolis. Trinity also became a gathering place for Lutheran and Episcopal clergy from around the state to meet, discuss, and learn, which led to the Call to Common Mission of Lutherans and Episcopalians, a major ecumenical milestone. Additionally, Trinity provided leadership for the diocese in founding the first new congregations since the 1960s, including Holy Family, Fishers, Indiana.

During 1984–1985, Trinity became heavily involved in aiding refugee families who were forced to flee their native countries. The director for the Presiding Bishop's Fund for World Relief, Marnie Dawson Carr, was well-acquainted with Father Lemler and asked him whether the Diocese of Indianapolis and Trinity would serve as a test model diocese and parish for the resettlement of refugees in America. Father Lemler agreed, and Trinity began its program of resettling refugee families from Poland, South Africa, Vietnam, and Nigeria in Indianapolis. Trinity also aided the founding of the Diocesan Refugee Resettlement Commission, with Father Lemler serving as its first chair. This commission later grew into Exodus Refugee Immigration ministry in Indianapolis, about which more will be said in Chapter 19.

When a group of 10 churches formed the Consortium of Endowed Episcopal Parishes in January 1985 at the House of the Redeemer in New York City, Father Lemler (then Trinity's associate rector) and Trinity Senior Warden Ed Burns were Trinity's representatives. Father Lemler was chosen to serve as the Consortium's first vice president. He subsequently became the Consortium's president, holding that position until 1992, and guiding the Consortium's growth to more than 25 members. With Father Lemler playing a leading role, the Consortium became a solid organization.

In 1985, Trinity once again proved its dedication to the immediate neighborhood. The church and others nearby—North United Methodist Church, Tabernacle Presbyterian Church, Broadway United Methodist Church, and Our Redeemer Lutheran Church—together with the Mapleton-Fall Creek Neighborhood Association formed the non-profit organization, Mapleton-Fall Creek Development Corporation (MFCDC). MFCDC became dedicated to increasing the Mapleton-Fall Creek neighborhood's quality of life by providing safe and affordable housing and working to stimulate economic opportunities for its residents.

*The Rev. Dr. James B. Lemler, tenth rector of Trinity (seated),
with associate rectors, the Rev. Nancy Ferriani and the Rev.
William Hibbert, and Trinity's director of music, Barry Gibble.*
Trinity Episcopal Church

Thanks to Father Lemler's initiative, nearly 10 years after women were first ordained as priests in Indianapolis, the parish welcomed female clergy. Nancy Ferriani, the first female deacon at Trinity, was hired in 1986. After ordination to the priesthood in April 1987, Mother Ferriani was successively promoted in turn to curate, assistant to the rector, associate rector, and senior associate rector. Lisa Kraske Cressman was hired as the second female deacon in November 1992. After her ordination, Mother Cressman also rose through the ranks of curate, assistant to the rector, and associate rector.

During this time, Trinity also was a critical partner in forming or assisting with the formation of several important ministries in the city which would later become Diocesan Cooperative Ministries. In 1989, Trinity provided leadership when a renovated building adjoining All Saints on 16th Street opened as Dayspring Center Emergency Shelter, a resource to assist homeless families with children. The Diocese of Indianapolis thereupon made Dayspring Center a Diocesan Cooperative Ministry along with two other ministries that had come before in the 1970s, The Julian Center and Alternatives, Inc., both of which combatted sexual and domestic violence.

Additionally, the diocese created another Diocesan Cooperative Ministry about the same time as Dayspring Center, that being Damien Center, which brought relief and sought prevention from the Human Immunodeficiency Virus (HIV) after the Acquired Immune Deficiency Syndrome (AIDS) crisis erupted. Trinity was actively and cooperatively involved with other churches in the formation of both The Julian Center and Damien Center.

Another major project was the increase of the physical space of St. Richard's and Trinity. In 1985, Trinity purchased the St. Edward's House at 3256 North Pennsylvania Street, just south of 33rd Street. In 1987, the parish initiated a $5 million capital campaign ($11 million in 2019 dollars) for additional building expansion. Trinity pledged to contribute half of that amount, most of it from the Benefaction. Additional gifts came from the Lilly Endowment, the Clowes Fund, and many generous individuals. The project resulted in new buildings along 33rd Street, a new interior quadrangle, a multi-purpose room (i.e., the gymnasium), labs, and meeting rooms. St. Richard's was expanded to include seventh and eighth grades. In addition, the parish house was extensively remodeled.

Under Father Lemler, Trinity flourished in its leadership in the creation or co-creation of yet more major ministry programs in the community. Shortly after Bishop John Pares Craine died in 1977, the Diocese of Indianapolis had created John P. Craine House (generally known as, simply, Craine House) in downtown Indianapolis. It was a facility for women who would soon be released from the prison system that would give them a second chance at rehabilitation. Craine House gave them the support and tools they needed to make positive steps toward law-abiding lives and reintegration into the community. Craine House, however, was forced to close in 1980 after the Indiana General Assembly pulled funding for work-release programs in the state.

In 1990, though, Craine House was reopened and, thanks largely to an initiative by Trinity, was relocated a short distance from Trinity's campus. (In 2013, Craine House would leave Trinity's neighborhood for much larger facilities at 6130 North Michigan Road.) The Diocese of Indianapolis also made Craine House a Diocesan Cooperative Ministry. In 1993, Craine House's mission was expanded to include the women's children, the unintended victims of the criminal justice system. Women sentenced to Craine House then could serve their sentences along with their preschool aged children. Craine House became the only facility in the Midwest, and one of only six facilities in the nation, that allowed incarcerated women to do that.

Another important mission of the parish was developed during this time by Katherine Tyler Scott, a Trinity parishioner who was director of the Lilly Endowment Leadership Education Program, a statewide leadership development program for professionals working in youth programs. Ms. Tyler Scott and four of the 52 Lilly Fellows trained in the program were asked to develop educational resources for boards of directors of not-for-profit organizations. These resources were developed and field-tested with 70 Indiana organizations. The response was such that the Lilly Endowment provided funding to disseminate the resources more widely. This was the genesis of Trustee Leadership Development (TLD).

As TLD grew, it required an affiliation with an organization that could assist it with administration and bookkeeping. Because TLD's philosophy of leadership focused on character as well as competence, and because TLD wanted an organizational affiliation whose mission and values were compatible with its own, Ms. Tyler Scott approached Father Lemler and asked whether Trinity would serve as the administrative institution for TLD. In 1989, TLD became an official program of Trinity.

In 1998, TLD was incorporated to enable it to strengthen its governance and financial oversight. TLD became funded by the Lilly Endowment and also obtained revenues from fees for services and sales of TLD educational resources. During TLD's first 10 years of existence, more than 15,000 individuals and 800 organizations across the country, including Trinity, St. Richard's, and the Diocese of Indianapolis, received training and services from TLD.

During this time, Trinity began the process of becoming a steward for the neighborhood and providing space for important services. In 1994, Trinity purchased for $1.6 million ($2.76 million in 2019 dollars) the office building and parking lot at 3333 North Meridian Street, half a block north of its sanctuary. The previous owner and occupant had been Anthem Life Insurance Company. Trinity refurbished and leased the building to Wishard Health Services, part of Wishard Memorial Hospital (later renamed Eskenazi Hospital), to be used as the largest of Wishard's Midtown Community Mental Health Centers and the largest mental health center of any kind in the city. Although Wishard would be a rent-paying tenant for Trinity, the clergy and vestry of Trinity felt strongly that the presence of a mental health center was an important contribution for the people living in the neighborhood. For the next 10 years, 3333 North Meridian Street was both a revenue-producer for Trinity and a genuine benefit to the community.

It was during this time that Father Lemler and director of Christian education, Kim McPherson, introduced many innovations in adult and children's formation at Trinity. Journey in Faith (JIF) became a new opportunity for parishioners to deepen their faith in community by exploring together the history, practices, and theology of The Episcopal Church. The introduction of JIF resulted in one of the largest numbers of adults being received and confirmed at Trinity in its recent history. The Lenten Series turned into an annual multi-night program during Lent on a variety of topics created jointly with Christ Church Cathedral. Sunday Adult Forum provided learning opportunities on Sundays after worship services on a wide variety of subjects.

New children's ministries also were varied and effective. Trinity introduced Godly Play, a new program for teaching young children in Sunday school developed by the Rev. Dr. Jerome W. Berryman, an attorney and Episcopal priest. Trinity also initiated an innovative program for teenagers in the parish created by The Episcopal Church called Journey to Adulthood (J2A). The J2A program consisted of a complete youth ministry program of spiritual formation for sixth through twelfth graders. The program encouraged relational ministry and used Bible study, prayer, rites of passage, outreach ministries, and serious and fun activities to underscore the two guiding principles of the program: first, manhood and womanhood are free gifts from God; second, adulthood must be earned.

In 1996 after 15 years at Trinity, Father Lemler—in spite of the fact he was the rector of a parish within the diocese—was one of five priests nominated as a candidate for bishop coadjutor of Indianapolis. Father Lemler was not elected to that position, however, and the Rev. Catherine M. "Cate" Waynick, the rector of All Saints, Pontiac, Michigan, was elected on the third ballot. Bishop Waynick became the first female bishop of Indianapolis and the fifth female Anglican bishop in the world. The following year, Father Lemler was again nominated as a candidate for a bishop coadjutor position, this time of New York, but he withdrew his name from nomination for that position during the election process.

By then it was clear to everyone that Father Lemler, one of the bright stars in The Episcopal Church, eventually would receive another call that he would accept. This happened in April 1998, when he accepted a call to become dean and president of Seabury-Western Seminary in Evanston, Illinois. As he was leaving Trinity, Father Lemler and his wife, Sharon, were given an emotional leave-taking for which the Trinity choir commissioned

The Rt. Rev. Catherine Maples Waynick,
tenth bishop of Indianapolis.
Lindsay Haake

a hymn by composer Cary Ratcliff, *Love Simple Things*. Father Lemler then departed Trinity for Seabury-Western in August 1998. Numerous Trinity parishioners and the Trinity choir traveled to Evanston to participate in Father Lemler's installation at the seminary.

After his time at Seabury-Western, Father Lemler continued his career as director of mission for The Episcopal Church in New York City and then as rector of Christ Church, Greenwich, Connecticut. In 2018, he and his wife, Sharon, returned to Indianapolis, where Father Lemler became president of the Allen Whitehill Clowes Charitable Foundation, Inc., about which more will be said in Chapter 19. Father Lemler and his wife also made Trinity, once again, their church home in Indianapolis.

After Father Lemler left and in response to new trends for Episcopal schools, St. Richard's School began making changes that would have ramifications for the school and Trinity in the future. Under the school's original articles of incorporation, a majority of the school's board of directors were required to be members of Trinity, new members of the board were subject

Palm Sunday procession from the Lemler Garden,
a gift of parishioners in honor of
Father Jim and Sharon Lemler, 1999.
Trinity Episcopal Church

to the approval of Trinity's vestry, and the vestry could dismiss the entire board with or without cause. Under the school's bylaws, the rector of Trinity automatically was president of the board and an ex-officio member of the board.

In 1998, however, the board of directors of St. Richard's adopted, and the vestry of Trinity ratified, a reorganization plan whereby Trinity's rector would no longer be president of the board but would remain a voting board member. By this time, only about 20 percent of the enrollment at St. Richard's was Episcopalian, and for various reasons—including capital formation, which the school felt was hampered as long as it was part of a church—the board had a strong desire to become more independent, a fever that was evident in other Episcopal schools nationally. Other significant changes in the relationship of the school and the church would occur in the next few years.

Previously, when a rector left Advent or Trinity, the vestry would hire a new rector as soon as possible. After Father Lemler left, however, the vestry used the fairly new concept of hiring an interim rector while a search for a new permanent rector went on. The notion of an interim ministry during a time of transition in an Episcopal parish had begun to develop in the 1960s.

The concept of interim pastor began to take hold in The Episcopal Church in the mid-1970s. Finally, the position of interim pastor was formalized at the General Convention held in Detroit on July 2–11, 1988, by the following resolution:

> *An interim pastor is a priest with parish experience and interim*
> *ministry skills and training, who can give guidance to parishes which*
> *are between rectors, and who understands and is trained to respond*
> *to dynamics and issues which come into operation during the interim*
> *period. . . . The interim pastor is not a candidate for the permanent*
> *position.*

Warren Smith, Trinity's senior warden at the time of Father Lemler's departure, learned that the Rev. Earl Wepley, who had previously worked at both St. Paul's and Christ Church Cathedral in Indianapolis, was available for such a position. The vestry interviewed Father Wepley and unanimously approved offering him the position of interim rector. Father Wepley accepted and started in that position, the first ever interim rector of Trinity, in August 1998.

Father Wepley, a native Yankee from New England, was extremely forthright in manner and speech. Everyone in the church soon understood from Father Wepley that Trinity had two jobs to do: first, carry on as a functioning parish; second, start the search for a new rector.

The last years of the millennium were good ones for Trinity. During the period 1984–1998, the number of households and membership in the parish (especially of young families with children) grew substantially despite a fall in Episcopal affiliation in Marion County as a whole. During 1990–1998, the number of communicants in good standing officially grew from 604 to 678, and the number of baptized members officially grew from 832 to 1,036. Membership also became more diverse, Trinity's worship services became ever more beautiful, and the parish's music program flourished. In addition, Trinity's Benefaction grew to be greater than $26 million.

Through the work of Father White, Father Lemler, Mother Ferriani, Mother Cressman, and numerous other members of the parish, Trinity had become a recognized leader of the Diocese of Indianapolis and The Episcopal Church. In essence, Trinity had become less inward-looking and had started to think more about its role in the city, state, nation, and world. The parish had begun its mission of benefiting people in need in many ways and in many places, albeit mostly through funding and providing space for projects managed by people outside the parish. Without question, these efforts were hugely important and impactful. In future years, Trinity would continue to build on this foundation of good works and enlightened mission.

Part Five

The New Millennium: 2000–2019

Sunday Worship Service
at Trinity Episcopal Church
Trinity Episcopal Church

Chapter 15

The City in the Twenty-First Century:
2000–2019

Strong leadership and smart business sense took Indianapolis from sleepy backward India-no-place in the 1950s and 1960s to a more vibrant progressive Indy by the 1970s. Fortunately, those trends continued into the following decades. Many cities in the industrial Midwest and Northeast dealt with Rust Belt issues beginning in the 1980s, but Indianapolis and Columbus, Ohio, were the only two cities in that region whose populations grew during that time.

In 2019, Indianapolis was ranked as the thirteenth largest city in the country. According to the 2000 U.S. census, Indianapolis's population was 781,926. The 2010 U.S. census had this number pegged at 829,718. This number seemed to continue to grow at a rate of about 8,000 people per year. At that rate, the population of Indianapolis in 2019 could have been 870,000 to 900,000, a far cry from the population of 500 who settled there 200 years before.

The area around Indianapolis also grew with new suburbs to the south, west, and north. By 2015, the 11 counties surrounding and including Indianapolis had an estimated population of about two million and was the thirty-fourth largest metropolitan area in the country. According to projections by the Indiana University Kelley School of Business, the Indianapolis metropolitan area should be Indiana's primary source of population growth over the coming decades and could grow to 2.5 million by 2050. If the Indianapolis metro area's population reaches that level, its share of the total Indiana population will be over one-third.

*Monument Circle with Christ Church
Cathedral in the foreground and the
Indiana Statehouse in the background, circa 2000.*
Harold Lee Miller

Indianapolis's growth in the twenty-first century was fueled in part by the city's historic connection to sports dating back to 1909 and the construction of the Indianapolis Motor Speedway. Starting with the 1982 National Sports Festival and the 1987 Pan American Games, city leaders set a goal of Indianapolis becoming a nationally prominent sports hub. In 1997, the National Collegiate Athletic Association (NCAA), the most important organization in collegiate athletics, asked for bids to build a new headquarters to replace its outmoded one in an outlying suburb of Kansas City. The NCAA was a massive organization that regulated more than 1,200 institutions in the United States and Canada and more than 480,000 college athletes participating in three divisions and 19 men's sports and 21 women's sports.

Naturally, Indianapolis submitted its bid to be the new headquarters city for the NCAA. The NCAA was exactly the kind of organization Indianapolis thought would be a perfect fit for its vision of being a national sports center. Several other cities competed to be the new location, as well. After all the bids were evaluated, the two finalists were Kansas City and Indianapolis. In the end, the NCAA chose Indianapolis and moved its 300-member staff to new headquarters in a 140,000 square foot building in the city's downtown White River State Park. The reasons for the NCAA choosing Indianapolis were many: Indianapolis had closer proximity to more NCAA members, its central city was closer to its airport, and its downtown 50,000-seat RCA Dome was perfect for hosting major college tournaments.

Partly because of the NCAA's headquarters in Indianapolis and partly because of the quality and convenience of the many athletic facilities in the city, Indianapolis has been the location for some of the biggest athletic events in the country. The city has hosted the NCAA Division I Men's Basketball Championship a total of four times and was scheduled to host it again in the year 2021. The city also has hosted the NCAA Division I Women's Basketball Championship three times. These tournaments have been very big business for the city. In its 2016–2017 fiscal year, the NCAA took in $1.06 billion in revenue, more than 80 percent of which was generated by the Division I Men's Basketball Tournament.

The Big Ten Conference, the oldest college athletic conference in the country and based in suburban Chicago, has held the Big Ten Football Championship in Indianapolis from 2011–2018, and was scheduled to hold it in the city at least through 2021. The Big Ten Men's Basketball Championship has been held 10 times in Indianapolis, and was scheduled to be held in the city in 2020 and 2022. The Big Ten Women's Basketball Championship has been held in Indianapolis an amazing 21 times, and was scheduled to be held in the city at least through 2022.

The Indianapolis headquarters of the
National Collegiate Athletic Association
and the Hall of Champions.
Jason Lavengood

At about the turn of the century, the Indianapolis Colts of the National Football League (NFL), who had moved to Indianapolis in 1984 and been consistent losers for years, became an NFL powerhouse. The team's success, culminating in winning Super Bowl XLI in 2006, helped turn Hoosiers into passionate football fans as well as basketball fans.

By 2007, Indianapolis's growing convention and sports traffic had made the home of the Colts, the 24-year-old RCA Dome, obsolete. In 2008, the city undertook the huge project of constructing the $720 million Lucas Oil Stadium in downtown to replace the dome. Although many people thought the prime mover for the new stadium was the Colts organization, the real force behind it was the city, which wanted to build the stadium as part of a $275 million expansion of the Indiana Convention Center completed in 2011.

Indianapolis was rewarded for its efforts when the NFL's Super Bowl XLVI was held at Lucas Oil Stadium on February 5, 2012. It was only the fourth Super Bowl out of 46 that had been held in a city outside the Sun Belt. Indianapolis benefited greatly from being the host of one of the largest televised events in America with additional televised coverage to 32 foreign countries. The central location, smooth operation, close proximity of restaurants and hotels to venues, and novel activities (e.g., a downtown zip line!)

*Indianapolis at night the week
before Super Bowl XLVI, 2012.*

Jason Lavengood

for the Super Bowl made Indianapolis a winner with the national media. Moreover, hosting the two-week-long event boosted the local economy by an estimated $324 million.

Although sports venues became a primary part of the evolving Indianapolis cityscape, city leaders also knew they had to deal with a growing population and an aging infrastructure. In 2011, public utility Citizens Energy Group began DigIndy, a $2 billion construction project to correct Indianapolis's combined sewer overflows (CSOs) by 2025. When completed, the DigIndy Tunnel System should be a 28-mile long network of 18-foot diameter deep rock tunnels 250 feet beneath the city. Along with other projects including two advanced wastewater treatment plants, the DigIndy program should reduce CSOs into area waterways by up to 97 percent.

A surprising contributor to the success of Indianapolis during this time period was the rise of the technology industry in the city. The creation of local tech millionaires by the acquisition of Software Artistry by IBM in 1997 was referred to in Chapter 12. This was followed by other acquisitions of local tech companies, including the purchase of Indianapolis-based Aprimo by Teradata for $525 million in 2000, the $2.5 billion acquisition of Exact Target by Salesforce in 2013, and the $1.4 billion acquisition of Interactive Intelligence by Genesys in 2016. The Indianapolis metropolitan region during the years 2010–2015 gained 9,200 technology jobs, doubling the number in previous years. Indeed, by 2015 Indianapolis had become acknowledged to be an important, growing technology center.

Life sciences were another significant contributor to the city's growth. The presence of Eli Lilly and Company in Indianapolis had made it a significant player in the health field for many decades. Moreover, Indianapolis had long been the home of several important hospitals. By the twenty-first century, Indianapolis and Indiana also had become home to more than 1,600 life sciences companies, plants, and offices in the fields of medical laboratories, pharmaceuticals, medical devices and equipment, health information technology, and agriculture. A large number of these were centered around Indianapolis, including—in addition to Eli Lilly and Company—Roche Diagnostics, Dow AgroSciences (renamed Corteva), Anthem, AIT Laboratories, Exelead, Envigo, Covance, and Beckman Coulter.

The traffic and dollars that came into downtown Indianapolis as a result of sports, conventions, and business activity resulted in a downtown that was the envy of mid-sized cities across the country. By 2019, more than 150,000 employees worked in downtown Indianapolis, and the number of downtown residents had grown to nearly 30,000.

The headquarters of Eli Lilly and Company.
Jason Lavengood

Indeed, the influx of downtown housing and a youthful population changed the city's vibe remarkably. Indianapolis experienced growing numbers of hotels, theaters, concert halls, restaurants, museums, shopping areas, fitness facilities, spas, schools, places of worship, and other amenities, all within a short distance of Monument Circle. The city got a further boost in 2013 with the completion of the $63 million eight-mile Cultural Trail, a walking and bicycling path that connected all six of Indianapolis's cultural districts from Massachusetts Avenue to White River State Park to Fountain Square.

The $1.1 billion Colonel H. Weir Cook Terminal at Indianapolis International Airport was another major construction project completed in 2008. Indianapolis first started to grow as a railroad center in the 1840s and had remained a transportation hub ever since, but the modern means of transportation had become airplanes and trucks rather than railroads. From the time it first opened in 2008, Indianapolis International consistently would be acknowledged as the best passenger airport in the country.

In addition, Indianapolis International became a major commercial air traffic center. FedEx Express, the cargo airline, operated its national hub out of Indianapolis International, which became the second largest hub operation in the world behind only FedEx's Superhub in Memphis, Tennessee. FedEx operated flights directly from Indianapolis to FedEx hubs in Europe and Asia.

Historically, Indianapolis had an extensive network of streetcar routes, and up until the early 1940s, the state was tied together by an interurban light rail network. In 1953, streetcars stopped running in Indianapolis, and trolleybuses made their last run in the city four years later. As a result, the city was left with an all-bus public transit system. In 1975, the Indianapolis Public Transportation Corporation was established by the city as a municipal corporation to take over the privately owned Indianapolis Transit System. The corporation initially operated as Metro but in 1997 changed its operating name to IndyGo.

In the 2010s, the city made efforts to improve public transportation in the city. The Julia M. Carson Transit Center at 201 East Washington Street in downtown Indianapolis was constructed during 2014–2016 for $26.5 million. (The late Julia M. Carson was the U.S. representative for Indiana's 7th congressional district during 1997–2007 and helped secure federal funding for the transit center.) Formal bus service started on June 26, 2016. IndyGo's 31 routes had a total of 7,000 stops; 26 of the routes offered transfers at the center.

Part of the Cultural Trail.
Jason Lavengood

Monument Circle in the twenty-first century.
Jason Lavengood

In the late 2010s, Indianapolis began its most ambitious public transportation plan, a $1.2 billion project to create a network of bus rapid transit lines, bikeways, and walkways. The first stage to be constructed was phase one of the Red Line, an electric rapid bus line that was to extend fourteen miles from the north side of the city to the University of Indianapolis on the south side. Construction began in June 2018 and became operational in September 2019.

Much of Indianapolis's success in the first 20 years of the twenty-first century could be attributed to the continuation of its string of highly competent mayors. Mayor Barton R. "Bart" Peterson served two terms from 1999–2008. Mayor Peterson had practiced law and served on the staff of Governor Evan Bayh, eventually becoming the governor's chief of staff. He was the first Democrat to be elected mayor of Indianapolis since John J. Barton in 1967. Peterson was mayor during many of the major construction projects of the first decade of the century, including Indianapolis International Airport and the expansion of the Indiana Convention Center. He merged the Indianapolis Police Department and the Marion County Sheriff's Department to form the Indianapolis Metropolitan Police Department. In addition, he combined several township fire departments with the Indianapolis Fire Department.

The Indiana Convention Center.
Jason Lavengood

Peterson's successor as mayor of Indianapolis, Gregory A. "Greg" Ballard, a Republican, was a surprise dark horse winner over Peterson in 2007 in what was one of the biggest upsets in Indiana political history. Peterson had won his first two elections by landslides and personally was very popular. He had a $4.4 million war chest, while Ballard's was a mere $300,000. Peterson had a problem, however, which was that taxes and crime had increased during his tenure. As a result of those matters, and perhaps overconfidence on the part of Indianapolis Democrats, Ballard was elected by a 50 percent to 47 percent margin.

Mayor Ballard also served for two terms, from 2008–2016. One of his attributes was he was a 23-year decorated veteran of the United States Marine Corps. At the time of his election, though, he was a self-employed consultant with no government experience. He ran against Peterson because no other Republican was willing to do so. After his surprise victory, he astonished everyone by proving to be a very competent and effective mayor. Among other personal strengths, he was willing to listen to people who knew more than he did, a most welcome trait in any elected official.

Under Mayor Ballard, Indianapolis underwent many improvements in infrastructure. He sold the city's water and sewer systems to Citizens Energy Group and issued bonds, all of which raised $504.4 million to be used in the city's RebuildIndy program of street, bridge, and sidewalk improvements.

The city also completed its Convention Center expansion begun under Mayor Peterson.

After Mayor Ballard declined to run for a third term in 2015, the people of Indianapolis elected another Democrat, Joseph H. "Joe" Hogsett, as mayor. Hogsett, a lawyer like Mayor Peterson before him, took office on January 1, 2016, and was reelected in November 2019. Prior to his election, Mayor Hogsett had extensive experience in politics, having served as secretary of state of Indiana from 1989–1994, as chair of the Indiana Democratic Party from 2003–2004, and as the U.S. district attorney for the Southern District of Indiana from 2010–2014. He had other kinds of experience in politics, as well, having run unsuccessfully for the U.S. Senate in 1992, for Indiana's 2nd congressional district in 1994, and for attorney general of Indiana in 2004. Mayor Hogsett commendably continued the initiatives begun by Mayor Ballard for the good of the city of Indianapolis.

But not all the changes in Indianapolis during this time period affected the city's streetscape or skyline; some were purely social in nature. One of the most significant things to happen in the years 2014 and 2015, in not only Indianapolis but throughout the country, was the legalization of same-sex marriage. In Indiana, as in many states, laws on the books restricted marriage to "one man and one woman" and denied recognition to same-sex couples legally married in other states or Canada. But a growing number of state courts were declaring such laws unconstitutional, and legislatures were legalizing same-sex marriage.

In March 2014, the American Civil Liberties Union (ACLU) of Indiana, the national ACLU, and the Lemieux Law Office of Indianapolis filed a lawsuit, *Fujii v. Commissioner of the Indiana State Department of Revenue*, on behalf of six couples, a widow, and two children of same-sex parents. Three members of Trinity Episcopal Church, Indianapolis, were plaintiffs in this lawsuit: longtime parishioners Steven Stolen, Rob MacPherson, and their daughter Abbey had been approached by the ACLU of Indiana to serve in that role. Eventually, the MacPherson Stolens were front and center as spokespersons for the case, including media appearances, public-speaking events, and multiple press conferences. When asked why they were involved, Mr. Stolen consistently remarked that the prohibition against same-sex marriage and how it was defended by some "misrepresents all the good people we know in Indiana. Enough is enough."

In June 2014, in a decision involving *Fujii* and two other lawsuits, *Baskin v. Bogan* and *Lee v. Abbott*, the Indiana Supreme Court issued an opinion written by Chief Justice Richard Young ruling that Indiana's ban on same-sex marriage violated the Due Process and Equal Protection Clauses of the Fourteenth Amendment to the U.S. Constitution. Indiana's executive branch at that time was led by Governor Michael R. "Mike" Pence, self-described as "a Christian, a conservative and a Republican, in that order." Indiana Attorney General Gregory F. "Greg" Zoeller immediately took the matter to federal court, and the U.S. Seventh Circuit Court of Appeals in Chicago stayed the Indiana Supreme Court's order.

A three-judge panel of the Seventh Circuit heard arguments in the appeal of the Indiana case and a similar Wisconsin case in August 2014. Concerned people had lined up outside the courtroom beforehand and filled it to capacity. After deliberation, in the following

Steven Stolen, Abbey MacPherson Stolen, and Rob MacPherson in Chicago, 2014.
Towne Post Network Inc.

month, the Seventh Circuit affirmed the Indiana Supreme Court's decision that banning same-sex marriages would violate the Equal Protection Clause. Writing for the unanimous three-judge panel, Judge Richard Poser explained:

> *[M]ore than unsupported conjecture that same-sex marriage will harm heterosexual marriage or children or any other valid and important interest of a state is necessary to justify discrimination on the basis of sexual orientation. As we have been at pains to explain, the grounds advanced by Indiana and Wisconsin for their discriminatory policies are not only conjectural; they are totally implausible.*

Governor Pence's administration then appealed the case to the U.S. Supreme Court. The Supreme Court in October 2014 denied a hearing on the case, which kept intact the Seventh Circuit's affirmation of the Indiana Supreme Court's decision in support of same-sex marriage. Attorney

General Zoeller immediately informed county clerks across Indiana that they were required to issue marriage licenses to same-sex couples. Then, finally in 2015, the U.S. Supreme Court decided the landmark decision, *Obergefell v. Hodges*, which ruled that all bans on same-sex marriages were unconstitutional.

Religious conservatives were not finished, however. When the members of the Indiana General Assembly returned in session in 2015, the Republican majority adopted Indiana's version of the Religious Freedom Restoration Act (RFRA). But the real controversy erupted when Governor Pence signed Indiana's RFRA into law on March 26, 2015. Why would this cause the uproar for Indiana that it did? After all, the U.S. Congress had adopted a federal Religious Freedom Restoration Act in 1993 that was signed into law by Democratic President Bill Clinton.

The differences in the federal RFRA and Indiana's RFRA, although seemingly subtle, were significant. The federal RFRA applied only to federal and state government infringement of an individual person's religious freedom: it prohibited any agency, department, or official of the United States or any state from substantially burdening an individual's exercise of religion. The law was partially limited in 1997 when the U.S. Supreme Court ruled in *City of Boerne v. Flores* that the federal RFRA's prohibitions could apply only to the federal government, not to state governments. This led to 21 states passing their own Religious Freedom Restoration Acts.

Then, in 2014 the U.S. Supreme Court handed down the landmark decision in *Burwell v. Hobby Lobby Stores, Inc.*, recognizing a for-profit corporation's claim—as opposed to an individual person's claim—of the capability of having religious belief. What made Indiana's RFRA different from any previous version was its extension of the protection against infringement of religious belief, based on *Hobby Lobby Stores*, not only to any individual but also to "a partnership, a limited liability company, a corporation, a company, a firm, a society, a joint-stock company, an unincorporated association," or any other entity claiming to be guided by religious belief, "regardless of whether the entity is organized and operated for profit or nonprofit purposes."

The outcry and opposition to Indiana's RFRA was immediate. Many people saw the new law as granting *carte blanche* to any entity to discriminate against LGBTQ people based on a claim of religious beliefs. Those in favor of the law pointed to the U.S. Constitution's First Amendment's Establishment Clause and its protection of freedom of religion. Those opposed pointed to the U.S. Constitution's Fourteenth Amendment's Equal Protection Clause and its protection against discrimination.

Overall, however, national and local reaction was extremely negative. Companies and universities immediately issued travel bans to Indiana. Conventions and trade shows threatened to cancel their plans to come to the state. Sporting events put Indianapolis on notice that they would not consider the city if Indiana's RFRA remained in place. Major companies in Indiana began to worry about recruiting and retaining employees. Even so, Governor Pence seemed oblivious to the storm of controversy that Indiana's RFRA had caused and defended it on national television.

Then-serving Indianapolis Mayor Greg Ballard, a Republican, lent his voice to the opposition. Four other living former mayors of Indianapolis—Republicans Richard Lugar, Bill Hudnut, and Steve Goldsmith, and Democrat Bart Peterson—stated that they were "distressed and very concerned" at the negative impact on Indiana resulting from the bill.

Mitchell E. "Mitch" Daniels Jr., former Republican governor of Indiana and then-current president of Purdue University, stated that the university was opposed to any governmental measure that interfered with its anti-discrimination policy. The presidents of Indiana University and Butler University issued similar statements in opposition to Indiana's RFRA.

Nine CEOs from companies with presences in Indianapolis—Angie's List, Salesforce Marketing Cloud, Anthem Inc., Eli Lilly and Company, Cummins Inc., Emmis Communications, Roche Diagnostics, Indiana University Health, and Dow AgroSciences—called on Republican leadership in the state to enact legislation to prevent "discrimination based upon sexual orientation or gender identity." Several other corporations with ties to Indiana did likewise, as did numerous professional sports organizations in the state, and so on, and so on.

The result was that the Republicans in the Indiana General Assembly quickly acted to amend Indiana's RFRA. (Democrats in the General Assembly, who wanted to repeal completely Indiana's RFRA, were excluded from the negotiations.) Governor Pence signed the amendments into law on April 2, 2015. As reported by the *Indianapolis Star*:

> *The proposed new language—worked out during private, marathon negotiations on Wednesday between Republican legislative leaders, key business and sports officials and the governor's staff—would alter the Indiana Religious Freedom Restoration Act, or RFRA, to ensure*

it does not discriminate against gay and lesbian customers of Indiana businesses. But it stops short of providing statewide protections against discrimination of gay, lesbian and transgender people.

Overall, most people were satisfied with the revisions to Indiana's RFRA, but there were lingering fears that significant damage had been done to the state's reputation for Hoosier Hospitality with corresponding economic damage for years to come.

At the least, however, after all of the effort that had been waged on their behalf by advocates of every description, same-sex couples finally could have a traditional church wedding at Trinity. In fact, there have been two joyous and celebratory same-sex weddings at Trinity since the LGBTQ-landmark year of 2014.

By 2019, even with all the overall positive things that had happened in Indianapolis in the past 20 years, there were still many problems facing the city. Crime in Indianapolis still had not been remedied, and the city's crime rate remained one of the worst in the country. Hunger was another major problem, with the number of the people in the city facing food insecurity approaching nearly 175,000, more than 18 percent of the population. Drug addiction, especially opiates, and homelessness also continued to be major concerns for the city. With all of these, it would be safe to say that the social fabric of the city was still far from being fully mended.

Fortunately, by the beginning of the new millennium, Trinity was eager to bring its dedication to mission in the city up to a new level.

Chapter 16

Embracing the Neighborhood:
2000–2005

While Indianapolis was growing at the turn of the millennium, Trinity Episcopal Church also was poised for significant changes. Some of these changes would take years to mature and fully develop, but by 2000, church leaders were planting the seeds. Trinity's story during the early years of the new decade is highly impressive because, not only did the church endure extremely challenging economic times, it continued to grow and improve its already impressive programs.

One such planted seed had to do with Trinity's location. Since the time that the Mission to the North created the Church of the Advent at 33rd and Meridian Streets, the church's location had evolved from an upscale suburb to an older inner city neighborhood. Rather than cause parishioners to flee to churches far from the urban core of the city, however, the changes would be seen by those parishioners as a reason for more personal outreach to the immediate community.

To its great credit, Trinity always had been generous with its money for mission and outreach, particularly after it received Mr. Eli Lilly's bequest. As part of the budget process in most years during the 1980s and 1990s, the vestry would approve a large sum of money to be distributed to worthy causes. Applications for financial grants then were solicited, considered, and recommended to the vestry by the Outreach Grants Committee, which was made up of parishioners who were appointed by the rector and approved by the vestry. The vestry also created guidelines for the committee and set a goal for grants to be divided equally among four classes of recipients: international, national, regional, and local. Trinity saw itself as a force for good in many far-flung places, not just the local neighborhood.

By 2000, Trinity's use of money as its primary tool of outreach had reached a high point. The budget for that year called for outreach grants totaling nearly $228,000. Shortly thereafter, however, the use of money in this manner would change dramatically.

In January 1999, Trinity's vestry began the search for a new permanent rector to succeed Father Jim Lemler. First, the vestry selected a consultant for the search from outside the diocese, the Rev. Dr. Richard J. Kirk, the recently retired rector of the Church of the Advent, Kennett Square, Pennsylvania. Next, the vestry chose a Search Committee from members of the congregation, first considering more than 60 names, then narrowing those to 25, and finally selecting 15 members, two of whom—parishioners Steve DeVoe and Rilla Murray—were to serve as co-chairs. Shortly after the committee was established, Ms. Murray relocated to West Virginia with her husband, and the committee determined to proceed with just 14 members. Vestry member Natalie Boehm was selected by the committee to take Ms. Murray's place as one of the co-chairs. The committee also quickly decided that it could function without the consulting services of Father Kirk and proceeded without his assistance.

The Search Committee targeted mid-2000 as the time it would recommend a candidate for rector to the vestry. An important tool in attracting candidates was a written detailed description of Trinity called the *Parish Profile*. The committee studied the profiles developed by similar congregations at that time to create something that potential candidates would recognize and appreciate. It then gathered information and opinions from a parish-wide survey, discussions groups among parishioners, and interviews with church and community organizations. Out of all this, the committee fashioned Trinity's unique profile. A number of very frank impressions of the church, both from the inside and the outside, were revealed by that research.

A large majority of parishioners seemed to think that Trinity was headed in the right direction. The greatest attraction to parishioners at the time was the beauty of the traditional worship service. There also was a strong sense of family. But many parishioners thought some things needed improvement.

Interviews with leaders from government, business, social services, and churches—including but not limited to the governor's and mayor's offices, the Lilly Endowment, the United Way, the Indianapolis Public Schools, the Catholic Archdiocese, the Mid-North Church Council, and the Mapleton-Fall Creek Neighborhood Association—revealed an overall positive impression of Trinity. Flattering descriptors used by those groups included "positive," "caring," "educated," "intellectual," "stressed arts," and "well-respected."

But certain not-so-flattering terms also emerged from these interviews: "elitist," "insular," "rich," "removed," "snooty," "sleeping giant," and "tends to use money, not people." Suggestions on ways to make the parish better included, "provide more volunteers (not just money) to community efforts at improvement" and "provide greater use of facilities for the neighborhood." The Search Committee concluded, "The hope from many sectors is that Trinity will boost volunteerism overall as well as direct 'bold' sums of money to really try to accomplish things in the local neighborhood."

To be fair, however, Trinity had never been absent from the neighborhood at any point in its history. The parish had founded St. Richard's School and was instrumental in establishing the Midtown Mental Health Center and Craine House nearby. But it was clear that the message that it cared about its neighbors was not making it into the community. More work needed to be done.

The Search Committee sent information about Trinity and its objectives for a new rector to The Episcopal Church's Deployment Office in New York City. In response, the committee received a total of 112 names of possible candidates. The committee members trimmed this list first to 30 candidates and then to seven. Groups of Search Committee members thereafter visited, interviewed, and observed these remaining candidates, each over the course of an entire weekend.

During 1999, more change happened in the clergy of Trinity as Associate Rector Lisa Kraske Cressman left to accept a call as rector of St. Thomas Episcopal Church in Whiteland, Indiana. Father Earl Wepley and Mother Nancy Ferriani consequently doubled their efforts and cared on their own for a parish in transition. Fortunately, Father Wepley and Mother Ferriani worked together well and continued to provide stability for the parish while the Search Committee carried on its work.

The vestry also continued hard at work on other important matters. After it ratified the changes in the St. Richard's bylaws that created a new governance structure for the school, the vestry held joint meetings with the St. Richard's board of directors to bring into focus the new relationship between the school and the church. Up to this point, the school had been governed by the rector and vestry of Trinity. Moreover, the church still owned all of the real property used by the two institutions, and there was concern by both whether this would be workable in the future. As a result, Trinity and particularly St. Richard's felt there was a need to evaluate the governance of the school and explore the nature of its relationship with the church. During this discernment process, Karen King Dorfman (later Karen E. King), a Trinity parishioner, was elected president of the St. Richard's board and became the first person who was not the rector of Trinity to hold that position.

Senior Warden Sally Morton reported, "Our main goal is to be certain that the relationship between the School and the Church is maintained in a manner consistent with Trinity's objectives of outreach and mission." Father Wepley noted that there was "a mutual recognition by the Board and the Vestry of Trinity of the need for better communications between the two governing bodies concerning the life and direction of the School" and a need "to assure [*sic*] better communications and understanding of the School as a mission outreach of Trinity Church."

The years 1999 and 2000 also saw changes in lay leadership at the church when two giants of the parish stepped down from long-held positions. In August 1999, Thomas F. "Tom" Whitten retired after serving many years as treasurer of Trinity and was succeeded in that role by parishioner John Craun. Mr. Whitten had served on the vestry numerous times, had served as senior warden twice, and had been instrumental in every aspect of the construction projects for Trinity and St. Richard's in the 1980s. Along with Father Wepley, he had overseen the completion of the construction of the new wing of St. Richard's in 1999.

In January 2000, William R. "Bill" Ehrich retired as clerk of the vestry. Mr. Ehrich had served many three-year terms on the vestry, served as senior warden four times, and always served as the corporate memory of the parish. Mr. Ehrich was a professional photographer, and many of his uncredited photographs can be found in the parish archives and in this book. He also was the official photographer of the fiftieth-anniversary history, *Trinity Episcopal Church 1919–1969*, and was author of another history of Trinity, *A Revised and Updated History of Trinity Episcopal Church, Diocese of Indianapolis.*

With this shift in lay leadership, the two new financial leaders, Treasurer John Craun and Finance Committee Chair Jay Simmons, began to make innovative changes to the financial picture of the parish. In December 1999, they gave the vestry a proposed consolidated budget for 2000, which brought together all sources of revenue as well as expenditures previously shown separately in the parish operating budget, the Memorial Fund budget, and the Benefaction budget. The vestry approved the new consolidated budget, and Mr. Craun presented it at the annual parish meeting the following month.

At the same Annual Meeting, Interim Rector Earl Wepley made his final official report to the parish, in which he identified four challenges that he felt Trinity would face in the coming years: developing a role that was separate from its relationship with St. Richard's; at the same time, strengthening its relationship with a more independent St. Richard's; continuing financial stewardship in order to lessen its dependence on the Benefaction; and strengthening ties with its immediately surrounding neighborhood. Father Wepley was most perceptive, for these were the challenges that Trinity would deal with for the next two decades.

The Rev. Earl Wepley,
first interim rector of Trinity.
Trinity Episcopal Church

In the spring of 2000, the Search Committee invited five final candidates for the position of permanent rector to meet the vestry and be interviewed by the committee. After deliberation, the Search Committee presented to the vestry the name of the Rev. Thomas "Tom" Kryder-Reid as its candidate for the position of rector. The vestry thereupon voted its intention to call Father Kryder-Reid as rector and so notified Bishop Catherine Maples Waynick. The bishop approved, the vestry called Father Kryder-Reid to be rector of Trinity, and he accepted the call.

Previously, Father Kryder-Reid had served as rector of St. Bartholomew's, West Baltimore, Maryland, but he had resigned and moved with his family to Indianapolis in support of his wife Elizabeth "Liz" Kryder-Reid, who had accepted a position as a professor at Indiana University-Purdue University Indianapolis.

Father Kryder-Reid began work at Trinity on August 1, 2000, and performed his first worship service on Sunday, August 6. The church celebrated his new ministry on September 17, 2000, and Father Kryder-Reid thereupon became the eleventh rector of Trinity. If the years of Rector Jim Lemler's tenure had been a time when Trinity shone brightly at the diocesan and national levels, the era of Rector Tom Kryder-Reid would be a period when Trinity intentionally shifted its focus to local issues and the immediate neighborhood.

This new era also would see an increased focus on finances. In 2000, the year of the parish's first consolidated budget, the vestry budgeted for $300,000 in pledges, but members pledged only $292,000. The situation improved somewhat the following year. For 2001, the vestry set

The Rev. Thomas Kryder-Reid,
eleventh rector of Trinity.
Trinity Episcopal Church

an aggressive budget of $338,000 in pledges. While the actual pledges of $316,000 again fell short of the budget, the parish could boast 123 new and increased pledges.

Other positive news was that the Memorial Fund was valued at $1.1 million, and the Benefaction was valued at $26.5 million. The not-so-good news, however, was that 60 percent of the expenses in Trinity's budget still came out of the Benefaction. Father Kryder-Reid told the parish, "We are an endowed church. And we are tipping ever more precariously toward total reliance on our endowment to pay for everything."

Even with that dire warning, Trinity still generously pledged $500,000 to the capital campaign of the diocese's Waycross Camp and Conference Center, a pledge it would not finally pay off until seven years later in 2008. Prior to that final payoff, however, the parish would learn hard lessons about its dependence on the Benefaction.

In other respects, 2001 was a positive and productive year for the parish. The 2001 Annual Convention of the Consortium of Endowed Episcopal Parishes was held in Indianapolis and was hosted by Trinity, St. Paul's, and Christ Church Cathedral. Many volunteers from Trinity helped in the organization and running of the convention.

Progress also was made on revising the relationship between the church and St. Richard's School. The Trinity vestry and the St. Richard's board formed the Joint Trinity-St. Richard's Governance Task Force, which consisted of seven people from the two institutions. After deliberation, the task force's recommendations to each group were to revise the school's mission statement to reinforce its commitment to Episcopal values and to change the school's organizational documents to reflect the school's desire for more independence. The task force also recommended enhancing the school's shared responsibility for the buildings and grounds by making the school a joint owner of the property with the church. In 2002, both the church and the school would experience the challenges of implementing these proposals.

For the first time in some years, the clergy and staff at Trinity decided to review in detail the church's rolls of members, households, and communicants. The results of these revelations were that the number of baptized members increased from 1,068 to 1,085, the number of confirmed communicants in good standing went up from 705 to 709, but the number of households dropped significantly from 467 to 425. Average Sunday attendance in 2000 and 2001 held steady at 302 and 297 per Sunday, respectively.

Trinity was stable at this time, but it soon became shockingly clear that the world was not. On September 11, 2001, terrorist attacks on the World Trade Center towers in New York City and the Pentagon in Washington, D.C., devastated the nation's morale and jolted its economy. Indeed, the political, economic, and personal aftereffects of those traumatic events would be felt for years to come, not the least of all in seemingly endless warfare in the Middle East.

But even though the events of 9/11 shook America to its core, the parish continued on. Near the end of 2001, Trinity held forums focused on outreach, the results of which were much the same as the Search Committee had found in 1999: enthusiastic support was evident for using the parish's time and resources, both human and financial, to respond to the needs of the local community. Trinity also restructured the Outreach Grants Committee to consist of a smaller membership of six parishioners and changed its name to the Outreach Committee. The reconstituted committee completely changed its focus, worked on how the church should respond to and work with the local community, and put into motion the reduction of most grants to regional, national, and international charities. Implementation of plans to achieve all of this would begin in 2002. In addition, the vestry committed to hiring a third priest in 2002, an associate rector who would focus on mission and outreach.

During this tumultuous period, Trinity also managed to expand what it would start to think of as its campus. The parish purchased two residences in 2001–2002: what would become known as the Corner House, at the intersection of 33rd and Pennsylvania Streets, and the Alley House, at 32 East 32nd Street. The Outreach Committee expressed its desire to use both of these buildings to expand Trinity's mission in the neighborhood.

It was still the case, however, that Trinity's outreach during 2001–2002 consisted largely of making grants of money to worthy causes. Indeed, while the budget for outreach grants dropped in 2002 to $160,000, the amount of outreach grants made that year was considerably over-budget at $189,000.

Even with the continued emphasis on donating money, the people of Trinity still were determined to create more hands-on opportunities for mission work, and the parish began the first of a number of strategic planning sessions that would bear fruit months later. Some parishioners, though, already were making offerings of their personal time and efforts. A small number were working at the Mid-North Food Pantry, which at that time was located in a building in the Mapleton-Fall Creek neighborhood owned by Tabernacle Presbyterian Church.

The greatest sign that Trinity was serious about becoming more personally involved with outreach was the hiring of the Rev. Karen L. King (not to be confused with parishioner Karen E. King) as the new associate rector for mission and outreach on July 1, 2002. Mother King, the first full-time African-American member of Trinity's clergy, renamed the Outreach Committee the Mission and Outreach Committee and worked with it to continue integrating the church into the neighborhood. The committee focused on revitalization of the Corner House, participation in a Meridian Park Neighborhood Association Tour, organization of clean-up and fix-up days, recruitment of volunteers at the Annual

The Rev. Karen L. King,
senior associate rector of Trinity.
Trinity Episcopal Church

Mozel Sanders Thanksgiving Dinner, and implementation of the Magi Tree for providing gifts to needy recipients at Christmastime. The committee also linked parishioners to opportunities in the neighborhood and outreach grants to organizations for which parishioners could participate.

While parishioners were putting into practice their goal of personally serving their neighbors, one negative circumstance manifested itself in 2002 that would affect Trinity for the next several years: the stock market's plunge in value that would not completely right itself for nearly a decade. The cause was a combination of shock to the country and the world by the terrorist attacks on 9/11 in 2001 and, even more seriously, the bursting of what became known as the Tech Bubble—the cumulation of overaggressive investments in speculative high-tech and internet-based companies—which precipitated a plunge in the value of the entire stock market.

Trinity instantly experienced a steep decline in the values of both the Memorial Fund (from $1.1 million in 2001 to $830,000 in 2002) and the Benefaction (from $26.5 million in 2001 to $20.5 million in 2002). These losses put great pressure on the parish's budget, programs, and stewardship. Everyone was hit by financial hardship. In 2002, parishioners' pledges, which had been growing for years, went down both in numbers and dollars while Trinity's overall expense budget, which was keeping pace with the church's growing membership, increased from $2.27 million in 2001 to $2.37 million in 2002.

To help matters after the Tech Bubble crash in 2002, the vestry approved what was intended to be a temporary increase in the draw on the Benefaction from 5.75 to 6 percent. In addition, the trustees of the Benefaction, with the advice of their investment advisor Morgan Stanley, adopted more of an Endowment Model approach to the Benefaction with a focus on diversification of assets, tactical asset allocation, and alternative investments in order to better preserve and grow assets. The trustees of the Benefaction used this investment model for the next 15 years.

Despite the financially challenging times Trinity then faced, the clergy and parishioners continued to focus on achieving goals previously set. In early 2002, Father Kryder-Reid, together with Senior Warden Erick Ponader and vestry member Nedra Feeley, met with a consultant to form a Strategic Planning Committee to work with a similar committee being formed by St. Richard's. The idea was for the church and the school to work separately, but with close communication, to develop complementary long-range plans for budget, space usage and development, education, school and congregation population growth, outreach, and worship. Both groups would put special emphasis on defining the governance and property relationship of the church and school. Another objective was to enable St. Richard's to develop its full financial potential while maintaining its Episcopal identity. In the fall of 2002, 114 parishioners attended 21 meetings to discuss Trinity, its operations, and its mission, after which feasibility teams turned the parishioners' ideas into concrete proposals.

At about the same time, the vestry approved amended and restated articles of incorporation for St. Richard's, and the St. Richard's board of directors changed its name to the board of trustees. Originally, a majority of the St. Richard's board of directors were required to be members of Trinity; under the new governing document, a majority of the St. Richard's board of trustees had to be Episcopalians, but not necessarily members of Trinity.

Trinity's vestry also decided that the shared facility used by St. Richard's should be owned jointly by the church and school. St. Richard's also was to own property in its name, and Trinity was to retain property in its name. The Trinity vestry and the St. Richard's board of trustees agreed on the legal documents needed to accomplish these matters, and Trinity executed and recorded them. The result was a campus where some property was in the name of each of the two institutions individually and the title of some property was held in common. The two institutions formed a Joint Property Committee and approved and signed an operating agreement. The hope was to create clear expectations and shared responsibilities between the school and the church. Senior Warden Erick Ponader and vestry members George Plews and Fred Roetter, all of whom were attorneys, worked diligently on this process.

Why, after more than 40 years of being an important mission of Trinity, did St. Richard's initiate these actions? According to *Behind these Walls, the Story of St. Richard's Episcopal School* by Alexandra Lombardo, St. Richard's '10, and Andrea Neal:

> *The shifts in governance were considered to be vital for the school's long-term health. Both school and parish wanted a continued Episcopal presence on campus but a broadening of that identity beyond the Trinity congregation. . . . By loosening the bonds with Trinity, it was hoped that the school would have an easier time raising funds for capital and other needs. A false perception that the school was bankrolled by wealthy Episcopalians had limited its ability to solicit donations.*

If 2002 was about issues related to financial crisis, real estate, and governance, 2003 would see technological, organizational, and social justice changes that would affect the par-ish. In May, Trinity launched its website, *www.trinitychurchindy.org*, which would help bring Trinity into the twenty-first century's digital age. (*The Trinity E-pistle*, another digital milestone, would make its debut two years later in 2005.) Staffing also took a large step forward. Father Kryder-Reid hired Kevin DePrey, an experienced administrator for the Catholic Church in Indianapolis, as Trinity's first parish administrator. It is safe to say that Mr. DePrey's title did not do justice to the large number of responsibilities that he would assume over the course of the next 15 years.

Kevin DePrey,
parish administrator of Trinity.
Trinity Episcopal Church

The year 2003 also saw yet another gain for social justice that would have profound effects on The Episcopal Church as a whole. The Rev. V. Gene Robinson was elected bishop of the Diocese of New Hampshire on June 7, 2003, and was consecrated as bishop on November 2, 2003. Bishop Robinson was the first openly gay priest to be elected and consecrated as a bishop in the Anglican Communion. After his election, a number of Episcopalians who disagreed with his consecration for theological or other reasons abandoned The Episcopal Church, formed the Anglican Church in North America, and aligned themselves with bishops outside The Episcopal Church in the United States, a process referred to as the Anglican Realignment. Although this schism was unfortunate, Bishop Robinson's consecration was a clear bold step forward for the recognition of the importance of lesbian, bisexual, gay, transgender, and queer (LBGTQ) members of The Episcopal Church.

Amid these changes, Trinity continued to focus its efforts on more hands-on outreach than in the past. In August 2003, the parish hosted the first Community Picnic and Fun Day for people in the neighborhood with 150 neighbors joining for an afternoon of games and food. Some parishioners started working at the Open Door Program at Tabernacle Presbyterian Church in the neighborhood, helping to serve hot meals to 200 people per day three days a week. Grants of money were still important, however. The vestry approved recommendations from the Outreach Grants Committee for grants of $81,000 to 19 organizations in the spring and $82,000 to 15 organizations in the fall.

The year 2003 also saw Trinity continue to be engaged in significant amounts of strategic planning. In early 2003, the church conducted a time and talent survey to determine what people wanted in the way of outreach. In February, the results were tabulated, and it was clear that parishioners were most interested in short-term volunteer opportunities outside the walls of the church.

In the spring and summer of 2003, the feasibility teams working on Trinity's strategic plan came up with initiatives developed with broad parishioner involvement over 16 months that called for clergy-staff-lay action. The initiatives consisted of three components with two specific recommendations in each. The first initiative was ministry to others, which included recommendations for outreach and hospitality; the second was ministry to one another, which included recommendations for spiritual growth and pastoral care; and the third was for institutional stewardship, which included recommendations for more participation and year-round stewardship. By all appearances, the parish was seriously trying to address the challenges that Father Wepley had identified four years earlier.

Although the stock market improved somewhat in 2003–2004, it was still considered a bear market. The improving stock market, though, boosted the value of both the Endowment (as the Benefaction had come to be known about this time) and the Memorial Fund. The vestry, faced with the need to fund the church's many programs with diminishing parish support over the previous two years, approved a budget for 2004 that called for the Endowment to provide a whopping 80 percent of needed revenue and for parish support to provide only 20 percent. Outreach grants was one line item that took a big hit in the new budget, getting trimmed to $100,000 after years of being closer to $200,000.

It was clear that parishioners also were feeling financially stressed. In that same year of 2004, there was a slight increase in membership at Trinity but not enough to cause increased parish financial support. As a result, only 51 percent of members pledged for 2004. In fact, some parishioners decreased their pledges and made note that the reason was the increase in the draw on the Benefaction of the previous year, which they felt was financially irresponsible.

The year 2005 would be both a tough and a historic one for Trinity. Without question, the parish's financial position was weaker by 2005 than it had been in 1999. To help matters, the clergy and staff—through a team effort—managed to cut $66,000 from the church's budget for 2005. Capital expenses also were trimmed. Improvements and repairs to the parish's physical structures had been significant in the years 2000–2002, with the high point being $124,000 spent in 2002. Expenses for such, however, were slashed in the next three years with a low of $11,000 in 2004.

While times were tough, members began to pledge as they could and parish support increased. For the year 2005, 61 percent of the members pledged compared to 51 percent the year before, and pledges surpassed $400,000 for the first time in the parish's history. In addition, parish support reached 25 percent of the revenue side of the budget compared to only 20 percent the year before. In the period 1999–2005, despite worsening economic conditions, overall parish support (including unpledged contributions) had grown from $346,000 to $446,000—an increase of $100,000.

But financial challenges were not the only ones Trinity tackled in 2005. There were theological barriers to break through, too. Open Communion, the practice of offering communion to people who were not baptized, was one matter to resolve. Traditionally, only baptized Christians were welcome to take communion in The Episcopal Church. Trinity's Worship Committee, upon Father Kryder-Reid's recommendation and with Bishop Waynick's understanding, endorsed the practice of open communion at Trinity as a theologically radical welcome to the not-yet-baptized who were seeking God and were drawn to Christ.

That same year, 2005, Trinity crossed another theological hurdle. A gay male couple at Trinity, both of whom were committed Christians, asked not for a wedding ceremony (as discussed in Chapter 15, same-sex marriage would not be legal in Indiana for another nine years) but simply for a blessing of their union in the church's sanctuary with the support of the congregation. For about the previous 10 years, some of Trinity's clergy had presided over the blessings of same-sex unions, but only outside Trinity's sanctuary. The question of whether Trinity's members were ready to support such blessings in the church itself had come up in 2004. With the issue squarely on the table in 2005, Father Kryder-Reid asked the parish to read, pray over, and respond to the couple's request.

The parish's response was overwhelmingly, but not unanimously, positive. A few, but very few, parishioners left Trinity over the issue, but most who disagreed with the propriety of the blessing remained. Father Kryder-Reid acknowledged those who stayed in the parish despite their disagreement, referring to "the love of God that calls us together as a congregation and sends us forth to serve in spite of our inevitable differences." In mid-June, with the explicit support of Bishop Waynick, a full sanctuary recognized and gave thanks for God's blessing on the lifelong union of the two men who courageously had sought it.

At the same time Trinity was dealing with these critically important matters, its members' volunteerism continued on a steeply upward trend. In 2005, parishioners not only continued to help at Mid-North Food Pantry, to host another Community Picnic and Fun Day, to help serve at the Open Door Soup Kitchen at Tabernacle Presbyterian, and to organize another Magi Tree, but they also made multiple distributions of food from Gleaner's Food Bank to more than 400 people, began the program of serving dinners to families at Dayspring Center each month, and helped tutor children at Indianapolis Public School 60 in the neighborhood. When Mid-North Food Pantry ran out of food just before Thanksgiving, Trinity's clergy and staff organized an emergency food drive supported by parishioners and St. Richard's to replenish the food pantry's stores before the holiday. Trinity people had become far more personally involved in outreach than they had been only a few years before.

But other kinds of changes occurred during this time, as well. One of Trinity's established, successful outreach efforts, Trustee Leadership Development (TLD), left the church in 2004. TLD had reached its fifteenth anniversary in that year. During its time with Trinity, the organization had provided leadership skills training to more than 47,000 individuals working in nearly 1,000 not-for-profit organizations across the country. But in 2004, Katherine Tyler-Scott announced that she was leaving TLD to form another company, and TLD became independent of Trinity.

Having engaged in a number of productive strategic planning projects since 2000, in 2005 Trinity turned its attention to its buildings and grounds. In that year, capital spending was only a tenth of what it had been in 2002. To determine the best way to tackle the parish's property concerns in 2006 and beyond, Father Kryder-Reid formed a Campus Master Planning Committee for that purpose. The impetus was the need to address what were considered urgent space needs for children's, youth, and music ministries as well as for staff offices and parish gatherings. St. Richard's put together a similar team that was to work closely with Trinity's committee and "develop a coordinated plan for growth in mission as well as campus." As it would turn out, work on this initiative would continue for a number of years.

Despite the financial hardships during this period experienced not only by Trinity itself but by its parishioners, the church's programs continued to flourish. Trinity's choir—in addition to performing regular church services including multiple services during Christmastime and Holy Week—sang at a number of music festivals, including the Two Choir Festivals with the choir of St. Paul's, and performed significant choral masterpieces such as Brahms's *A German Requiem* and Mozart's *Grand Mass in C Minor*.

In 2000, the choir made a pilgrimage to sing at the National Cathedral in Washington, D.C. In 2002, it made a pilgrimage to England to sing at Winchester and Chichester Cathedrals. In 2005, the choir made another English pilgrimage to sing at Bristol and Durham Cathedrals. Choir pilgrimages would remain a regular part of the musical life of Trinity in the years to come.

The choir also was involved in a number of special anniversary celebrations. In 2004, Dr. Michael Messina celebrated his tenth anniversary as Trinity's organist and director of music. An anniversary celebration was held on January 9, a gift was made to the choir of his alma mater, St. Olaf College in Minnesota, and a concert was held in his honor in May. In 2006, the parish celebrated twentieth ordination anniversaries for both Father Kryder-Reid and Mother Ferriani, and Dr. Messina composed two hymns for the occasions: *We Would Honor* for Mother Ferriani and *A Wreath of Light* for Father Kryder-Reid.

Trinity's youth program also continued its successful ways during this time. In 1999 and 2001, the Journey to Adulthood (J2A) group and its chaperons made pilgrimages to New Mexico and the Black Hills of South Dakota, respectively. In 2003, the J2A group and chaperons made a pilgrimage to Anchorage, Alaska, and in 2005 journeyed to a Native American reservation near Cody, Wyoming. Moreover, in 2005 the youth started their annual Souper Bowl of Caring at which bowls of soup were sold around the time of the NFL's Super Bowl to raise money for outreach.

One of the key elements of the J2A pilgrimages was the youth raising the money for the trips themselves, largely through annual Christmas cookie bakes and sales. Over the years, the J2A members would raise thousands of dollars each year, in some years more than $10,000, from impressively planned and executed cookie bakes and sales. The group also conducted car washes (with car blessings by the clergy) and sold springtime flower baskets—those activities together would generate additional thousands of dollars.

At the beginning of the new century, Trinity was determined to build upon its reputation in Indianapolis as a place with beautiful worship services and a solid children's and youth program by becoming more actively involved in its neighborhood. Despite the financial challenges caused by overdependence on an Endowment experiencing stagnant growth, the church's good programs only improved, and its new volunteer activism firmly took root. The years to come would bring continuing and additional challenges, some as daunting as the parish had ever faced, but Trinity's clergy, staff, and congregants would be ready to meet them.

Chapter 17

Trinity in the Great Recession: 2006–2009

I n the years 2006–2007, life at Trinity Episcopal Church, Indianapolis, seemed to be getting back to normal. Average Sunday attendance was up, membership was up, pledging was up, and more parishioners were pledging. The economy and stock market had improved somewhat in 2005 and would continue to do so in the following two years. With parishioners feeling more financially secure, Trinity set a new record of $467,000 in parish support for 2006 and went over $500,000 in parish support for the first time in 2007. Clergy, staff, the Finance Committee, and the vestry continued to cut budgeted and actual expenses and, as a result, achieved budget surpluses in both years.

Trinity was still highly dependent on what had become an annual $1.3 million draw on its Endowment, but there finally was some good news, too. Endowment earnings were up in 2005 after slumping for several years. Moreover, for the 2006 budget, the Endowment was to contribute 72 percent of parish expenses compared to 76 to 80 percent in the previous two years. For the 2007 budget, the draw on the Endowment was reduced to $1.28 million, the lowest since the year 2000, and was to contribute the relatively low, but still risky, 70 percent of the total budget.

Trinity continued to make progress on the on-going strategic plan that was formally adopted by the parish at the 2007 annual parish meeting. Teams of clergy, staff, vestry members, and selected parish leaders developed elaborate, detailed Guiding Principles and Action Steps for the church to follow. These included proposed outcomes for liturgy, music, and arts; pastoral care; Christian education and formation; invitation and incorporation; outreach; and parish stewardship. Trinity also created a new mission statement, "As a worshipping community of diverse Christians, we accept, nourish, and send all to do God's work," and a new vision statement:

> *To build and enhance connections with God, with one another, and with communities around and beyond us. To be an urban center of Christian ministry sought after by anyone on a quest for a deepened relationship with God.*

One of the important recommendations of the Guiding Principles and Action Steps was to spend capital related to worship space, including repairing windows, improving lighting in the nave, improving the sound system, providing equipment for the hearing impaired, renovating the organ, and enhancing the Fortune Room and Cloister Room. After the past few years of belt-tightening and reduced capital spending, this was a bold plan. Unfortunately, intervening events would cause the delay of these improvements for nearly a decade.

But one of the other recommendations of the Guiding Principles and Action Steps was immediately put into action: the action step of eradicating hunger under the guiding principle of outreach. Mother King and parishioner Diana Creasser spearheaded the formation of a Food Security and Hunger Relief Visioning Work Group. The group researched nearby hunger-relief programs and found that a midday meal of soup, bread, salad, and pastry was being provided to anyone in need of a meal by two soup kitchens just a few blocks from Trinity, one at Tabernacle Presbyterian Church at 34th Street and Central Avenue and the other at North United Methodist Church at 38th and Meridian Streets. There was one day of the week in which no meal was available at either church, however, and that day was Sunday. Trinity's Food Security and Hunger Relief Visioning Work Group became determined to fill that gap.

In a very short time, the group—and especially Mother King and Ms. Creasser—established logistics for food delivery with Second Helpings, a non-profit food rescue and preparation training program, and wrote program directions, recruited volunteers, coordinated work schedules, and much more to put together a Sunday feeding program. On Sunday, October 21, 2007, the greatest Trinity-born outreach program up to that time—the Sunday feeding ministry—was introduced. Food was served in the church's Fortune Room to people from the neighborhood from 12:30 p.m. to 2 p.m. Parishioners, with some grumbling, willingly gave up their space for after-worship coffee and socializing to make room for this important new mission.

The years 2007–2008 saw another important development in outreach. The building at 3333 North Meridian Street, which had been purchased by Trinity in 1994, was fully leased through February 2006 to Wishard Health Services, the organization that provided mental health services in the neighborhood. Upon the expiration of the Wishard lease, however, the building became unoccupied.

With the church's tenant gone, the clergy and vestry had to determine what to do with the building. It may have been prescient that in his annual report to the parish made in January 2006, Father Kryder-Reid stated, "I'm heartened by the passion I hear expressed by many parishioners, including key lay leaders, that our time is past due to commit more of our budget and our caring presence to the needs of people beyond our parish, especially the poor and hungry in our own neighborhood."

In September 2007, parishioner Diantha Daniels and vestry member Robert Wilson chaired a task force charged with examining the possibilities for 3333 North Meridian Street. The task force gave special consideration to prospects for urban mission and ministry as well as the possibility of temporarily relocating the Trinity staff there. When the task force reported to the vestry in January 2008, it recommended that the building be used to house agencies with proven track records in addressing education and hunger, priorities identified by earlier strategic planning initiatives. The group also recommended borrowing $750,000 from the Endowment to pay for upgrades to the building. The vestry approved these recommendations and appointed an implementation team chaired by John Craun.

In 2006, the vestry appointed a separate task force, the Campus Master Plan Task Force, to conduct interviews with parishioners, learn their insights and priorities, and, based on that information, develop a wish list for the parish's existing and possible future properties. St. Richard's also appointed a similar group. Both the Trinity and St. Richard's task forces continued their work through 2007.

The year 2007 also saw two important ordinations at Trinity. In 2004, Grace Burton-Edwards, an ordained Baptist pastor who was confirmed into The Episcopal Church that year, became the chaplain of St. Richard's on a part-time basis. In November 2007, she was ordained as an Episcopal priest and became the full-time associate rector of Trinity and chaplain of

St. Richard's. Mother Burton-Edwards would bring many talents to her work for the parish, including an exceptional ability to connect with newcomers.

The Rev. Grace Burton-Edwards, Mother King, and Father Kryder-Reid leading worship.

Casey Cronin

In 2006, Jeffrey "Jeff" Bower became a deacon at Trinity and, in February 2007, also was ordained as an Episcopal priest there. Father Bower also would prove to be a gifted priest, particularly with outreach ministries. Both Father Bower and Mother Burton-Edwards later became rectors of other churches.

Trinity parishioners continued to be involved in worship and ministry with many finding service opportunities through the church's historic guilds. The Altar Guild was responsible for clearing and setting the altar for each worship service with flower arrangements and everything else necessary for the Eucharist. St. Stephen's Guild was in charge of lectors (i.e., scripture and prayer readers), for worship services. The St. Francis Guild was responsible for the gardens. The Guild of the Holy Cross helped with pastoral care, flower deliveries, and baby visits. St. Monica's Guild prepared food for meetings, offered fellowship, made outreach donations, and hosted speaker programs. St. Ursula's Guild was in charge of the library, helped with clergy discretionary funds, and made outreach donations. Trinity Women arranged speakers, outings, and receptions.

But the period 2006–2007, when Trinity was progressing financially and making plans for the future, was just the calm before the storm. The year 2008, an important year for the entire country, was notable both for the highs and lows experienced by the parish.

In 2008, the United States and Western Europe suffered the greatest financial catastrophe since the Great Depression of the 1930s, an event that became known as the Great Recession. The catastrophe was linked to what was commonly referred to as the subprime mortgage crisis. In essence, with the housing boom of the 2000s, mortgage lenders became less restrictive as to whom they would lend money. As housing prices rose, other financial institutions acquired investments in risky mortgages in bulk, usually in the form of mortgage-backed securities.

In February 2007, the Federal Home Loan Mortgage Corporation (Freddie Mac) announced that it would no longer purchase risky subprime mortgages or securities backed by them. In April of that year, subprime mortgage lender New Century Financial declared bankruptcy. In the summer, rating agencies Standard and Poor's and Moody's reduced ratings on bonds backed by subprime mortgages and put more than 600 such securities on credit watch. Suddenly, the market for these securities dried up.

Meanwhile, in October 2007, the U.S. stock market reached its all-time high as the Dow Jones Industrial Average exceeded 14,000 for the first time. That, however, was the last bit of good news the U.S. economy would have for some time. Over the course of the next 18 months, the Dow would lose more than half its value, falling to 6,547 points. The net worth of American households and not-for-profits declined by more than 20 percent, from $69 trillion in the fall of 2007 to $55 trillion in the spring of 2009, a loss of $14 trillion.

In March 2008, Bear Stearns, a prominent investment banking firm, collapsed due to its holdings in subprime mortgages. A few months later, financial giant Lehman Brothers declared itself bankrupt for the same reason, creating the largest bankruptcy filing in U.S. history. Within days, the U.S. government agreed to lend insurance and investment company AIG $85 billion so it could stay in business. From then on, the U.S. economy and much of the world's economy were in free fall.

The effect on Trinity was two-fold. First, the Endowment, after gaining $1.89 million in value in 2007, lost $8.11 million in value in 2008. The value at the end of 2007 was $25.85 million; the value at the end of 2008 had fallen to $17.74 million. The Endowment, however, was still paying 71 percent of the church's budget; the draw on the Endowment in 2007 and 2008 was still in the range of $1.3 million.

Second, due to the economy and stock market spiraling downward, parishioners defaulted on pledges more than in the past, and parish support dropped from $501,000 in 2007 to $489,000 in 2008. So, as a result of the Great Recession, in 2008 Trinity suffered the double whammy of a 30 percent drop in the value of its Endowment and an eight percent drop in parish support.

Although the economic picture was grim, Trinity's parishioners still were able to celebrate great accomplishments. In 2008, the church's most ambitious advancement yet in reaching out to the needs of the community opened—the Trinity Outreach Center in the building at 3333 North Meridian Street that formerly was leased to Wishard Health Services. In June, the Neighborhood Christian Legal Clinic (NCLC) became a tenant. NCLC, which had begun as a mission of Tabernacle Presbyterian Church, provided free legal services to more than 8,000 clients per year. In September, Precious Gifts Visionaries Childcare also became a tenant. Precious Gifts provided daycare for 75 children in ages from infancy to 12 years. Trinity and Mid-North Food Pantry made plans for the food pantry to occupy space in the building in 2009. The church also started making plans to relocate its Sunday dinner ministry there.

The opening of the Trinity Outreach Center came at a financial cost. Wishard Health Services had paid market-rate rent for its Mid-Town Mental Health Clinic at 3333 North Meridian Street, but the church generously decided to charge below-market rent to tenants it now regarded as its partners in outreach. To cover the deficit in revenues and fund its initiatives at the Outreach Center, Trinity had to shift $45,000 from what it would have made in outreach grants. As a result, the parish had to reduce its outreach

Entrance to the Trinity Outreach Center,
3333 North Meridian Street, Indianapolis.
Trinity Episcopal Church

grants by half to $43,000 donated to just 10 recipients. Nevertheless, Trinity deemed the benefits to the neighboring community provided by the Outreach Center worth the financial sacrifices necessary in order to provide them.

Trinity and St. Richard's continued their cooperative efforts in 2008 by forming a new 11-member Joint Campus Planning Steering Committee to replace their separate campus planning committees that had begun work in 2006. As the new committee reported to the church's vestry and the school's board of trustees:

The purpose for undergoing a joint planning process was for both institutions to develop a long-term vision of how they might each expand according to programmatic needs within the two block area they occupied between 32nd and 34th Streets along the Meridian Street Corridor.

Despite the financial challenges it faced, Trinity established another partner in outreach in 2008. A group of young professional women who were unaffiliated with the church were eager to start a unique but needed ministry and approached Trinity about possibly using its Alley House at 32 East 32nd Street. The ministry they had in mind was a home for unwed, pregnant, homeless, teenage girls—clearly one of the most vulnerable groups of people imaginable.

The new ministry, named Project Home Indy (PHI), sought and obtained approval by Trinity's vestry for its use of the Alley House and entered into a triple-net lease for use of the dwelling at a token amount of rent. The city of Indianapolis later awarded Trinity a grant in the amount of $195,000 to renovate the house for occupancy by Project Home Indy by mid-2010.

Meanwhile, Trinity completed the first full year of its weekly Sunday feeding ministry, during which it served more than 3,900 hot meals, and continued serving monthly Sunday dinners at Dayspring Center. Volunteers also still worked at the Mid-North Food Pantry and participated in six Gleaners food distributions. At Christmastime, the parish again contributed gifts to young people through the Magi Tree project. Finally, Trinity also paid the last installment of its 2001 pledge of $500,000 to the capital campaign for Waycross Camp and Conference Center.

Thanks to an initiative from the diocese, the church and St. Richard's formed a task force in 2008 co-chaired by parishioners Christine Plews and Kathy Watson to work for the preservation of the environment, affectionately referred to as the Green Team. The Green Team immediately took a number of steps to decrease pollution, save energy, and improve the environment, including performing an energy audit and engaging in recycling initiatives.

Through all of the chaos of the Great Recession, almost miraculously Trinity's wonderful existing programs held together. Its children and youth ministries, mission and outreach programs, and music programs all continued to thrive. Journey to Adulthood (J2A) entered its eleventh year as strong as ever. By 2006, Trinity's J2A program was the largest and oldest J2A program in the state.

In 2007, the J2A group traveled to the Dominican Republic for its spiritual pilgrimage, the first time the group had made such a trip outside the United States. In 2009, the group traveled to Pemberton, British Columbia, Canada, where the teens worked closely with the Lil' Wat First Nations of Mount Currie, British Columbia, as part of their mission work on the pilgrimage.

Trinity's choir also continued its magnificent work throughout the church year. In 2006, the choir observed the two hundred fiftieth anniversary of the birth of Mozart by presenting three of his Masses with orchestra on three Sundays. The choir also sang Mozart's *Requiem* with the choir of St. Paul's and made a video of Christmas music for the Diocese of Indianapolis with the choirs of St. Paul's and Christ Church Cathedral. In 2007, the choir premiered a new work, *Evening Service* by Richard Webster, commissioned in memory of two beloved choir members, Paul Stewart and former Senior Warden Mary Stewart, who were not related but did share the same last name.

In 2008, the choir and choristers traveled to New York City, where they sang a Friday noon Eucharist at Trinity, Wall Street; a Sunday morning Choral Eucharist at St. Thomas, Fifth Avenue; and a Choral Evensong at the Cathedral of St. John the Divine. In December 2009, the choir released its CD titled *From Advent to Trinity*, a recording of seasonal anthems, hymns, and organ music. These events, of course, are only a sampling of the numerous and varied activities of Trinity's choir during this time period.

In large part, these programs survived because of the heroic response of Trinity's clergy, staff, and parish during 2009, a challenging year in which the parish would celebrate its ninetieth anniversary. Early in the year, the Endowment trustees and the Finance Committee, led by Treasurer Kay Whitaker, reviewed the parish's financial situation and recognized that significant budget adjustments were necessary. The vestry thereupon appointed a Spiritual Stimulus Committee to work during Lent to explore options. In

April, Father Kryder-Reid and the committee hosted four Sunday morning open forums to chart out and seek parishioner input about the possibilities and hard choices ahead.

In May 2009, the vestry met in executive session to determine a course of action. A letter to the parish was then followed by four more open forums. On July 1, a number of drastic, but carefully considered actions, were put into effect, including $207,000 of budget cuts, an Endowment spending policy of a set $975,000 per year, closing the Trinity bookstore, reducing staff, an across-the-board pay cut for remaining staff, and more use of parishioner volunteers for support functions. The remaining staff, of course, continued to work with great commitment even as their responsibilities were expanded, their pay reduced, and positions in some cases significantly altered or downsized.

Parish members as a whole also did their part and responded to the call for better stewardship. One of the goals of Trinity's Guiding Principles and Actions Steps was improving stewardship. In June 2008, the church established its first Stewardship Commission, and the commission started meeting monthly in September. In October, the commission organized the church's first annual appeal with a goal of $468,000 in pledges for 2009.

The vestry, however, recognizing the realities of the dire economic situation for the entire country, reduced the budget for pledges to $425,000, a decrease after years of ever-increasing goals. Nevertheless, the parishioners rallied—including 79 households who increased their pledges by an average of 17.6 percent—and Trinity exceeded the vestry's goal with $442,000 in pledges for 2009.

The vestry took another stewardship initiative by creating a Planned Giving Committee chaired by parishioner Mary DeVoe. The committee was tasked with finding ways to encourage Trinity congregants to remember the church in their wills and trust instruments as Mr. Eli Lilly had done in 1977. On November 9, 2009, Mrs. DeVoe presented to the vestry the proposed Tree of Life Society, which was "to acknowledge gratefully those persons who have made provisions to leave a documented gift of a portion of their accumulated assets at the end of their lives." The vestry officially chartered the legacy society at that meeting, and plans were begun to present it to the parish as a whole.

Other important developments included the formation of a group for parents of young children at Trinity, Parents Raising Episcopal Preschoolers (PREP), which was later expanded to include somewhat older children and renamed Parents Raising Exceptional People. The parish also established the

Collaborative Outreach Ministries Oversight Team, chaired by parishioner Ed Stephenson. This group's responsibility was to provide opportunities for parishioners to meet and work on issues with liaisons from the outreach partners located on Trinity's campus, specifically, Mid-North Food Pantry, Precious Gifts Visionaries Child Care Center, Neighborhood Christian Legal Clinic, Horizons at St. Richard's, and Project Home Indy.

Despite the good things going on at Trinity, Sunday worship attendance continued to drop slightly in 2009. Undoubtedly, this was caused to some degree by the nation's malaise, which understandably was felt by parishioners. Even in this stressful time, though, 43 baptisms were enrolled at the parish in 2009, including for adults who would go on to have significant leadership roles at Trinity. Moreover, summer attendance benefited from yet another innovation: the addition of a 9:15 a.m. informal Eucharist outdoors in the Lemler Garden during the summer months.

Membership rolls were refined in 2008 and again in 2009—this second time through use of new computer software. Trinity households, which had been thought to be 425 in number in 2003, were now determined to be only 350. Likewise, the number of baptized members in 2003—1,100—were now counted as 807, and the number of communicants in good standing in 2003—737—were now 698. The parish, it appeared, could be shrinking.

But the key thing was that the parish, unlike many other congregations during this time, continued to thrive. One of the highlights of the period was the dedication of the Trinity Outreach Center on Sunday, October 18, 2009. The celebration, titled Miracle on Meridian Street, began with worship and a sermon by Bishop Catherine Maples Waynick, in which she reminded the congregation, "Without hope there can be no vision, and without vision the people perish." Following the worship service, the choir led the congregation outside to the Outreach Center for the dedication, singing the hymn, *We are Walking in the Light of God.*

Thankfully (and it is appropriate to exclaim at this point, "Thanks be to God!"), after 2009, Trinity started the process of recovering from the financial debacles of the first years of the twenty-first century. It is impossible to overemphasize the effects that 9/11, the Tech Bubble, and the Great Recession had on the parish; they dominated life at the parish for the entire decade—often referred to as the Lost Decade due to the failure of anyone to make any economic headway during that time—and in particular for the vestry, the clergy, and the staff.

In the words of parishioner Mark Green, chair of Trinity's Endowment trustees at that time, "Market historians still have not figured out what to

Trinity's choir singing at the dedication
of the Trinity Outreach Center.
Trinity Episcopal Church

make of the early 2000s. Lost Decade, Tech Bubble/Crash, Financial Crisis/ Great Recession, it all runs together." One of the things that made living through the early 2000s so difficult for Trinity was that, as we have seen, the stock market seemed to recover in some periods, only to decline precipitously again.

During what may have been the most challenging years for Trinity since the years of the Great Depression in the 1930s, the parish still achieved many of the community outreach goals it had set for itself at the beginning of the decade. This was an outstanding accomplishment by any measure.

Chapter 18

The Strife Is O'er:
2010–2015

During the Lost Decade, Trinity Episcopal Church, Indianapolis, often was on the brink of financial disaster, but, at the start of the new decade, the parish finally seemed poised for recovery. The clergy, lay staff, Finance Committee, and vestry created a balanced budget for 2010 thanks to total parish support of $478,000. The clergy and staff again cut expenses, this time by $150,000, which put parish spending at $313,000 less than in 2008. The clergy and lay staff even took another decrease in salaries, this one by five percent. But enough was enough. In April, the vestry approved an amount to reinstate three percent of that reduction.

Because of increased parish support and reduced expenses, the parish could begin to reduce its dependence on the Endowment. While in the recent past the Endowment had accounted for up to 80 percent of Trinity's budget, in 2010 the Endowment draw of $975,000 paid for 63 percent of the budget, and parish support paid for 32 percent. (The balance always came from other sources.) In addition, the Endowment's value began to rise again, gaining $1,000,000 after losing a total of $8,000,000 in 2008–2009.

Membership also started to rise with 22 enrolled baptisms and 24 transfers. Baptized members were up to 831, and communicants in good standing were up to 722. According to the new parishioners, the things that were bringing them into the parish were Trinity's education and music ministries, its outreach to the wider community, and its traditional worship that incorporated innovative expression. All of these characteristics would be important for the church's growth in the coming years.

In 2010, Mother Nancy Ferriani, who had spent her entire life as a priest at Trinity, announced that that she was retiring as senior associate rector. In her 23 years at the parish, Mother Ferriani had brought warmth and stability through transition and financial crisis. She was also a strong advocate for LGBTQ inclusiveness.

In honor of her service, Mother Ferriani's five daughters announced that they would be making a gift to honor her, specifically a new west window in the sanctuary. The window proposed by the Ferriani daughters would feature the figure of a lamb etched in a center pane representing the subject of a beloved sermon given by Mother Ferriani at Christmastime for many years. The new window also would let in significantly more light than the existing aged window.

After this generous offer, Father Kryder-Reid and the vestry determined that all of the other windows in the sanctuary needed replacing. In keeping with the colorless glass found in most English churches (much stained glass was

Mother Nancy Ferriani,
senior associate rector of Trinity.
Trinity Episcopal Church

destroyed by the Puritans during the English Civil War in the seventeenth century), Trinity's sanctuary windows, including the west window, all were made of colorless glass with plexiglass covers on the outside. The plexiglass had darkened considerably with age, and all the windows had started to leak.

To pay for the window replacement project, the parish began the first of its mini-capital campaigns. By April, parishioners and friends of Trinity donated sufficient funds to replace all 41 windows in the sanctuary. Installation of the new windows commenced in June during the relatively calm summer months. When done, the effect of seeing for the first time a Sunday worship service in the formerly semi-dark sanctuary newly filled with light was awe-inspiring. The new windows, without question, at that time were a sorely needed morale booster for the parish.

After so many difficult years, 2010 brought several other positive events to the parish. First, St. Richard's School celebrated its fiftieth anniversary and officially changed its name to St. Richard's Episcopal School. Again quoting from *Behind These Walls, the Story of St. Richard's Episcopal School*, this name change was to "affirm [St. Richard's] identity, and to distinguish itself from the myriad Roman Catholic schools in Indianapolis . . . ." Second, Project Home Indy completed the renovation of its new home for teenage mothers in the Alley House on 32nd Street with plans to open the following year in 2011.

Third, Mother Karen King launched the first Senior Luncheons for and in appreciation of elderly parishioners who could not attend church services on a regular basis. Fourth, the vestry approved $77,000 to repair the console of the organ, which had suffered shorts in its circuitry; work on the console would commence in 2011. And fifth, creation of the Tree of Life Society for planned giving for the church was announced on All Saints Sunday, November 7, 2010.

Additionally, the Trinity/St. Richard's Joint Campus Planning Steering Committee again started to work on the church's and school's Campus Master Plan, work that had begun four years earlier but had been put on hold during the Great Recession. In January 2010, the committee began a year-long process of working with two architectural firms, Axis Architecture & Interiors, LLC, and Rundell Ernstberger Associates, LLC, to put the wish list developed during 2006–2007 into actual plans.

The committee held a Sunday morning of dialogue, conducted surveys of St. Richard's parents and Trinity parishioners, and hosted focus group discussions for parents and parishioners with the architects. As a result, it received more than 1,000 different suggestions on ways to improve the campus. It then distributed several variations of possible plans to parents and parishioners for review. Eventually, the committee created three alternative plans. From May until the fall, constituents from the school and church weighed in with their thoughts concerning which plan they preferred. Finally, the committee began putting together its proposal to present to the vestry and the St. Richard's board of trustees in 2011.

Even with its renewed concern about real-estate matters, Trinity continued to grow its outreach programs during this time. The Sunday feeding ministry, then in its third year, was bolstered by 35 new volunteers, raising the total to more than 100. This group served over 4,000 meals to guests from the neighborhood and surrounding areas in 2010. In addition, a large number of parishioners helped with four distributions of food from Gleaner's Food Bank that served 590 households, almost all in the neighborhood. Outreach grants continued to shrink in amount with only 11 grants awarded totaling $44,500. Even so, the church sent a special gift of $22,000 to Haiti for relief from the devastating earthquake that hit there.

As the year 2011 began, the Trinity/St. Richard's Joint Campus Planning Committee presented its final proposal, which was approved by the vestry on January 17 and by the St. Richard's board of trustees on January 24. One of the radical ideas contained in this final proposal included construction of a new building running along Meridian Street north of 33rd Street that would connect the Trinity Outreach Center to the north entrance to the church. This new building would house church offices, a fellowship hall, and education and meeting rooms. It also would require the city to agree to close 33rd Street east of Meridian Street.

Another idea was to construct new buildings for St. Richard's along Meridian Street between the church and 32nd Street. This would provide a music center to be used by both Trinity and St. Richard's, a performing arts center, and needed science labs and additional classrooms. All of this, it was believed, would enhance both institutions' visibility along Meridian Street and would make the church's sanctuary the center hub and heart of the entire campus.

Trinity acolytes preparing for a procession.
Casey Cronin

Unfortunately, the economy, although improving, would continue to be an issue for Trinity in 2011. The values of both the Endowment and the Memorial Fund dropped again. Pledges were slightly down, and parish support still counted for only 31 percent of the parish budget. Capital expenses for building repairs and improvements also went down in 2011, but were still higher than at any time during 2002–2010.

Still, many reasons existed for optimism in 2011. The church again was able to create a balanced budget. Pews were more crowded with average Sunday attendance on the rise again, and the numbers of households, baptized members, and communicants in good standing were all up. Things definitely were looking better, and the vestry approved raising the salaries of the clergy and staff up to the levels they had been in 2009.

Trinity's music program also was active as usual. In February 2011, the choir hosted its first Cabaret to raise money for its next pilgrimage to England the following year where it would sing in residence at Coventry and Norwich Cathedrals. Goulding & Wood Pipe Organ Builders completed the new organ console, and Dr. Michael Messina played the first concert with it in October. Trinity also had two other musical programs in residence at this time, the Ensemble Voltaire instrumental group and parishioner Steven Stolen's Meridian Song Project.

Outreach also continued to go well in 2011. The Sunday feeding teams served more than 4,900 meals and recruited 20 new volunteers. With the Endowment trustees' recommendation, the vestry provided a $300,000 bridge loan from the Endowment to the Mapleton-Fall Creek Development Corporation for the rebuilding of vacant homes in the neighborhood.

The Outreach Grants Committee still awarded a total of $45,000 to 15 different organizations in Indianapolis, but traditional outreach grants were being reduced significantly as Trinity's outreach focus turned to the Sunday feeding ministry and the partner ministries on its campus. Most parishioners probably did not realize that the subsidized rents to Neighborhood Christian Legal Clinic, Previous Gifts, Mid-North Food Pantry, and Project Home Indy were a major contribution to outreach that did not appear on Trinity's financial statements. The city of Indianapolis as a whole, however, was beginning to recognize the parish as a developing center for urban ministry.

After a bit of a dip in 2011, the nation's economy continued to improve in 2012 and was the best it had been since before 2008. Finances at Trinity also were recovering nicely. The Endowment's earnings were up 10.9 percent, which put the value of the Endowment above $20 million again. The ratio of Endowment budget support to parish budget support seemed to be holding at a fairly steady 65 percent/35 percent ratio, where it had been since 2010. Both pledged income and total parish support were up again. Parish revenues were above budget, and expenses were below.

At the same time, though, the parish appeared to continue to shrink. The parish's rolls were reviewed in detail once again, which showed numbers of households, baptized members, and communicants in good standing all down significantly. But interestingly, both average Sunday attendance and the number of pledging households went up in 2012; if the parish was shrinking overall in some sense, its members were becoming more involved.

The Trinity/St. Richard's Joint Campus Plan Steering Committee was very active in 2012. It organized and conducted meetings with 89 parishioners consisting of vestry members, choir members, and large pledging households to discuss the campus plan in order to determine parish satisfaction with it and the will to move forward with next steps. The committee expressed that its job was to determine whether the parish thought the project was worthwhile, not whether the parish could pay for the project. After much discussion, the committee determined that there was near unanimity that the project should move forward.

Nevertheless, the committee picked up concerns from Trinity members about the parish's capacity to fund the far-reaching campus plan. It also determined that no one saw a reason to improve the sanctuary itself and that the priorities for improved spaces in the church included youth and adult music programs, parking, meeting spaces, and administration offices.

The committee concluded from its research, however, that the absolutely most pressing need for improved space was for youth and adult education and formation. Education and formation always had been important at Trinity, and the programs offered at that time were representative of opportunities the church had made available for some time.

Journey in Faith (group size, three to 28 in the period 2009–2012) was a ministry that gave adults an opportunity to deepen their faith by exploring the history, practices, and theology of The Episcopal Church in conversation with others through the cycle of the church year. Adult Forum gatherings (group size, 15 to 75 in the period 2009–2012) were learning opportunities presented after church services on Sundays.

Education for Ministry (group size, four to 16 in the period 2009–2012) was a four-year course that offered intense theological training and formation for leaders in the parish. The Lenten Series in 2012 was a series on

The Rev. Gordon Chastain,
one of Trinity's affiliated priests, leading Adult Forum
with Mother Burton-Edwards.
Casey Cronin

spiritual practices inspired by the book, *Strength for the Journey*. Julian Gatherings was a group that offered a time of centering prayer and reflection on the writings of Julian of Norwich. The Rector's Study Group (group size, five to 18 in the period 2009–2012) was a Bible study group led by the priest many thought was a natural-born teacher, Father Kryder-Reid.

Meanwhile, the Journey to Adulthood (J2A) teens and their chaperons continued their biannual pilgrimages. During the period in question, the J2A members made pilgrimages to Iona, Scotland, in 2011; to Juneau, Alaska, in 2013; and to Rome, Italy, in 2015. On their visit to Rome, the pilgrims were fortunate enough to have an audience with the Pope. They also spent time at the Anglican Center in Rome and met refugees from the Middle East and Africa at the Joel Mafuma Refugee Center.

During July 5–12, 2012, the Diocese of Indianapolis hosted the 77th General Convention of The Episcopal Church at the Indiana Convention Center in downtown Indianapolis. The General Convention had upwards of 200 active and retired bishops and more than 800 clergy and lay representatives from the 110 dioceses of The Episcopal Church. Numerous volunteers from Trinity served numerous different functions for the diocese during the week-long meeting.

Outreach continued to hum along at its new pace in 2012. The Sunday feeding ministry surpassed its record of nearly 5,000 meals in 2011 by serving more than 5,500 meals in 2012. The other newly-established outreach projects also still thrived. Meanwhile, outreach grants continued to decline, totaling only $15,000 for only four missions: Gleaners Food Bank, Second Helpings, Mid-North Food Pantry (all related to battling hunger), and the Global Missions Commission for the benefit of Trinity's two sister parishes in Brazil and Bor, South Sudan. The Outreach Grants Committee, however, also donated $10,000 to the Diocese of Indianapolis to help defray the costs of the General Convention hosted by the diocese.

Sunday dinner team members ready to serve their guests at the Trinity Outreach Center.
Trinity Episcopal Church

The year 2013 got off to an encouraging start for the parish. Numbers were up: households (333 from 320), membership (809 from 781), and communicants in good standing (718 from 690). The Endowment's value was up to $22.4 million, and the draw had leveled off at $1 million, which constituted a draw of only 4.8 percent—a number finally below the five percent level thought to be financially sustainable. The value of the Memorial Fund went up to $745,000. Expenses continued to be under budget.

In January 2013, after 15 months' work, the Trinity/St. Richard's Joint Campus Plan Steering Committee made its presentations to the vestry. The committee's report had three key findings. First, in the collective mind of the parish, the most important considerations in any building program were children's education and the music program, with parking and access coming next in importance. Second, $4.5 million would be necessary for a Phase I construction project north of the church building, but estimates were that only $2 million could be raised in a capital campaign at that time. Third, there was $1.2 million in deferred capital and maintenance expenses that would go unaddressed if the capital campaign focused only on building new space.

Given those grim but realistic findings, the committee recommended to the vestry that the parish spend $2 million (the benchmark for what was thought could be raised in a capital campaign) on improving Sunday school space, improving parking and access, and making improvements in existing structures, including the Tudor House, the Fortune Room, and the sanctuary. The committee pointed out that, while looking into the need for capital improvements of existing structures was not part of its original charge, members of the vestry and other parishioners had raised the issue of the need for such improvements during the committee's planning process.

Despite this being the sole recommendation by the committee after 15 months of work, the recommended capital campaign was not initiated by the clergy or the vestry, nor did they tap into the Endowment for the recommended improvements. Was this the result of the parish no longer being made up of the wealthy and socially elite—names like Clowes, Ayres, Stokley, Frenzel, Noyes, Fairbanks, Pulliam, Fortune, Griffiths, and others—who had built new church and school buildings in the decades of the 1950s through the 1980s? Was this the result of the aftereffects of the Lost Decade and the Great Recession and the parish's collective exhaustion from worrying and thinking about finances? Or could it have been both? Whatever the reason, the known needs for improvements to the parish's physical structures went unmet in 2012.

A few months later, Father Kryder-Reid announced his decision to retire from his position as rector in a year's time in 2014. Father Kryder-Reid had served as rector for nearly 13 years, well more than the average tenure for a rector in The Episcopal Church. In his time at Trinity, the parish had made good on its expressed desire to become more involved with the neighborhood. Under his leadership, the parish had weathered the Lost Decade and the Great Recession with all of its excellent programs intact. Both of these accomplishments were crucial for the continued good works of Trinity in the future.

But Father Kryder-Reid and the vestry were not finished. In May 2013, the two together created a new Mission-Focused Financial Master Plan Task Force charged with developing a Master Plan for the overall financial structure of the parish. The Financial Master Plan was to contain scenarios to reflect how the parish's money would support its overall mission and how that mission would inspire the giving of money.

Ideas for the Financial Master Plan included reviewing the mission and purpose of the Endowment, the Memorial Fund, and giving opportunities;

assessing the pros and cons of merging the Endowment and the Memorial Fund; and reviewing whether there should be separate endowments for different purposes, such as capital expenses, continuing education, ministry initiatives, and outreach. The targets for completion were to have recommendations ready for the vestry in April 2014 with presentation to the parish in May or June 2014.

A major change to the Trinity and St. Richard's campuses also occurred during this time of transition. The church and school went together to purchase the Atkinson Building, a multi-story former apartment and office building to the immediate south of the Tudor House. A generous donor had made a six-figure gift to help fund the purchase, and the remaining expense of the acquisition and demolition of the building would be shared by Trinity and St. Richard's. The school indicated that its goal, again, was to expand its campus and increase its visibility on Meridian Street.

Artwork for the Tree of Life Society.
Trinity Episcopal Church

Improvements in stewardship also continued apace. The Tree of Life Society created three levels of membership: Legacy, Founding, and Sustaining. The members of the Society did research to determine who the Legacy members were, performed a drive to initiate new Founding members, and finalized the design of the Tree of Life Sculpture for the Wall of Recognition in the Fortune Room.

Trinity's other outreach missions also made advancements. Volunteers built two Habitat for Humanity houses and organized a Magi Tree to provide Christmas gifts for residents of Craine House. The Dayspring Dinner team and the Sunday Dinner teams continued to feed the hungry, Sunday dinners reaching more than 5,900 in number. A new mission of the church had its first stirrings when vestry member Jim Purucker began special cook-out meals and breakfasts for events on a fairly regular basis.

The Collaborative Outreach Ministries Oversight Team addressed several issues that arose in the operation of the parish's outreach ministries with its mission partners on the church's campus, particularly in the Trinity

Outreach Center. The oversight team established tenant rules, revised leases, planned a walk-in refrigerator for the Mid-North Food Pantry, planned a renovation of the east end of the Trinity Outreach Center, developed a cleaning schedule for the Outreach Center's kitchen, worked with the Neighborhood Christian Legal Clinic for use of the Corner House by its interns during the summer, and—upon the departure of Precious Gifts Visionaries Childcare from the Outreach Center—explored finding a new high-quality, affordable childcare facility for the building.

The Mid-North Food Pantry kicked into high gear in 2013. Working with Gleaners Food Bank, the food pantry distributed more than 416,000 pounds of food, double what it was able to do only two years before. It also recruited many more volunteers, achieving a total of 25, up from six volunteers a few years before.

*Father Tom Kryder-Reid
at the celebration of his time at Trinity.*
Trinity Episcopal Church

The year 2014 ushered in great changes in the lay and clergy staff at Trinity. In February, Mother Grace Burton-Edwards accepted a call to become rector of St. Thomas, Columbus, Georgia. Then, in June, Father Kryder-Reid departed for his new career as an interim priest for the diocese. The congregation showed its appreciation for his time as rector at a celebration after church on Sunday, June 15. One of the highlights of the event was the unveiling of the Tree of Life Wall of Recognition in the Fortune Room. The last clergy departure, albeit a temporary one, was by Mother Karen King, who had received a $50,000 grant from the Lilly Endowment to go on sabbatical and was gone during the entirety of April–July. Also during and shortly after this time, some of the lay staff retired or resigned.

Even with all of the leave-taking in 2014, things remained remarkably stable during an emotional time of transition. Senior Warden Jeff Brinkmann and Junior Warden Gloria Gangwer provided assurance and a feeling of continuity during the search for another interim rector for the parish. The Rev. Robert "Bob" Dekker was hired as interim associate rector for Christian education and brought with him sterling qualities of dignity and warmth.

Parish administrator Kevin DePrey and financial administrator Albie Marco ably managed the finances and numerous other details behind the scenes. Director of music Dr. Michael Messina and youth coordinator Missy Roetter kept their admirable music and youth programs going as strong as ever. Tracey Lemon joined the staff as an imaginative and creative director of communications.

But a strong clergy leader was necessary at this time, and, through the efforts of a Search Committee, the church got one. In August 2014, the vestry called the Rev. LaRae Rutenbar as interim rector of Trinity. Mother Rutenbar brought high energy and enthusiasm to her role. One thing she was determined to deal with very shortly after her arrival was the understandable distress that many parishioners were suffering due to the departure of a number of beloved clergy and staff.

The Rev. LaRae Rutenbar,
second interim rector of Trinity.
Trinity Episcopal Church

To do this, she scheduled three Holy Conversations so that parishioners could share their worries about the issues Trinity was facing. Giving people a chance to speak their minds in open forums with the clergy greatly helped heal the pain felt by many and brought the clergy, vestry, and parishioners closer together. Many congregants also gave valuable input concerning what they looked for in a new rector.

Mother Rutenbar as interim rector also took her role seriously in preparing the parish for the next permanent rector. One concern that she quickly decided needed remedying was the parish's physical plant. She turned again to the issue of deferred maintenance that had been pointed out by the Campus Planning Steering Committee two years earlier.

The vestry, the Finance Committee, and the Endowment trustees all agreed that the deferred maintenance and capital improvements of the parish's structures were mission-critical. The vestry estimated the cost of the needed work to be $1 million and decided, rather than raise the necessary funds in a capital campaign, to take them from the Endowment.

The Endowment trustees approved using money from the Endowment for the deferred maintenance as necessary because of special circumstances, including the search for a new rector. The trustees, however, cautioned that the draw was "above the long-term spending policy of the Endowment" and recommended and expected that the annual draw in future years would decline to levels consistent with a prudent long-term spending policy.

The vestry, with the help of director of facilities Dirk Edwards and parish administrator Kevin DePrey, identified two dozen projects requiring work that were divided into four categories. The vestry went on to appoint a Property and Deferred Maintenance Committee, led by vestry members Janet Craun and Rob McMath, and an Arts and Furnishings Committee, led by vestry member Christy Jacobi and parishioners Gayle Holtman and Peter Whitten.

The parish's finances took another dip in 2014. Pledges for the year, a period of great transition, were down; expenses for the year, a time of searching for a new rector, were up. The budget consequently had a $43,000 deficit. The value of the Endowment, which had gone over $22 million in 2013, went down to $21 million in 2014 as a result of flat earnings and the $1 million draw for deferred maintenance.

Even though Mother Rutenbar arrived relatively late in 2014, she single-handedly initiated a remarkable pledge appeal by the end of the year. The result was pledges for 2015 hitting $504,000, the first time pledges surpassed $500,000 in Trinity's history.

Innovations in the parish's stewardship program were made in the next pledge appeal in 2015. A number of parishioners hosted a series of house parties at which people could gather, socialize, and receive encouragement to support Trinity financially. The vestry and the Endowment trustees also approved a matching gifts program whereby any new pledge or 10 percent increase in a previous pledge would be matched by a gift from the Endowment to be used to fund special one-time projects selected by the vestry.

By the end of 2015, more than 200 households had pledged, and more than half of these had increased their pledges by more than 10 percent. The result was pledges for 2016 reached a new high of $523,000, and $61,000 in the matching gift from the Endowment was used for special projects. To everyone's credit, the program had the hoped-for effect of setting a base for parishioners' pledges in the future. Overall parish support, which included unpledged donations, also hit a new high of $535,000, which represented an increase of $62,000 in five years.

On January 18, 2015, the choir and parish of Trinity threw a celebration in honor of Dr. Michael Messina's 20 years of service as the church's organist and director of music. Dr. Messina received many gifts from the church and the people present, including a commissioned motet, *Locus iste*, by Frank Boles. The choir under Dr. Messina would be quite active in 2015, singing at Christ Church, St. Paul's, and Indianapolis Hebrew Congregation and making its fourth pilgrimage to England in July, where it sang in residence at Norwich and Lincoln cathedrals and visited the four churches in Norfolk and Suffolk in East Anglia that were the architectural inspirations for Trinity's church building.

Dr. Michael Messina,
Trinity's director of music.
Kyung-Won On

In February 2015, the vestry appointed a new Search Committee to find a permanent rector for Trinity. Unlike the last formal search in 1999 in which the vestry appointed Search Committee members, the vestry this time asked for parishioners who would like to participate in the search to nominate themselves. The vestry received 25 highly qualified self-nominations and chose from that group a committee of 11. Also, unlike in 1999 in which the chairs of the Search Committee were appointed by the vestry, the committee itself chose to be co-chaired by members Kathy Watson and Cathy Bridge, who would become known as the K/Cathys.

In anticipation of rector candidates touring and evaluating Trinity's facilities, in 2015 the parish underwent the greatest amount of construction since the new buildings for St. Richard's were built in the 1980s, a quarter century earlier. Projects included major upgrading of the Tudor House and Fortune Room; improvements in the HVAC system in the church, Tudor House, and Fortune Room; new roofs in many places; demolition of three buildings and other structures; new walkways; a new passenger elevator in the Trinity Outreach Center; and improvements in the Outreach Center's rear entry. The vestry took another special $352,000 draw on the Endowment for this work. Altogether, the various needs of the parish caused the draw on the Endowment in 2015 to reach nearly $1.7 million. This unprecedented figure was considered necessary in order to make up for the deficit from the year before, to pay for deferred maintenance and other capital expenses, and to pay for all things related to the search for a new rector, in addition simply to run the parish's regular programs and missions.

In the meantime, Trinity decided to examine what could be done with another piece of property the parish owned: the St. Edward's House on North Pennsylvania Street. Until recently, it had been used to house director of facilities Dirk Edwards and his large family. The house was zoned for residence, group home, or church use. Parishioners John Craun and Erick Ponader, two members of the Property and Deferred Maintenance Committee, spent much time and effort considering possible uses of the house. In November, Mr. Craun and Mr. Ponader recommended to the vestry that Trinity spend $40,000–$50,000 to put the house in good enough condition to use as "offices and meeting space by a charitable organization with a mission compatible with Trinity and St. Richard's . . . ." The vestry accepted that recommendation, but any actual expenditures were put on the back burner until a decision could be reached as to what exactly to do with the building.

In the midst of a rector search and a huge construction undertaking, the parish's efforts at outreach did not sit idle. Members of the parish, in fact, were able to build another new outreach mission from the ground up. In 2015, parishioner Jane Stephenson had a vision that the church could start its own childcare service for the Trinity Outreach Center to replace the departed Precious Gifts Visionaries Childcare. Soon she was joined by many others who were eager to help, and together they created the Trinity Childcare Committee to build such a mission for the Outreach Center. In April of that year, the vestry awarded the committee a grant of $30,000 as seed money for the project. The committee forged ahead and, in November, incorporated St. Nicholas Early Learning, Inc.

Parishioners kept coming up with creative projects, and another innovative mission was created in 2015, the Guild of the Unexceptionable Cuisiniers (*unexceptionable*: (adj.) not open to criticism; *cuisiniers*: (n) men who cook). The guild loosely was formed when a few male parishioners led by Jim Purucker and Rob McMath volunteered to prepare a brunch for one of the parish's Holy Conversations. After that, as the guild became quite active, its 27 initial members acquired two grills and other equipment to help them prepare professional-level culinary creations. They became a popular

Cuisiniers Rob McMath and Jim Purucker
with the Most Rev. Michael Bruce Curry,
twenty-seventh presiding bishop of The Episcopal Church.
Trinity Episcopal Church

mainstay at Trinity as they prepared food for a large number of events attired in their own logo-bearing hats, aprons, and chef coats.

To a great extent, Trinity during 2010–2013 went through a recuperation period after the Lost Decade and the Great Recession of the previous years. There were great planning efforts made with two significant results: a Campus Master Plan and a Financial Master Plan. Unfortunately, those plans called for more on-going work than parishioners were willing to expend at that time. The efforts spent on these plans were not completely in vain, however, as will be seen in Chapter 19.

The arrival of Interim Rector LaRae Rutenbar, though, definitely jolted the parish out of its doldrums. In one person's words, she was a "force of nature." She brought a new energy and sense of urgency to the parish, she empowered lay leadership, and, as a result, Trinity achieved many accomplishments during her term: continued strides and new beginnings in neighborhood outreach; three Holy Conversations about the parish and what was looked for in a new rector; table talks about violence in the neighborhood; visits by two Episcopal bishops; effective innovations in stewardship; numerous musical events; pilgrimages by the choir and J2A; noticeable improvements in the physical surroundings of the parish; and all this while the parish searched for a new rector. This dynamism would carry forward into the remainder of Trinity's first 100 years.

Chapter 19

Approaching 100 Years:
2016–2019

As Trinity began to reflect on its first 100 years and look ahead to its future, changes in the parish were evident since its incarnation as the Church of the Advent after the First World War. The parish may have begun as a mission for wealthy suburbanites, but it had grown into a center for inner city ministry. Even after nearly a century of change, 2016 was an exceptional year of transition for Trinity and the Diocese of Indianapolis. In that year, Trinity welcomed a new rector, and the diocese consecrated a new bishop.

In January, Trinity's Search Committee announced that it was approximately halfway through the rector search process. As it turned out, the committee members made faster progress than they anticipated. By the end of March, they completed video call interviews with candidates, discerned which candidates they would go to see, visited those candidates in their home parishes, and then asked four candidates to come to Indianapolis to meet with Trinity's vestry and Bishop Catherine Maples Waynick.

On March 30, 2016, the Search Committee recommended to the vestry its candidate for rector of Trinity, the Rev. Canon Julia E. Whitworth of the Cathedral of Saint John the Divine, New York City. The vestry unanimously approved the committee's candidate and obtained the blessing of Bishop Waynick. After prayerful discernment, Mother Whitworth accepted Trinity's call to be the twelfth rector of Trinity. The necessary papers were signed, and the call was announced to the parish on Sunday, April 10, 2016.

Mother Whitworth became not only the first female rector of Trinity, but the first female in that or a similar position at any of the Episcopal churches on Meridian Street in Indianapolis—Christ Church Cathedral, Trinity, or St. Paul's. She also would join a small group of women who had become rectors of churches in The Episcopal Church that were the size and scale of Trinity.

On Sunday, May 22, 2016, Trinity gave heartfelt thanks and bade farewell to Interim Rector LaRae Rutenbar, who returned with her husband Mark to their home in Michigan. It was an emotional moment for both Mother Rutenbar and the parish, as each had become very attached to the other.

Prior to the arrival of Mother Whitworth, the vestry appointed a transition team to assist her, her husband Ray Neufeld, and their children with their move to Indianapolis from New York City. Mother Julia's first Monday in the office was July 6, 2016, and her first Sunday in the pulpit was July 10. She held a fourth Holy Conversation on the following October 9, a joyful Celebration of New Ministry on November 12, and a large number of Meet the Rector gatherings in parishioners' homes.

Trinity was not alone in experiencing change. In the spring of 2015, the Rt. Rev. Catherine Maples Waynick announced that in two years she would retire as the bishop of Indianapolis. Her successor, therefore, would need to be elected at the diocesan Annual Convention in 2016. In April 2016, Trinity's delegates who would represent the parish at the convention attended a mandatory all-day diocesan leadership conference. They then attended the Mid-Central Deanery meeting in September, where the anticipated bishop election processes and procedures were discussed.

The Diocese of Indianapolis selected a Search Committee and a Transition Committee from clergy and parishioners in the diocese to facilitate choosing a new bishop for the diocese. The Transition Committee was chaired by Trinity parishioner Jeff Brinkmann. In

Bishop Waynick congratulating the Rev. Julia E. Whitworth, twelfth rector of Trinity, at her celebration of new ministry.
Trinity Episcopal Church

July, the diocese published the slate of four candidates for bishop of Indianapolis selected by the Search Committee. One of those candidates happened to be the Rev. Grace Burton-Edwards, formerly associate rector of Trinity and at the time rector of St. Thomas, Columbus, Georgia. In October before the diocesan Annual Convention, all four candidates for bishop came to Indiana to participate in a series of meetings held in Indianapolis, Greencastle, Evansville, and Columbus, Indiana, which were open to all members of the diocese.

The opening service for the Annual Convention was held on Thursday, October 27, 2016. Bishop Waynick gave an address emphasizing Episcopalians' responsibility to be stewards of each other and the Earth. The election for the new bishop was held the next day on Friday, October 28. For the delegates at the convention, the choice seemed to be abundantly clear.

On the second ballot, and very nearly on the first ballot, the Rev. Jennifer Baskerville-Burrows was elected bishop of Indianapolis. Bishop-elect Baskerville-Burrows would become the first African-American female diocesan bishop in The Episcopal Church and, by extension, the Anglican Church. Moreover, the new bishop-elect also would become the first female bishop to succeed a retiring female bishop in The Episcopal Church.

The election followed a number of other historical events in The Episcopal Church. Just a few years before, the Rt. Rev. Barbara Harris had been elected a bishop suffragan (a type of bishop that works for a diocesan bishop) and became the first female bishop in the Anglican Communion. The Most Rev. Katharine Jefferts Schori had been invested as the twenty-sixth, and first female, presiding bishop of The Episcopal Church. After Presiding Bishop Jefferts Schori retired, the Most Rev. Michael Bruce Curry was invested as the twenty-seventh, and first African-American, presiding bishop of The Episcopal Church.

On April 29, 2017, in Clowes Hall on the campus of Butler University, Bishop-elect Jennifer Baskerville-Burrows was consecrated as the eleventh bishop of Indianapolis. Trinity clergy, lay staff, and parishioners were highly involved in the ceremony: Jeff Brinkmann, chair of the Transition Committee, organized the ceremony; Dr. Michael Messina led the music; Eric Baiz oversaw the ushers; and Mother Whitworth emceed the ceremony. In addition, a lunch for all visiting bishops and other clergy, including Presiding Bishop Michael Bruce Curry, was hosted by Trinity with food prepared by that jolly band, the Guild of the Unexceptionable Cuisiniers.

With a new bishop and a new rector, Trinity dug deeper into exploring its role in an inner city neighborhood. In 2017, a group of parishioners led by Bill Coleman created an important new adult formation group called the Working Group on Race and Reconciliation. The new group hosted six weeks of Real Talk programs during the Lenten Series with many distinguished speakers, including Bishop-elect Baskerville-Burrows. It also offered a discussion on the book, *Waking Up White*. Finally, in the fall, the group offered a three week series on the documentary, *13th*, with panel discussions on local issues concerning incarceration and policing. As its range of topics expanded, the group changed its name in 2019 to the Working Group on Social Justice and Reconciliation.

The Rt. Rev. Jennifer Baskerville-Burrows, eleventh bishop of Indianapolis, at her consecration with the Rt. Rev. Barbara Harris.

Chris Denny

Trinity's outreach in 2016 continued to grow and thrive. The Sunday feeding ministry served more than 5,500 meals to people in the neighborhood. The Dayspring Sunday dinner team continued to serve meals on a monthly basis, and Trinity Comforters and Habitat for Humanity continued to perform good works. Parishioners' gathering of gifts under the Magi Tree, this time for Trinity's new Welcoming Team and Horizons at St. Richard's, remained a popular annual event. The Mid-North Food Pantry served more than 12,000 clients, a record number, while the number of Trinity volunteers at the pantry grew to more than 30. Project Home Indy welcomed 11 new teenage girls and their babies into its residential program.

But even with all of that activity, parishioners at Trinity wanted to do more. Trinity partnered with Gleaners Food Bank, the Indianapolis Department of Public Safety, the Indianapolis Metropolitan Police Department, the Indianapolis Fire Department, and the C.A.R.E. (Community Action Relief Effort) Mobile Pantry Program. Trinity joined IndyCAN (the Indianapolis Congregational Action Network, later renamed Faith in Indiana) to engage voters in upcoming elections and to work for economic opportunities for disadvantaged groups, criminal justice reform, and immigration reform.

Parishioners collected toiletries during Advent for Dayspring Center and the Mid-North Food Pantry.

One of the newest and most creative outreach ministries at Trinity, St. Nicholas Early Learning, Inc., was growing rapidly. Organized in less than a year by the Trinity Childcare Committee, its goal was to fill the gap created by the departure from the Trinity Outreach Center by Precious Gifts Visionaries Childcare. In May 2016, The Episcopal Church's United Thank Offering awarded a $39,000 grant to the new mission. In June, the St. Nicholas board of directors selected a new executive director, Dr. David Sandrick, the former director of the Indiana University-Purdue University Indianapolis Center for Young Children. In June, St. Nicholas achieved Section 501(c)(3) status under the Internal Revenue Code, making it eligible to receive tax-deductible charitable donations.

That summer saw Trinity volunteers working to get St. Nicholas's physical facilities ready and Dr. Sendrick and the Board busy recruiting families and hiring staff. In the fall, St. Nicholas passed its state inspection and opened in September with three children and four staff. The new mission hosted a grand opening ceremony on December 6, 2016, which a proclamation by Indianapolis Mayor Joe Hogsett declared to be St. Nicholas Early Learning Day. By the end of the year, after four months of operation, St. Nicholas had grown to 27 students and 10 staff members.

Trinity created yet another new outreach ministry in 2016, the Welcoming Team. In the previous year, the vestry had approved a proposal by Mother Karen King to welcome a refugee family to Indianapolis. It would be the first time since the 1980s that Trinity had undertaken such a project for refugees. A group of parishioners led by Elsa Sands created the Welcoming Team to ensure that the family would be well supported. Mother King's proposal included that Trinity should work with Exodus Refugee Immigration, an Indianapolis-based organization that provided legal and other support for refugees establishing new lives in Indiana and that had grown out of the Diocesan Refugee Settlement Commission described in Chapter 14. After undergoing a training program at Exodus, the Welcoming Team furnished and equipped an entire apartment, obtained clothing, and arranged English tutoring for Trinity's future assisted family.

A few days before Thanksgiving 2016, the Welcoming Team and Mother Whitworth went to Indianapolis International Airport to greet the newly arrived family from the Central African Republic: father Prosper Bessaguem, mother Sidonie Noudjounare, their children, and their nephew. Before long, with the help of the Welcoming Team, the family was settled in Indianapolis and became active parishioners at Trinity.

But Trinity's outreach initiatives continued. In August 2016, Mother Whitworth and the vestry created the 3256 Discernment Team, chaired by John Craun, and charged the team with identifying potential mission opportunities for the St. Edward's House at 3256 North Pennsylvania Street. Starting in September, the 3256 Discernment Team brainstormed, then reached out to potential community partners, and then assessed the possibilities it had identified. Beginning with a list of 15 ideas, the team members narrowed the list down to four. The team projected that it would make recommendations to the vestry and parish in the spring of 2017.

The program of catching up on deferred maintenance of Trinity's physical plant, which had begun in earnest in 2014, continued into 2016. Lighting throughout the Trinity/St. Richard's campus was switched over to LED lighting. New speakers were installed in the Fortune Room and the sanctuary, greatly improving audibility in those spaces.

One of the last items on the Deferred Maintenance Committee's list of things to do was the installation of new lighting in the sanctuary. In August 2016, the Deferred Maintenance Committee met with Shakespeare Lighting Design of Bloomington, Indiana, to discuss the church's lighting needs. In November, the committee and Shakespeare finalized the lighting design and chose Barth Electric of Indianapolis as the installation team. After obtaining approval from the vestry, the committee presented the design plans to the parish on Sunday, January 8, 2017.

Trinity organized another mini-capital campaign to help pay for the lighting similar to that done for the sanctuary windows in 2010. Approximately 100 donors, including Bishop Waynick and the Consortium of Endowed Episcopal Parishes, gave generous gifts in response to the campaign. The new sanctuary lighting was dedicated at a ceremony in May 2017. Immediately, parishioners could tell that the new lights dramatically illuminated the worship space in the sanctuary to an extent never seen before.

In August 2017, Mother Whitworth announced that, after much discernment and prayer, the 3256 Discernment Team had concluded its search for an appropriate use for the St. Edward's House. The team, with strong leadership by Junior Warden Leigh Ann Hirschman, had determined that the best use for the St. Edward's House was as a safe, welcoming abode for homeless LBGTQ youth. The reasons were manifold. Approximately 40 percent of homeless youth identify as LGBTQ. Between 75 percent and 85 percent of homeless LGBTQ youth were forced out of their homes by their parents or were fleeing rejection and abuse at home. With not a single shelter for these young people in the state, the available shelters were unsafe and unable to protect them from sexual, physical, and verbal assaults.

The 3256 Discernment Team finally settled on the name Trinity Haven for the project that would utilize the St. Edward's House and changed its name to the Trinity Haven Implementation Team. The team actively worked on its plans for Trinity Haven with Indiana Youth Group (IYG), an organization that provided effective programming for LGBTQ youth and that had moved its headquarters to just a few blocks north of Trinity. The plans were that, with IYG's involvement, Trinity Haven would provide the LGBTQ youth staying there with access to legal services, education, job placement, classes teaching life skills, and support from IYG staff.

The Trinity Haven Implementation Team anticipated that Trinity Haven would open in the St. Edward's House in the fall of 2018. The team also hoped that the mission, which it had started from the ground up, could serve as a model for and be replicated by other faith-based organizations throughout the city. In furtherance of this goal, the team sought and was awarded a $20,000 grant by the new Faith and Action Project at Christian Theological Seminary in Indianapolis, which had been founded to help eradicate poverty in Indianapolis in innovative ways.

At this time, other Episcopalians also were bringing innovative changes to worship and service in central Indiana. Trinity always had been active in the formation of new parishes in the diocese, including St. Alban's in Indianapolis and Holy Family in Fishers, Indiana. Both of these were traditional churches with sanctuaries, rooms for meetings and education, and administrative offices. In September 2017, the vestry committed financial support for a completely different kind of church, Good Samaritan Episcopal Church, in Brownsburg, Indiana. Good Samaritan was a recently established but vibrant and growing church without walls in Hendricks County, an Indiana county where previously there had been no Episcopal church. Good Samaritan's worship services took place in a variety of places, none of which was a church sanctuary, and its members were highly motivated to do good works.

But Trinity was, if nothing else, a traditional church with all the trappings. In October 2017, Trinity was granted $182,000 by the Allen Whitehill Clowes Charitable Foundation, Inc., for the renovation of its organ and a celebratory concert series during the summer of 2019. Allen Clowes was the younger son of Dr. George H.A. Clowes and Edith Whitehill Clowes, who were so important in the design and building of Trinity's church building.

Welcoming worshipers at Trinity.
Trinity Episcopal Church

During his lifetime, Mr. Clowes was at all times a Trinity parishioner. In fact, he was the one member of the Clowes family who officially served on the Building Committee with overall responsibility for the construction of Trinity's church building. Carrying on the philanthropic tradition of his parents, he made generous contributions to a number of charitable organizations, mostly in central Indiana, that promoted or preserved fine arts, music, literature, education, science, and history.

At the end of the parish's first 100 years, Trinity's finances appeared at last to be again on a solid footing. Parish support at Trinity had grown from $500,000 to more than $600,000 during 2014–2017, a period of just three years. In 2018, Trinity achieved total parish support in the amount of $627,000, which was $22,000 more than budgeted. The next pledge campaign set a goal for 2019 of $636,000 in pledges alone, but pledges surpassed that goal and hit $644,000. In the years since the beginning of the new millennium, the number of pledging units had stayed relatively constant, but the total dollar amount of pledges by those units had doubled.

Meanwhile, the draw on the Endowment, which had reached a staggering $1.7 million in 2015, dropped to $1.5 million in 2016 and to $1.2 million in 2017. The draw was budgeted to be slightly more than $1 million in 2018, which would be more in line with previous years' draws. The same draw was budgeted again for 2019.

In addition, the Trinity clergy and staff continued to manage the parish's budget well. The treasurer of the vestry, the Finance Committee, and the Endowment trustees interacted on a regular basis with the vestry regarding issues such as budgeting, spending policy, and investments. The vestry, with the advice of the trustees, for many years had appointed an investment advisor to the trustees who also served as a custodian of the marketable securities held by the Endowment. For the 10 years since 2007, that advisor had been Morgan Stanley. In dealing with the Endowment, the trustees and the investment advisor were bound to follow investment guidelines approved by the vestry.

Beginning in 2017, however, the trustees began to review their traditional policy of investing and spending, asset allocation, and benchmarking. The reasons were that the philosophy behind investment guidelines had changed slowly since the Lost Decade and Great Recession of the 2000s. The reality was that mainstream investment thinking had become more in line with the innovative tenets of the Financial Master Plan conceived in 2013 by the task force appointed under Father Kryder-Reid. The trustees also decided that it was time to consider reviewing a change in the position of investment advisor, and so they started a Request for Proposal (RFP) process to determine whether such a change was warranted.

The year 2018 would be notable for many reasons, most of which were extremely positive, but some of which generated mixed emotions. In May, Trinity gave bittersweet goodbyes to two beloved, long-time leaders. The first was Mother Karen King, who had come to Trinity in 2002 to head up the parish's fledging neighborhood outreach program and had spearheaded the Sunday feeding ministry. When she arrived at Trinity, people said that the parishioners would not personally get involved in mission. Mother King, however, persuaded people to use their hands and their hearts to serve the people in the community and, by doing so, reap the benefits of doing good works themselves.

The second leader to leave was Kevin DePrey, Trinity's parish administrator, who came in 2003 and worked tirelessly and effectively to keep the books and records straight, everything else in order, and all of the balls in the air. It is doubtful that anything happened at Trinity in the 15 years Mr. DePrey was there with which he did not have some significant involvement. Mr. DePrey's main goal was to make sure the parish ran smoothly, which sometimes involved intervening to prevent people from trying to do harm to each other. But he always performed his role with gentle humor and a never-failing positive attitude.

Certainly, the most dramatic events of the year occurred in the area of outreach. The established outreach missions all were doing well. Trinity Haven had incorporated and had achieved Section 501(c)(3) status, but in

2018 it hit an unexpected snag. Despite the best efforts of Trinity to inform the St. Richard's stakeholders of the upcoming establishment of Trinity Haven in the St. Edward's House, a significant number of St. Richard's parents—none of whom were affiliated with Trinity—strongly objected to the St. Edward's House being used in the manner intended by Trinity.

Everyone at Trinity—the clergy, the vestry, and the Trinity Haven Implementation Team—were caught off guard by this reaction. After all, Trinity's campus had become the home for a number of other outreach ministries that welcomed the desperately needy onto Trinity's campus, including Project Home Indy, the Neighborhood Christian Legal Clinic, and the Mid-North Food Pantry. The specific problem for the concerned parents seemed to be the proximity of the St. Edward's House to the St. Richard's playground. Trinity, of course, had taken that into consideration but concluded it was not a real concern for the reason that the youth staying at Trinity Haven would be in school somewhere else while St. Richard's was in session.

To Trinity's credit, rather than exacerbate the situation by moving forward with its original plans, the implementation team searched for and found an even better house for Trinity Haven a few blocks away. The new house was larger, was more accessible and visible, had a better floor plan, and needed much less rehabilitation. Trinity's vestry approved financing the purchase with a loan from the Endowment. Clearly, miracles do happen.

After that, Trinity Haven received a truly remarkable reception from a number of places. Media from around the country gave the new mission great recognition and positive coverage. The Lilly Endowment awarded Trinity Haven a $300,000 grant to support its mission. Trinity Haven also received a Change Maker Award in the amount of $100,000 from Impact 100, an all-women philanthropy based in Indianapolis, which Trinity Haven announced it would use in conjunction with IYG.

In addition, Trinity's vestry approved a matching challenge grant of up to $50,000 to go along with its funding of the purchase price for the house. The Mike and Sue Smith Family Fund, St. Paul's, and St. Richard's provided other significant grants. All Saints, Everhart Studios, Ice Miller, the Coalition for Homelessness Intervention and Prevention of Greater Indianapolis, and a number of Trinity parishioners also gave donations to Trinity Haven.

To top off everything else, the Diocese of Indianapolis made Trinity Haven a Diocesan Cooperative Ministry, thus adding it to St. Richard's, Craine House, and Dayspring Center as such ministries that Trinity was instrumental in creating. In fact, Trinity Haven became the first new such ministry in nearly 20 years.

While Trinity Haven was attracting generous sums of grant money, St. Nicholas Early Learning also received a grant from Blue Cross/Blue Shield, and Project Home Indy received a grant from The Mary Alphonse Bradley Fund.

It should be noted that an interesting turn-around was occurring in the direction that grant money was flowing. Before the turn of the millennium, Trinity had granted great sums of money to other charitable organizations, but since 2000, it had achieved the position of creating and working with missions to which other organizations were granting their money.

Trinity's other outreach ministries also continued to thrive. In 2018, the Sunday feeding ministry served hot meals every Sunday of the year and, in 2018, served more than 5,800 guests, including more than 600 children. The ministry continued to work with six teams, but the total number of volunteers who worked on the teams over the course of the year had grown to 125 adults and 30 children and teens.

The Mid-North Food Pantry served more than 11,000 households in 2018. The pantry was able to serve eggs with grants received from Trinity and the Indianapolis Rotary Foundation. More fresh food was available through partnerships with Whole Foods, Second Helpings, and Gleaners Food Bank, as well as from its own garden.

In 2018, St. Nicholas Early Learning achieved full enrollment with children from diverse racial and socioeconomic backgrounds, a waiting list, a balanced budget, a scholarship fund, and increased family and community engagement. Things were going so smoothly, in fact, that plans were begun to move St. Nicholas into the full first floor of the Trinity Outreach Center.

As Trinity approached its hundredth anniversary, it could look back on the importance not only of legacy but of legacy gifts. The vestry, upon the advice of the Endowment trustees, merged the Endowment and the Memorial Fund into the Trinity Church Legacy Fund. The RFP process begun in 2017 also resulted in a change in investment advisor from Morgan Stanley to two new advisors in early 2018: Church Investment Group (CIG), a non-profit advisory firm focused exclusively on endowed Episcopal churches, and Hirtle, Callaghan & Co., LLC, an investment advisory firm that served as the outsourced chief investment officer of CIG.

Drawing upon lessons learned from the Financial Master Plan of 2014, the Endowment trustees developed and the vestry approved a new investment policy called A Faith and Goals Based Approach to Investment. The basic premise of the new policy was not just to maximize investment returns in one large portfolio to achieve an optimal total return on investment but to manage Trinity's investments in ways that ensure consistency with Episcopal values and alignment with the parish's budgeting process and enhance the likelihood of achieving the desired outcomes and overall mission of the church.

The goals, generally, were ministry (providing worship space, paying associated bills and expenses, clergy and administrative staffing, and all related programming); outreach and justice (one thing that sets Trinity apart and is a core mission); buildings and properties (another thing that sets Trinity apart given the size and complexity of its overall campus); direct mission investments (direct placement of capital, similar to Trinity's traditional outreach grants and loans for various projects); and funds for future generations (a powerful expression of intergenerational equity).

Under the new policy, funds for each of these separate goals would be set up in separate portfolios, which would be invested more conservatively or more aggressively depending on the need for liquidity of the funds. The parish's budget would be aligned with these goals. Equally significantly, the Trinity Church Legacy Fund would be invested in the utilization of Environmental, Social, and Governance (ESG) criteria in choosing investment vehicles.

Why was all this so important? If you look back on this story of Trinity, you will see the responses to the Lost Decade and the Great Recession: budget cuts, staff reductions, and deferred maintenance and capital expenditures. But you also will see all the good that was done at Trinity: outreach and more outreach, with major projects such as the formation of St. Richard's, the Trinity Outreach Center, the Sunday feeding ministry, St. Nicholas Early Learning, and Trinity Haven. In the past, Trinity had spent almost $8 million on property acquisitions and building support and had spent $2.3 million on support of missions.

None of these good things, however, were ever captured anywhere in the concept of total return on investment, yet all of it was fundamental to the identity of Trinity. Going forward, Trinity's parishioners have to remember that they are a body of Christians and that they have been blessed with the gifts they have received in order to fulfill their obligations as Christians.

The first 100 years of Trinity Episcopal Church, Indianapolis, ended on April 6, 2019, so most of the story of the year 2019 will have to be written by the next person continuing the story of the church. Suffice it to say that Trinity in 2019 remained extremely strong. It could be argued that the parish had shrunk slightly or at least just stayed about the same during the previous 10 years. In 2009, the number of households in the parish was determined to be 350, and in 2019, it was counted at 345; in 2009, the number of baptized members was calculated at 807, and in 2019, it was 793.

But other numbers told a completely different story about the strength and vibrancy of the church at 33rd and Meridian. The number of congregants in good standing went from 698 in 2009 to 793 in 2019 (an increase of nearly 14 percent), and the amount of pledges went from $442,000 in 2009 to $645,250 in 2019 (an increase of over 45 percent). And the very important average Sunday attendance figure, which was 255 in 2009 and had shrunk to 234 in 2015, grew to 274 in 2019—an increase of 17 percent in five years. In fact, the clergy deemed the 10 a.m. Sunday service to be effectively at maximum capacity. Although a nice problem to have, near-capacity attendance created challenges to serving existing congregants and welcoming newcomers at the same time.

The reasons for these improvements had bases in several other strengths of Trinity. The church had an energetic and talented clergy—Rector Julia Whitworth, Associate Rector and Chaplain for St. Richard's Episcopal School Benjamin J. "Ben" Anthony, and Associate Rector for Community Engagement and Vitality Erin Hougland—an exceptional staff, and the same

Mother Whitworth, the Rev. Dr. Benjamin J. Anthony, and the Rev. Erin Hougland ready to lead Sunday worship.
Kelly Kennedy Bentley

outstanding lay leadership that it has always enjoyed. It was part of a vibrant diocese led by a dynamic bishop, Bishop Jennifer Baskerville-Burrows. It was located in a city that had made great strides in recent decades and seemingly was determined to continue to improve.

It also must be recorded that the parish celebrated its first 100 years well.

On Saturday, May 11, 2019, the sanctuary held the Trinity Centennial Celebration, a Holy Eucharist at 1 p.m., at which the celebrant was Bishop Baskerville-Burrows and the preacher was the Rev. Canon Scott Gunn, executive director of Forward Movement, an evangelical ministry of The Episcopal Church. An anthem, *O Blessed Holy Trinity*, was performed by Trinity's choir. Trinity had commissioned the anthem from Robert and the Rev. Victoria Sirota, who were present to witness its premiere.

Trinity also celebrated its centennial with three inspiring and spiritually powerful pilgrimages.

The first such pilgrimage took place from February 20–March 5, 2019, and, fittingly, was to the Holy Land, the epicenter of the three Abrahamic religions, also known as the Religions of the Book: Judaism (since the seventh century BCE), Christianity (since the first century CE), and Islam (since the seventh century CE). There, Solomon built the First Temple, in which God resided. There, Christ was crucified, rose from the dead, and ascended to heaven. There, Muhammad left on his night journey to heaven to talk with God. More than half of the people in the world adhere to one of these three religions. The pilgrims consisted of 21 people, most of whom were Trinity parishioners (led by Mother Whitworth), and the rest were friends and family of the Trinity pilgrims.

Trinity's pilgrims to the Holy Land
at St. George's Cathedral, Jerusalem.
Trinity Episcopal Church

Trinity's J2A pilgrims on the island of Iona, Scotland;
youth coordinator Missy Roetter stands third from the right.
Trinity Episcopal Church

The pilgrims visited almost every site that was significant to the life of Jesus and the Holy Family. These included where tradition holds that the following occurred: the annunciation to Mary, the birth of Jesus, the baptism of Jesus, the Sermon on the Mount, several miracles, the procession of Jesus into Jerusalem on Palm Sunday, the last supper of Jesus and His disciples, His crucifixion on Good Friday, His resurrection on Easter Sunday, and His appearance to the disciples on the road to Emmaus. The pilgrims stayed and worshipped at the Cathedral of St. George in Jerusalem, the seat of the Province of Jerusalem and the Middle East, and worshipped at a number of other churches, including St. Andrew's Episcopal Church in Ramallah in the Occupied Territory. Without question, the pilgrimage was transformative intellectually, emotionally, and spiritually.

The second pilgrimage was of seven J2A teens and five adults accompanying them (led by Father Ben Anthony and youth coordinator Missy Roetter) to Scotland from May 30–June 9, 2019. The pilgrims first spent five days on the holy island of Iona, lodging at the youth hostel near the coast of the island. The teens prayed the daily office, prepared their meals, and learned to live in a community. While staying on Iona, the pilgrims traveled to the island of Staffa to view puffins and the famous Fingal's Cave. This was the eleventh youth pilgrimage in the past 20 years and the second time to Iona.

The next four days of the pilgrimage were spent in Edinburgh, where the pilgrims joined the Anglican bishop of Edinburgh at St. Mary's Cathedral on Pentecost Sunday. Some of the other sights taken in were the Queen's residence in Edinburgh and Edinburgh Castle, where the Black Watch Guards performed drills and music with pipes and drums. Again, the pilgrims benefited immensely from their journey together.

Trinity's choir and clergy in Ely Cathedral, England.
Kyung-Won On

The third and largest pilgrimage was taken from July 3–15, 2019, to Paris, France, and Ely, England, by 76 Trinity choir members and choristers, parents, spouses, parishioners, and friends. Of that large group, a total of 49 were singers (12 of whom were teens and younger). This was the seventh choir pilgrimage in the past 20 years, the fifth to England, and the first to France.

The choir sang the Saturday evening mass at Paroisse Saint-Étienne-du-Mont and Sunday morning Eucharist at the American Cathedral of the Holy Trinity in Paris. The choir then traveled to the cathedral town of Ely in England, where they sang six services of daily choral Evensong and Sunday morning Eucharist at the Cathedral Church of the Holy and Undivided Trinity of Ely. The choir performed works by a varied group of composers, including the English composers William Byrd, Herbert Howells, and Hubert Hastings Parry; French composer Maurice Duruflé; Estonian composer Arvo Pärt; and many others.

The choir, of course, was received enthusiastically by the people who heard them, and all the pilgrims were treated as fellow Anglicans by all of the people who met and hosted them. The pilgrims also were able to do sightseeing and dining in Paris and the countryside surrounding Ely. Vestry member Bill Mirola led day trips to Cambridge, London, Lincoln, Peterborough, Burghley House, and Market Day in Stamford, England. The pilgrims also again were able to visit the four parish churches in East Anglia that served as the architectural models for Trinity's own church in Indianapolis.

This final pilgrimage of the centennial year 2019 gave the choir members an opportunity to rehearse together daily and offer daily choral worship at a high level of artistic achievement; gave all pilgrims a deeper appreciation and understanding of their Anglican liturgical, musical, and architectural heritage; and increased greatly their fellowship.

Epilogue

How did struggling, underfunded Advent turn into diverse, dynamic Trinity? There were many factors. The church was blessed with a fortunate location on Meridian Street, the most prominent street in Indianapolis. Although its first 35 years witnessed financial hardship and struggle, the parish benefited from solid and continuous lay leadership. After that time, the parish also enjoyed energetic, charismatic, and competent leadership by its clergy. In addition, the enlightenment and generosity of Mr. Eli Lilly provided the Diocese of Indianapolis, Trinity, and the other Meridian Street Episcopal parishes—Christ Church and St. Paul's—with what should be permanent financial strength.

Over time, all of these blessings came together to help inspire an engaged group of congregants at Trinity. Unfortunately, churches such as Trinity are becoming scarcer. It is common knowledge that mainline Protestant churches, at one time the dominant religious group in America, have been in serious decline for some time. In 2014, the Pew Research Center in its Religious Landscape Study found that Americans who identified as mainline Protestants had dropped to just 14.7 percent of the U.S. population while 25.4 percent identified as evangelical Protestants and 22.8 percent identified as unaffiliated (the religious "Nones"); in Indiana, the results were even more extreme, with 16 percent identifying as mainline Protestants, but 31 percent as evangelical Protestants and 26 percent as Nones.

The Episcopal Church is not immune from this phenomenon of shrinking affiliation. According to its own statistics, average Sunday attendance throughout The Episcopal Church dropped 24.9 percent during 2008–2018 and dropped 17.4 percent in the Diocese of Indianapolis during that time. Also during that period, the number of baptized members in The Episcopal Church dropped 17.5 percent while the number in the Diocese of Indianapolis dropped 16.5 percent.

Trinity, however, has been successful in keeping consistent average Sunday attendance, numbers of baptized members, and numbers of communicants in good standing since the start of the new century. In other words, Trinity has bucked the trends that other mainline Protestant churches have been experiencing. How can this be?

It seems to be that three things draw people to Trinity. First, newcomers are attracted by the beauty and holiness of Trinity's sanctuary on a Sunday morning filled with people celebrating the glory of God in a traditional and music-filled Anglican worship service. The Sunday services at Trinity certainly are some of the most spiritually nourishing experiences I have ever had.

Second, newcomers are attracted to the numerous ways to provide service to others through Trinity's ever-expanding outreach ministries, which are offered by Trinity on its own as well as in collaboration with other city and neighborhood organizations.

Third, they are attracted to the learning and formation opportunities offered to them and their children that help facilitate their individual faith journeys.

Eventually, though, what keeps people at Trinity is the friendship and fellowship with others living Trinity's mission to accept, nourish, and send all into the world to do God's work. So, worship services and programs bring newcomers in, but warm, welcoming, and accepting clergy and congregants at those services help bring people back after their first visit. Trinity's existing parishioners—the heart and soul of the church—are critical to turning those newcomers into new Trinity parishioners.

For Trinity's programs, having a Legacy Fund, or Benefaction or Endowment as it was called in the past, also is a huge advantage—but it also is a disadvantage. The Legacy Fund has provided stability, but it also has caused complacency. Trinity struggled to increase monetary pledges from parishioners over its history, but important advances in this regard occurred during 2000–2019. Pledges by Trinity parishioners went from $330,000 for the year 2000 to $645,000 for the year 2019, very near a doubling in amount. Meanwhile, during the same time the draw on the Benefaction/Endowment/Legacy Fund declined from $1.231 million to $1.088 million, the lowest of any time during the period except for two years in the Great Recession. Again, this financial strength enabled by the generosity of parishioners is a direct result of the rich programs and service, outreach, and formation opportunities provided by Trinity. People put their money where they think it will do some good and do not put their money where they think it is not needed.

As I tried to make clear in this story of Trinity, the parish has weathered numerous crises in the past, some financial, some theological, some cultural, some political. We all know that great challenges exist in 2020, and many more are on the horizon. As I write this epilogue, the world is in the midst of one of the greatest catastrophes in many years, another world pandemic. The COVID-19 pandemic of 2020 is being called by some the worst world crisis since the Second World War. Already it has forced great changes in peoples' lives, our healthcare systems, our businesses, and our economy. The numbers of illnesses and deaths is unknown, but they are already tragically high. The economic and financial devastation the pandemic will cause cannot be measured in total probably for years. Moreover, America is engulfed in its most widespread, sustained period of racial unrest and protests since the late 1960s. Again, as I write this, the changes in our society that people are demanding must be made are yet to be seen. But I am confident that the strong clerical and lay leadership of Trinity, as in the past, will help lead the solution of these and any other future challenges, just they consistently have done before.

And, finally, I am confident that someone will have much more to say in the next story written about Trinity Episcopal Church, Indianapolis.

Appendix A

Episcopal Glossary

The following glossary contains some of the more important Episcopal terms used in this story of Trinity Episcopal Church, Indianapolis.

Anglican Church

St. Augustine, a Benedictine monk from Rome and the first Archbishop of Canterbury, brought Christianity to Anglo-Saxon England in 597. During the Middle Ages, churches in Europe were described by the regions they served, such as the Gallican Church and the Spanish Church. References to the English Church, or the Church of England, date from at least 1246. In the Latin of the time, it was *ecclesia anglicana*, hence the *Anglican Church*. In the sixteenth century, the English Reformation began as a series of political and theological events that resulted in the Church of England breaking away from the authority of the Pope and the Roman Catholic Church and declaring the Sovereign of England to be the Supreme Head of the Church. Over time, the Church of England would develop aspects of Protestantism and Catholicism in its theology and practices. According to The Episcopal Church's website, "Anglicanism stands squarely in the Reformed tradition, yet considers itself just as directly descended from the Early Church as the Roman Catholic or Eastern Orthodox churches."

Anglican Communion

In the following centuries, missionaries expanded the Church of England around the globe both inside and outside the growing British Empire. Anglican worship outside Britain began in Canada in 1578 shortly after the English Reformation. The start of The Episcopal Church in the United States was a first step in the breakup of the worldwide Church of England into autonomous *member churches* (also called *provinces*) which keep the Archbishop of Canterbury as their spiritual head and stay in communion with each other, hence the *Anglican Communion*. Member churches exercise jurisdictional independence but share a common heritage concerning Anglican identity and commitment to scripture, tradition, and reason as sources of authority. Member churches in the Anglican Communion continue to reflect the balance of Protestant and Catholic principles of the Church of England. The Anglican Communion has 40 member churches and six other extra-provincial national churches with tens of millions of members in more than 165 countries. *See* **Episcopal Church.**

Bishop

Each diocese has a *diocesan bishop*. Diocesan bishops are charged with the apostolic work of leading, supervising, and uniting the church and providing Christian vision and leadership for their dioceses. The Episcopal Book of Common Prayer states that such a bishop is "to act in Christ's name for the reconciliation of the world and the building up of the church; and to ordain others to continue Christ's ministry." Other types of bishops are a *bishop coadjutor*, who will succeed a sitting diocesan bishop upon the latter's retirement or resignation, and a *bishop suffragan*, who is elected to assist the diocesan bishop. The Episcopal Church's General Convention of 1835 adopted a canon permitting the election of a *missionary bishop* to exercise Episcopal functions in states and territories not organized into dioceses, which led to the election of the Rt. Rev. Jackson Kemper as missionary bishop of Indiana and Missouri. Each kind of bishop is elected by representatives of the parishes in the diocese at a convention. As at General Convention, the representatives vote for a bishop in two separate bodies, the clergy and the laity, and a candidate for bishop must be approved by a majority of both bodies. Episcopal and other Anglican bishops stand in the apostolic succession, meaning that even after the Reformation, they trace their authority back to Peter, the first bishop, and maintain continuity in the present with the ministry of the Apostles. Although the Church of England has two archbishops (of Canterbury and of York), The Episcopal Church has no archbishops. The head bishop of The Episcopal Church is called the *presiding bishop*. *See* **Dioceses.**

Book of Common Prayer

A unique feature of the member churches in the Anglican Communion, including The Episcopal Church, is the *Book of Common Prayer* of each church, which is that church's official book of worship. Thus, the Anglican

Church of Canada, the Anglican Episcopal Church of Brazil, the Anglican Church of Kenya, the Anglican Church of Korea, and each other member church of the Anglican Communion has its own Book of Common Prayer. The Book of Common Prayer of each member church provides liturgical forms, prayers, and instructions so that all congregants and orders of that church may share in common worship. Anglican liturgical piety has been rooted in the prayer book tradition since the publication of the first English Prayer Book in 1549 shortly after the English Reformation. The original Episcopal Book of Common Prayer was ratified by the first General Convention of The Episcopal Church in 1789. Subsequent revised editions of the Book of Common Prayer were ratified by General Conventions in 1892, 1928, and 1979. The Episcopal Church also may authorize services not in the Book of Common Prayer for use on a trial basis.

Broad Church

A *Broad Church* Episcopal church picks and chooses between High Church and Low Church aspects of its worship service. These middle-ground parishes are the most common in The Episcopal Church. Most people would have considered Advent and Trinity to be Low Church before 1980 and to be Broad Church starting in 1980 with the arrival of Father Roger White as rector. *See **High Church** and **Low Church**.*

Canon (Law)

The term *canon* has several meanings in The Episcopal Church. One meaning of canon is a written rule in the code of laws for the governance of the church. The canons of The Episcopal Church may be enacted, amended, or repealed only at General Convention. The canons of The Episcopal Church are organized by titles or sections concerning Organization and Administration, Worship, Ministry, Ecclesiastical Discipline, and General Provisions.

Canon (Title)

A *canon* on a cathedral staff is a person who assists the dean of the cathedral. A *canon* on a diocesan staff assists the bishop. Canons can be but do not have to be priests.

Cathedral

A *cathedral* is a church that contains the diocesan bishop's seat. The cathedral is the principal church of the diocese. The dean is the clergyperson with pastoral charge of the cathedral. The dean may be assisted by canons. Some cathedrals also have honorary canons who do not share in the daily pastoral responsibilities of the cathedral parish. Not all Episcopal dioceses have cathedrals, and most cathedrals are parish churches used for diocesan purposes.

Deacon

In The Episcopal Church, a *deacon* is a separate order of clergy, distinct from a priest and a bishop, who exercises a special ministry of servanthood directly under the bishop, serving all people inside and outside the church and especially those in need. In addition to those ordained as a deacon as a permanent vocation, *transitional deacons* are ordained as a deacon as a preliminary step toward ordination as a priest.

Dean

At a cathedral, the *dean* is the priest in charge, similar to a rector at a church, although the cathedral is the official headquarters of the bishop. At a seminary, a dean's function is like that of a president of a college or university.

Dioceses

The Episcopal Church is organized into geographical areas called *dioceses*. See **Bishop**.

Episcopal Church

No Anglican bishops existed for the Church of England in America during the colonial era; all such bishops were based in England. In 1783, following the Revolutionary War, the Anglican churches in Connecticut elected Samuel Seabury, an American, as their bishop. For the Church of England to consecrate Seabury as a bishop under its canons, though, he would have had to swear allegiance to the King of England, which would have been treason under U.S. federal law. Consequently, Seabury turned to the Scottish Episcopal Church, which under its canons could consecrate him without his swearing allegiance to the King of England—a move that marked the beginning of an Anglican Communion with autonomous member churches. By 1786, the American *Episcopal Church* (not called the Anglican Church of America, which would have sounded treasonous at that time) had succeeded in translating episcopacy for America and in revising its Book of Common Prayer to reflect American political realities, including more democracy in the selection of bishops and rectors. The Episcopal Church today has two official names: The Episcopal Church (with a capitalized The) and the Protestant Episcopal Church in the United States of America. The Episcopal Church has had its disputes with its own member churches and other Anglican

Communion churches in recent years, particularly over the ordination of female and LGBTQ priests and bishops, but it nevertheless remains part of the Anglican Communion. *See Anglican Communion.*

Episcopal vs. Episcopalian

Episcopal always should be used as an adjective, as in an Episcopal church, an Episcopal worship service, and the Episcopal Book of Common Prayer. *Episcopalian* always should be used as a noun meaning a member of The Episcopal Church, as in "I am an Episcopalian," and never should be used as an adjective.

General Convention

The *General Convention* is the national legislative body of The Episcopal Church. It consists of a House of Bishops, which includes all active and retired bishops, and a House of Deputies, which includes four lay persons and four clergy from each diocese, each area mission, and the Convocation of the American Churches in Europe. The Convention meets every three years. The Houses meet and act separately, and both must concur to adopt legislation. The General Convention alone has authority to amend the Book of Common Prayer and the Church's Constitution, to amend the canons (laws) of the Church, and to determine the program and budget of the General Convention, including the missionary, educational, and social programs it authorizes.

High Church

A *High Church, High Anglican,* or even higher *Anglo-Catholic* Episcopal church has a worship service that is similar to the most traditional Roman Catholic service and rituals. *See Low Church* and *Broad Church.*

Low Church

A *Low Church* Episcopal church has a worship service that is similar to the most traditional Protestant service. *See High Church* and *Broad Church.*

Parishes

At the local level, Episcopal congregations are called *parishes.* An Episcopal parish is not geographical but is largely synonymous with *congregation* or *church. See Rector.*

Priest

The term *priest* is derived from the Greek *presbyteros,* meaning elder. The Episcopal Book of Common Prayer refers to both *priests* and *presbyters* rather than to ministers or pastors. Priest is the more commonly used term. The Book of Common Prayer states that "the ministry of a priest or presbyter" is "to represent Christ and his Church, particularly as pastor to the people; to proclaim the gospel; to administer the sacraments; and to bless and declare pardon in the name of God." Several differences exist between Episcopal priests and Roman Catholic priests. Episcopal priests in America include women and people who are LGBTQ. Episcopal priests, and Anglican priests all over the world, are not required to take a vow of poverty or vow of celibacy and are free to marry. In most senses, then, Episcopal priests live more like the clergy in other Protestant denominations than like the clergy in the Catholic Church. Priests are one of the three distinct orders of ordained ministry in The Episcopal Church, along with bishops and deacons.

Pro-Cathedral

A *pro-cathedral* is a church named by a diocesan bishop to serve as a cathedral in the absence of a true cathedral in the diocese but which remains under the governance of the church's vestry and dean. It is used as a cathedral for diocesan purposes, but without the formation of a legal cathedral organization and without a cathedral chapter. It is not the official cathedral of the diocese. The church's status as a pro-cathedral ends when the bishop no longer holds the diocesan jurisdiction, and the pro-cathedral's status may or may not be extended by the next bishop.

Rector

Each parish elects a governing body called a *vestry*. Subject to the approval of its diocesan bishop, the vestry of each parish elects one priest, called the *rector*, who has spiritual jurisdiction in the parish and selects assistant clergy, both deacons and priests. The term *rector* comes directly from the Latin word *rector*, meaning leader. *See* **Vestry.**

Titles (Reverend, Very Reverend, Right Reverend, and Most Reverend)

The title for a priest in The Episcopal Church is *the Reverend*. The title for a priest with a Ph.D. in a religious subject is *the Reverend Doctor*. A priest canon of a cathedral is *the Reverend Canon*. (A lay canon's title is simply *Canon*.) A dean of a cathedral or seminary is *the Very Reverend*. A bishop is *the Right Reverend*. The presiding bishop is *the Most Reverend*. Reverend is usually abbreviated as *Rev.* or *Rev'd* in The Episcopal Church.

Titles (Father and Mother)

Before the 1980s, an Episcopal priest might be addressed as *Mr.*, *Reverend*, or *Father*, depending on how far up the High Anglican ladder the church, the priest, and the parishioner were. Before 1980, priests at Trinity generally were referred to as *Mister*. Parishioners at Trinity began referring to their priests more consistently as *Father* starting in 1980 with the arrival of Father Roger White as rector. With the arrival of female priests at Trinity later in the 1980s, parishioners naturally referred to them as *Mother*.

Vestry

The *vestry* is the legal representative body of the parish with regard to all matters pertaining to its corporate property. The number of vestry members and the term of office varies from parish to parish. Vestry members usually are elected at the annual parish meeting. The presiding officer of the vestry is the rector. There usually are two wardens: a *senior warden* (also known as the *priest's warden*), who is selected by the rector and who leads the parish between rectors and is a support person for the rector; and a *junior warden* (also known as the *people's warden*), who is selected by the lay members of the parish and who often has responsibility for church property and buildings. The basic responsibilities of the vestry are to help define and articulate the mission of the congregation, to support the church's mission by word and deed, to select the rector, to ensure effective organization and planning, and to manage resources and finances. The term vestry comes from when early Church of England parish meetings often were held in the vestry, the room off the chancel where the priests put on their vestments (i.e., their robes).

Vicar

Vicar has a meaning similar to rector, the difference having to do with finances. A vicar is the priest in charge of a parish that is supported financially from the outside, whereas a rector is the priest in charge of a self-supporting church. In England, most Anglican churches are supported by their diocese, so most of the priests in charge of English churches are vicars. In the United States, most Episcopal churches are self-supporting, so most of the priests in charge are rectors. In The Episcopal Church, the term usually used for a priest in charge of a non-self-supporting church is *priest-in-charge*, not vicar.

Appendix B

Miracles, Major and Minor

T he following memoir was written in 1953 by Edith Whitehill Clowes. She and her husband, Dr. George H.A. Clowes, were two parishioners of Trinity Episcopal Church, Indianapolis. They and other members of their family were intimately involved with the design and construction of the parish's church building during the immediately preceding years. In truth, there were many parishioners besides the Clowes family who were involved in the fund-raising, design, and construction of the church building.

But Edith Whitehill Clowes wielded great power in an age during which no woman served on the parish's vestry, junior vestry, or Building Committee for the new project—although her younger son, Allen Whitehill Clowes, did serve on that committee. Even so, she was the driving force of her family, and she was appointed as the official head of the very important—and all-female—Interior Decoration Committee for the building project. Her influence clearly extended far beyond just the interior of the structure, however.

In her memoir, Mrs. Clowes tells the extraordinary tale of her diligent study, boundless creativity, and detailed—one legitimately could say obsessive—supervision that resulted in the beautiful building in which Trinity's congregants have worshipped for over 50 years.

The version of Mrs. Clowes's memoir reproduced here is a typewritten manuscript in the Clowes Family Collection of the Indiana Historical Society. It is a piece of the period, and Mrs. Clowes's personality shines through clearly. A letter from Dr. Clowes to Mrs. Clowes in Trinity's archives reveals the poignant fact that Mrs. Clowes wrote her memoir at night while she was ill in a hospital, perhaps just to pass time during her recovery. Other documents in the archives make it evident that eventually she wished to have her memoir published and sought publication by The Bobbs-Merrill Company (a prestigious publishing company based in Indianapolis at the time), *The Atlantic Monthly*, and *National Geographic*. All of these turned it down. I believe, therefore, that this is the first time Mrs. Clowes's memoir has been published.

The Clowes Family Collection also possesses an earlier, original draft obviously produced on a different typewriter and which contains Mrs. Clowes's handwritten edits. Mrs. Clowes in all likelihood engaged two different typists for the two versions. Unfortunately, the finished memoir, which includes more details, also contains a number of typographical errors not found in the earlier, original draft.

In reproducing the finished memoir here, I have tried to leave it as unchanged as possible. I have indicated some misspellings and other typographical errors, and I have shown in footnotes what I believe was intended to be typed, in some cases by cross-referencing the earlier, original draft. (This draft is referred to in the footnotes as the "original draft.") Mrs. Clowes or her typists also occasionally used correct but alternative spellings (i.e., "33d" instead of "33rd"; "mediaeval" instead of "medieval"), and I have left those and the punctuation as they appear in the finished memoir. I also have added footnotes explaining many of the esoteric architectural and ecclesiastical terms used but not explained by Mrs. Clowes herself.

I am confident that a reading of this memoir will create a sense of awe toward the energy, intelligence, diligence, tenacity, and leadership of the amazing Edith Whitehill Clowes. All of us who love the beauty of Trinity Episcopal Church, Indianapolis, should be very grateful to her.

John B. Bridge
Indianapolis, 2020

MIRACLES, MAJOR AND MINOR

the story of

<u>Trinity</u> <u>Episcopal</u> <u>Church</u>
33d and Meridian
Indianapolis, Indiana

by

Edith Whitehill Clowes

MIRACLES, MAJOR AND MINOR

by

Edith Whitehill Clowes

* * *

Imagine yourself standing with me outside a modest frame church building with its young rector, looking with an appreciative eye upon its fine large corner lot on the main thoroughfare midtown in a growing city. To the south is the parish house, a transformed residence, somewhat Tudor in its brick and half timbering. Miracle of miracles, there is to be a new church and the old one will shortly be demolished! "The new building must be suitable in style to the parish house," we say. As we talk, I see before me, as if in a vision, a fine stone church with the simple lines of Early English Gothic, a square tower at the west end and entrance porches to north and south, thereby deadening the sound of outside traffic. From the south porch along the south wall runs a cloister,[1] which turns at a right angle to lead across to the back of the parish house. In the quadrangle thus formed, open to the west, is a mediaeval knot garden[2], geometrically laid out, its tiny paths bordered by dwarf evergreens and its beds set with herbs and hardy small creeping plants. The entrance from the street to the churchyard is through a lych gate from which lead walks to left and right to church and parish house respectively. The word "lych" means corpse—a "corpse gate," so called because in early days no coffin could be carried into the sanctuary without the presence of one in Holy Orders; therefore the covered gate provided a resting place until a priest arrived. Sometimes the lych gates were thatched and sometimes roofed in lead or slate. Our gate, roofed in slate like the church, is flanked by neat hedges and a tree overhangs it, throwing shadows and flickering lights across it.

In the Thirteenth Century there developed in England from the rounded Norman arches a new concept now called Early English, in which we first see the pointed arches and windows so characteristic of the Gothic Style. As our architect worked at the sketches, he outlined a church of Early English Gothic so simple as to be almost modern in design. Its nave[3] did not narrow

---

[1]A covered walk with a wall on one side and a colonnade open to an uncovered quadrangle on the other.

[2]A garden of very formal design in a square frame with a variety of aromatic plants and culinary herbs.

[3]The place in the church for the congregation, between the entry (i.e., the narthex) and the chancel.

at the chancel[4] and its north aisle balanced the cloister on the south. As the plans developed we realized that the east end of our church would be almost square. To use a dossal,[5] or hanging, would accentuate this, but to make a recess surrounded by a Gothic arch, within which would be a symbolic mural painting, would solve the difficulty. Careful reading of Webber's "The Small Church" and "Church Symbolism" provided much useful information and an idea for the mural grew from a picture of the decoration of a Twelfth Century Italian tomb in bas-relief of two peacocks, symbolizing immortal life, drinking the Waters of Eternity from a tall and graceful urn.

Just at this time I received a letter from a friend saying that she had mentioned my absorption in the new church to a young man, now an ecclesiastical artist, who, as a boy, visited her at the sea during the summer and often came over to our near-by house to talk to me. He was kind enough to express interest and to say that he would like to help if possible. I therefore wrote to ask his opinion of the idea of the recess above the altar containing a mural painting of such a subject as the peacocks, to which he replied enthusiastically endorsing it.

At this time our son returned from a meeting of the building committee greatly distressed by the obvious fact that there was no money for such plans as were contemplating [*sic*].[6] We wandered into the garden and finally, sitting in the late autumn sunshine, we spoke of the privilege and satisfaction it would be to help in making possible the building of a really beautiful church, an opportunity seldom offered to individuals nowadays. Finally we evolved the idea of giving the tower as our part of the project, which met with the approval of my husband and other members of the family. Then came a miracle indeed, when the most important foundation in our part of the country, hearing of our difficulty in carrying out our plans, gave an amount twice as large as any other donation, thus providing the balance needed beyond the gifts of the congregation, with the stipulation that the whole be carried out just as planned.

Activity became fast furious [*sic*].[7] Working drawings were begun and many talks given to various groups of the congregation to acquaint them with the outline of what was contemplated. Never in the whole course of the

---

[4]The place at the far end of the church for the choir, altar, lectern, pulpit, and seating for priests.

[5]A large cloth or piece of fabric that is hung on the wall behind the altar and may be decorated with religious symbols.

[6]The sentence in the original draft ends, " . . . as we were concocting."

[7]The sentence in the original draft reads, "Then the activity became fast and furious."

project, from start to finish, was there any difficulty or unkind criticism, but only enthusiasm and every possible aid from all concerned. What a major miracle for me that I should be the one with so glorious an opportunity to co-operate in such an inspiring undertaking with an architect like ours, so willing to accept suggestions when they were right and so adamant when they were wrong!

As the plans for the new building advanced, we became increasingly convinced that color should be used freely, as it had originally appeared in English churches before it was destroyed by the men of King Henry VIII, after 1534, and a century or more later by Cromwell's Roundheads. To poly-chrome[8] the beams and certain other members was our cherished plan, but the traditional use of color was a hard matter to run to earth. The Public Library offered nothing and it was only after much searching that I found in the library of the Art Institute a book called "English Church Woodwork," by Howard and Crossley, long out of print, containing a gold-mine of infor-mation in a chapter called "Color." Since I was much in need of advice, I addressed a letter to either of the two authors in care of the publisher in London. After an interval I received a reply in the shaky handwriting of a very old man, which began, "Your letter was the greatest surprise to me. My collaborator is long since dead" and which went on to encourage me to visit the remaining examples of the use of color in churches before undertaking any such plan as we were contemplating. Therefore, from the chapter on color, with the help of maps and guide books, I made a plan for a springtime motor trip through Norfolk and Suffolk, two counties on the east coast of England where there are churches scattered over the districts once so remote that they had escaped the marauders. Here are the glorious colors on roofs, tie-beams,[9] and cornices,[10] on rood screens[11] and pulpits, softened and beau-tified by time, but still there as examples of the traditional use of this kind of decoration. To these churches we planned to go.

On the steamer train to London—our first return since the War—by the merest chance we met two artists who, when they heard of our objectives, invited us to their house in London to meet one of the architects in charge of the fabric of Westminster Abbey. He, in turn, asked us to visit his office to see

---

[8]To paint in several colors.
[9]Horizontal beams connecting rafters in a roof.
[10]Ornamental moldings around the top of a wall in a room.
[11]Screens separating the chancel from the nave. As Mrs. Clowes explains later, *rood*—from Old English—means *crucifix* or *cross*.

a two-volume work called "Gothis [*sic*][12] Ornament," by James K. Kolling, containing beautiful colored plates of many details in churches that we were planning to see. He assured us that these books, printed well over one hundred years ago, were unobtainable, but our architect was lucky enough to find them by writing to the Times Book Club and they became our inspiration and mentor.

Before leaving London we presented a letter of introduction to a Canon of Westminster, with whom we discussed the problem of the proper colors to be used for the mock heraldic devices[13] of the Apostles. These are called <u>mock</u> heraldic devices because the College of Heralds presented them to the Apostles in the Middle Ages, probably believing that they should be included in the practices of heraldry. Our plan was to cover the lights along the walls of our church with shields, tipped slightly forward, upon which would be these mock heraldic devices, the light being cast upward as indirect lighting. The Canon had a clerical friend who had made a study of such matters. I wrote to him and he was kind enough to reply telling me that there was no rule for the colors used for mock heraldic devices, provided only that they should be the clear, true colors of heraldry. This was most satisfactory. Later, I found that some of the best examples of these devices of the Apostles were in a church in our own city and I spent a morning studying their use.

Setting forth from London with eager anticipation, we made our headquarters for our round of churches at an Elizabethan manor house, like a charming frame through which we looked at other glimpses into the far-distant past. The first church we visited was St. Mary the Virgin at Ufford. Its lovely tower is at the end of a quiet lane. We passed through the gate into the ancient churchyard, with its crumbling tombstones, and so entered the small church by the iron-studded oak doors of the south porch, where we paused in enchantment. Before us, rising to the roof, was the tapering, exquisitely polychromed, elaborately carved cover of the stone font.[14] The colors were those used in heraldry, clear bright red, blue, green, and gold, contrasting sharply with the dark oak of its delicate tracery and used in its interstices.[15] The rule for heraldic color is that red, blue, and green must always

---

[12]*Gothic.* The two-volume work referred to here, *Gothic Ornament*, is referred to but not named in the original draft.
[13]Coats of arms, essentially personal logos, often depicted on shields.
[14]A baptismal font.
[15]Small or narrow spaces between larger parts.

be separated by a tiny band or fillet of parchment-color or gold or perhaps black. On the wooden tie-beams or trusses spanning the narrow nave from wall to wall under the dark-timbered gabled roof, the colors are used in this way on moldings[16] suitably designed. A tie-beam, instead of being a long heavy piece of wood whose cross section is rectangular, is so made that its cross section is V-shaped, the narrow part pointing downward and the wide part toward the ceiling, with horizontal moldings for light and shade. Supporting the ceiling from the top of the side wall to the ridgepole are the rafters, which may be exposed. The barber-pole motif, like a black ribbon wrapped around a white pole, showing equal spaces of black and white, is universally used along the bottom edge of the V-shaped tie-beams, repeated again, perhaps in green and gold or in black and gold, higher up. The mold-ings are red, parchment-color, green, and a wide member with a graceful design of a vine having leaves and flowers done in gold on parchment-color. In the church at Ufford cresting[17] or dentils[18] top the whole, well spaced and delicately designed. The dark oak ceiling is divided into rect-angles of pleasing and uniform size by moldings of black and white barber pole. At the intersections are bosses[19] of the red rose on green leaves, sym-bolic of Mary, Mother of Christ. The triangular spandrils[20] where the tie-beams spring from the wall are carved and colored and between them is a cornice done to harmonize with the design described above. The roof of the chancel, beyond the chancel arch, is painted dark red, with IHS[21] and AΩ[22] alternating in silvery white, and around the chancel the cornice is more elab-orate than elsewhere. This little church was unequalled in my opinion as an inspiration for the decoration of the new church.

St. Peter's, Palgrave, has a very fine roof and trusses[23] elaborately done in red and shades of soft grey. At Woolpit the roof is magnificently carved

---

[16]A defining element that outlines a projection or cavity, such as a cornice or arch.

[17]Decoration at the edge of a ceiling or top of a wall.

[18]Decoration at the edge of a ceiling consisting of small, rectangular blocks resembling teeth.

[19]Knobs or protrusions of wood or stone.

[20]Triangular areas filling in between the tops of an arch and the horizontal roof or beam above.

[21]Monogram of Jesus taken from the first three letters of Jesus's name in Greek, which have been Latinized to *IHS*.

[22]*Alpha* and *Omega*, the first and last letters of the Greek alphabet, used in Christianity to designate the comprehensiveness of God.

[23]A framework of rafters, posts, and struts supporting the roof.

but there are no traces of color left. The roof at Knapton in Norfolk is supposed to have been made from the timbers of ships wrecked long ago on that grim coast. Its colors are yellow and red. At the center of each tie-beam is a delightful angel, with alternating red wings and green robe and red robe and green wings.

In many of the churches are partial remnants of rood screens between nave and choir[24] and in many there are recesses in the wall at the end of the screen, where the priest went up the spiral stair to the rood loft above to sing part of the service. "Roos" [*sic*][25] means "crucifix" and therefore originally each screen bore a cross, now no longer the case. At Ranworth and Tunstead are complete screens, each beautifully decorated with flower designs of great delicacy, the colors following the heraldic rules. The diaper work on the robes of the saints painted on the panels at the bottom is superb. Diaper work means a some-what triangular design, repeated over and over, either in color on a gold ground or in gold on color. The upper portions of the screens are delicately carved and open to permit the congregation to see and hear the service.

One of our objectives was to find a tiny country church at South Burlingham, which contains a famous decorated pulpit. I could find no mention of it in guide book, road map, or even footpath map and therefore we were delighted to see the name on a signpost on our right as we sped along one of the flat roads of Norfolk. We turned into a narrow lane and finally saw the church standing alone beyond hedges and a field. It was locked, but a shy urchin from a farmhouse on the other side of the lane brought us the huge hand-wrought iron key, which he handed to me, asking in his almost incomprehensible dialect that we return it later. A shilling persuaded him to wait and he stood motionless by the door, a stolid son of the hardy folk of Norfolk, his face giving no clue to his thoughts. The interior was bare of all beauty except for the wonderful pulpit, upon which the sunlight streamed from an adjacent window of clear glass. There was diaper work in gold upon the ancient oak panels and the surrounding moldings were done in designs of gold and black on parchment color, very handsome and unique.

I have always been charmed by the parish churches in the English countryside and moved by their bells peeling [*sic*][26] across the peaceful sunlit

---

[24]Another word for the chancel.

[25]The word is spelled correctly in the same sentence in the original draft: *Rood*.

[26]Removing a covering is *peeling*; ringing a bell is *pealing*. The original draft also uses the wrong word.

fields to call the people to morning prayer or evensong.[27] Members of my husband's family, father and son, were rectors of the same tiny church for nearly a century. Its parish register, from the time of Queen Elizabeth I, is among the oldest extant and the church itself is mentioned in the Doomsday Book, compiled after William of Normandy conquered the Saxons in 1066. Bullets used by Cromwell's men could still be found in the stout oak of an unused door against which their enemies were executed. The Bible, chained to the reading desk, dates from the reign of Charles the Second. I was told by the rector with a twinkle that it had to be chained because there were so many Americans about. The baptismal font is a very old seven-sacrament font of great beauty. When our sons were small, they and I used to imagine the perfect church by choosing from those we had seen each object that we liked best. We always chose St. Peter's seven-sacrament font to be incorporated in our imaginary church together with such wonders as the interlocking arches in the choir at Lincoln and the clock with many mechanical figures at Wells. The parish churches are so essential a part of English life and culture, having been in use since earliest Christian times, that to visit them, either in the country or on a picturesque village street surrounded by ancient houses, gives one a deep sense of the atmosphere of worship through the centuries and indeed of the very presence of God. We wandered on to Bacton, Loddon, Bramfield, Trimingham, Attleboro, Southwold, and many other churches, including the smallest one of all at Thornham Parva, where we crossed a field of buttercups and daisies to reach the thatched church containing a thirteenth-century reredos,[28] crudely representing saints, painted by the Norwich School. It is very striking that the churchyards of these old churches appear to have singularly few graves, although they have been used as burial places from earliest times. When I remarked upon this to the rector of St. Peter's, he pointed out that, after twenty-five years, all graves return to the possession of the church unless marked with a stone. Few of the humble people whose dead were interred out-of-doors could afford a marker and the tombs of the gentry were usually inside the churches. This explains why the grave-digger in "Hamlet" finds poor Yorick's skull, which he tosses out from its grave.

---

[27]Relatively brief but beautiful Anglican worship services held in the morning and evening, respectively.

[28]Decoration behind or above the altar, typically a screen, hanging, or panel consisting of stone, wood, jeweled metalwork, or drapery.

As we visited the various churches we were constantly looking for a lych gate suited to our needs. There are but few of them left and it was not until we were walking through a garden belonging to a treasure-filled house that we saw, close to the nearby church, a lych gate of such beautiful design and proportions that we hastened to photograph it. Our hostess explained that it was a memorial to the local men who fell in the First World War and I noticed a name which must have been that of her husband as the officer in command. She was a lady of great hardihood, for although the day was damp, cold, and gray, requiring layers of wool for some of us, she was wearing a thin silk dress and said, "I am no coat woman." As we walked she knitted constantly. From this chance discovery of the lych gate the architect was able from our photograph to design one like it for our purpose which was so beautiful that it was immediately given as a memorial.

Upon our return to America we found the bids in for the new church and the contracts ready to be signed. But how could we bear to build our beautiful church of smooth, rectangular stone blocks either four or eight inches wide? All honest building must be of native stone, but how could we accomplish the random look so greatly desired? It happened that the architect was motoring along a highway when he noticed a culvert not too far from out [*sic*]²⁹ city built of stone so ideal for our purpose that he immediately took steps to discover the whereabouts of the quarry from which it came. Its bearing strength, its resistance to heat and cold, and so forth were all determined by the necessary tests and all proved to be satisfactory. It contained enough flint in its lovely, rough, gray surface to give it a delightful gleam when struck by the sunlight and also to make the surface too hard to absorb dirt. We had found the ideal stone, whose lovely uneven planes cast changing shadows as the sunshine moved across them. But who knew how to lay such material to keep a semblance of the horizontal in its uneven courses and to fit in pieces of all shapes and sizes without allowing the mortar to show too much or too little? The sub-contractor for the stone work engaged an English mason who understood what was wanted and who finally produced a sample piece of wall, one of several, that was acceptable. He laid much of the stone himself, but finally was able to teach his skills to one or two others. The stone was lined with brick, suitably waterproofed. As

---

²⁹The word in the same sentence in the original draft is *the.*

the walls rose it became increasingly evident that the color and texture of the lovely light gray stone was perfect.

Having settled upon the symbolism and general idea of the mural to be used at the east end of the church in the recess above the altar, it became necessary to choose someone for its execution and to this end we asked a few artists to submit designs. Of those offered we preferred the one made by the young man who had first advised us on the suitability of the whole idea. From his first sketch in black and white he did a "rendering" in color, from which, after months of patient changes, we accepted the final sketch and at last the artist ordered the huge plywood panel upon which he would paint the mural. It was so large that it would not fit into the studio and therefore the artist rented an immense loft in an old building where the elevator for freight could accommodate the huge mural without damaging it when finished and crated. Its background of gold leaf, rubbed down enough to show the red ground[30] in places, glowed behind the Tree of Life, at the center of whose branches shone a gold cross in bas-relief. On either side of the trunk were the graceful peacocks drinking the Waters of Eternity from the tall stone urn in front of the dark trunk of the tree. Stylized red pomegranates, also symbols of eternal life, showed here and there. The sheaves of wheat below, and a handsome border of grapes surrounding the whole, meant the Holy Eucharist.[31] Below the wheat again, on a green ground, were small flowers, like those in a millefleurs tapestry,[32] each one with a tiny gold cross at its heart. Thus, as is essential, the symbolism of the whole mural was simple and unconfused.

Meanwhile, the roof of the church building was finished, spring had come, and suddenly a section of a tie-beam was strung up near the north door in what later became a coat room and there were the craftsmen who were going to polychrome the woodwork under my guidance. Out came books and notebooks, clear pur [sic][33] colors were chosen for our red and green, and we set to work. Nothing could be copied; everything had to be adapted to the sizes of our moldings. Neither the architect nor the painters

---

[30]The first layer or undercoat of paint applied to an artwork.

[31]Communion: the sacrament of Christ's body and blood, and the principal act of Anglican worship.

[32]A tapestry with a background of many different small flowers and plants, usually shown on a green background to create the impression that they are growing in a grassy field.

[33]The sentence in the original draft begins, "Out came books and notebooks; clear, pure colors were chosen . . . ."

had ever seen polychroming after the traditional heraldic manner of using color, and only by trial and error, by painting and repainting, by hauling up our sample to the height of the real tie-beams, looking and criticizing, hauling it down and beginning over, did we finally come to what seemed right and beautiful. The half-round member at the bottom proved large for the regular black and white barber pole and so we used longer black than white sections to reduce the apparent size. The barber pole, originally the insignia of the barber-surgeon, signified his spirally-wrapped bandages and therefore came to mean healing of the soul as well as of the body. This is its significance in church decoration.

From early morning until late afternoon, day after day, we sat on folding chairs on the uneven earth inside the unfloored building, working over the problem of the polychroming. First the whole surface of the sample section was painted with parchment-color and allowed to dry. Then the black spiral was painted on the bottom half-round member to make the barber pole. Above it came red, a fillet of parchment-color, green, again parchment, red, gold and black barber pole, then the wide parchment-color member gold-powdered in a graceful, running design of vine, leaf, and flower. This was hardest of all to achieve and we labored over it day after day, waiting for the inspiration which finally came. Above the wide member the colors were counterchanged, which means to be used in the opposite order: green, parchment, red, parchment, green, with the gold and green dentils or cresting running across the top. The width of each color band was determined by trial and error, but finally the short section, when hauled up to the height of the tie-beams, looked absolutely right as we peered at it through the almost solid scaffolding filling the interior. Then we gave the order to paint a whole beam exactly like the sample and members of the congregation came in to catch glimpses of it through the boards of the scaffolding and to get used to the idea of so much color.

The ceiling above the tie-beams was stained a fine dark oak color, against which the colors of the beams glowed. Black and white barber poles made rectangles on the ceiling with Mary's red rose at the crossings. It took the entire summer to paint beams and roof.

Without my committee the work could never have succeeded. One of them shared every decision and step of the way and often insisted that I was right when I doubted myself. All of them approved what was done and provided staunch support.

We decided to use the coloring of St. Peter's Palgrave on the ceiling of the cloister, which was accordingly painted in gray with large and small six-pointed stars in red alternating on the spaces between the rafters. The sides of the rafters were red and the lower face (gray to match the spaces between) was decorated with a charming design in darker gray. The effect from inside the church, when seen through the windows on the south side of the nave, is singularly pleasing. The heavy, hand-hewn timbers supporting the cloister roof were weathered to the color of old wood.

The problem of what to do with the roof of the north aisle was very difficult to solve. We tried blue with gold stars. We tried sections of it done like Palgrave, but it looked like an attic. We attempted the yellow and red of Knapton, which looked like a kitchen. Each effort required painting out a previous one and allowing a day for the coat to dry before making another attempt. Finally, I was inspired to stain the roof and sides of each rafter the same dark brown oak as the roof of the nave, and to paint the bottom of the rafters red, on which we used the ancient symbols of IHS and AΩ in parchment-color with a larger size of the same symbols in red on the brown spaces between the rafters. Small moldings in red, brown, and black and white barber pole where roof met wall gave the north aisle ceiling a handsome and churchly look. At the east end of the aisle, between the north wall and the door by which the choir enters, stands the baptismal font, its cover, similar to that at Ufford, reaching almost from font to ceiling. It tapers from its base to the small, graceful, gold pelican at the top. The panels are of a wonderful clear blue and the delicate moldings of gold, red, and green; the carving of dark oak, not polychromed.

The glass in the beautiful Gothic west window in the tower, as well as in the small windows in the clerestory[34] and those in the north and south walls, is all leaded in small diamond panes of sparkling, colorless glass, not wholly transparent, through which the sunlight streams to enhance the colors.

The walls are of gray plaster, uneven in texture, with no paint whatever, the color matching the stone of which are made the fine simple columns and pointed arches indicated along the south wall, like an echo of those dividing the nave from the north aisle. Against the gray plaster between the stone arches and also around the walls of the tower are the shields, alternating red and blue, with the mock heraldic devices of the Apostles. There are fourteen of them, starting with Christ on the north side of the chancel and ending with St. Paul on the south side. From behind them light, streaming upward,

---

[34]The upper part of the interior of a church with windows for lighting.

illuminates the ceiling and is sufficient for the use of the congregation at evening services.

We debated endlessly the question of the material of the floor, decisions being taken and rejected many times. Finally we decided upon green slate shading to black, in fourteen-inch squares. By the merest chance, a young English art authority came to tea one day after seeing the church. He liked it all immensely, including the floor. "You will have to employ an olive-oil girl," said he, "as they do at Petworth." Upon inquiry I found that the slate floors in that beautiful mansion were constantly rubbed with olive-oil to bring out the color and to protect against footmarks. We have tried this method with some success.

As I stood in the church in the early winter twilight, watching the end of the day's work, I saw a friend entering whose interest and enthusiasm had encouraged and supported me greatly. At the same moment in came an elderly man to whom we each spoke, as indeed I did to all the people who streamed through the church every day. He fell into conversation with us and said, "Please go and look at this church from down the street—pile of nothing, that's what it is, just a pile of nothing." But fortunately most people do not share his opinion, for we hear constantly expressions of approval and enthusiasm from our many visitors.

The outer doors are red, to signify Christ's sacrifice as the portal to salvation, and are most striking when they stand open against the gray stone of the outer walls. As one enters the church, one sees directly overhead the high, flat ceiling of the tower, separated from the nave by a pointed arch, above which is a small angel like those at Knapton, looking toward the altar. The background of the tower ceiling is red, with a green vine around a central coat of arms, carved and colored. Leaves and roses alternating in green and gold, both in the center square and in the triangles outside it, represent the people of the church, symbolized by the ever-flowing vine. The moldings are heavy and are done in heraldic colors with black and white barber pole at the bottom. As the men were trying to get the effect desired, I said to several of them, "You are rapidly becoming mediaeval craftsmen." "I don't know about the craftsmen," said Fred, "nor about the mediaeval—perhaps just evil." They seemed to be dedicated to their work in a very striking way and "Doc" and "Buck" often expressed their deep appreciation of being privileged to work at such an unusual task, saying that all jobs would be dull afterwards. Some of them say they plan to carry photographs of the interior of the church as long as they live. "Doc," the elderly foreman, was skilled in matching colors as well as in carrying out intricate directions. One day, as I sat watching him at work, he said, "If I can do it without crying, I'd like to tell you something that happened." The story was about an architect from New York, name unknown, who visited the church and who told Doc that the polychroming was the most beautiful thing he had seen on his journey. The little incident almost moved me to tears likewise, not because of the praise of our work from one who knew, but because of Doc's fervor and sincerity.

When the wood carver delivered the first section of the rood screen, the problem of its proper decoration seemed even more difficult of solution than had that of the tie-beams. First of all, it was painted entirely in parchment-color; then by dint of much cutting of beautiful stencils by our gifted painting contractor, Mr. Ralph Iula, flower designs of repeating small and simple pattern, used in various ways, were applied to the various moldings in different colors on different grounds. We used a small black and gold barber pole in each arch and the cresting on top of the screen was gold, black, and white. The solid panels at the bottom were of gold leaf with a diaper pattern in color, red in the first alternating with green in the second and so forth. The east side of the screen is parchment-color. Toward the nave, directly in front of an arch of the screen on the north side, stands the reading desk of carved wood, the reader standing inside the screen on the chancel side. The base is stone color and the eagle supporting the Bible is covered with gold leaf. On the south side, and entered through the last section of the screen, is the pulpit. It is not done after the one at South Burlingham, because I decided to reserve that handsome and dignified treatment for the altar and it is important for the pulpit to harmonize with the screen. Therefore the large panels are done in alternating red and green of a lovely tone, lighter than the colors used elsewhere, with gold diaper work. The separating moldings are all of parchment-color, some decorated in black and gold in small designs. The tiny panels in the carving just below the top are black, as are also those in the base, where appear the AΩ and IHS symbols. The pulpit is jewel-like in its beauty.

There is no color on the flat-topped altar, but a gold diaper pattern like that on screen and pulpit is used in the dark oak panels, the moldings being in parchment-color ornamented in black and gold, after the decorations on the pulpit at South Burlingham. The altar is in length exactly one-third the width of the sanctuary, which is traditional and proper. Above it is a five-panelled reredos of dark oak, in which is a brocade of muted silver and gold. A carved canopy runs the entire length at its top, coming just above the sill of the Gothic arch containing the mural. The altar ornaments are a pair of antique wooden Venetian candlesticks of silver gesso[35] and a cross with a matching base.

The installation of the new Cassavant [*sic*][36] organ was in progress as we worked at the decoration of the screen. When its "mighty harmonies" filled the church as the workmen tried its tone, it seemed the final touch of glory. The two large openings to the organ chamber above the console on the north wall of the chancel contain fine Gothic screens painted gray to match the walls. The pews of dark oak, of a very simple Twelfth Century design, complete the churchly atmosphere and provide the balance for the beautiful roof.

In order to avoid plates on any memorials,[37] we decided that the list of them should be inscribed in a Book of Remembrance, together with the names of the persons memorialized as well as those of the donors. It was difficult to find a book suitable to our purpose. The shops in New York where church equipment was available revealed nothing desirable, but on returning from the search the taxicab went through a side street where I spied a shop whose window was full of old tomes.[38] Calling to the driver to stop and to wait for me, I entered and asked for a large book with blank pages. One large and handsome volume they had, hand-tooled in gold on the red leather binding with "L" and the fleur-de-lis, indicating that it was made for King Louis XV of France. The price was within our range and this book has become our Book of Remembrance. The entries in it have been done by an artist after the manner of the mediaeval illuminated manuscripts over which the monks worked long and lovingly.

Out-of-doors, the planting—hedges, lawns, new trees—completes the picture of dignified and lovely simplicity. The know [*sic*][39] garden in the quadrangle formed by cloisters and parish house is the gift of the women of the church and its care will be their responsibility. In the center of the

---

[35]A white paint mixture consisting of a binder mixed with chalk, gypsum, pigment, or any combination of those.

[36]The correct spelling of the name of the company that made the organ is *Casavant*. The original draft also contains the incorrect spelling.

[37]Memorial plaques often attached to the walls of Anglican churches. Trinity consistently has declined to use these through the years.

[38]Books, especially large, heavy, scholarly ones.

[39]The correct word is used in the original draft: *knot*.

garden is a circle of flat stone where stands a simple sun dial. The four beds surrounding it, separated by narrow radiating gravel paths, form a Greek cross. In the same way, narrow paths separate the beds in the four corners of the rectangle from each other and from the border around the whole garden. All the beds are bordered by dwarf yew hedges and the four beds at the corners have knots of symmetrically intertwined dwarf hedges of different color and plant material. Between the taller planting fragrant small herbs cover the ground.

Here at last in reality stands the completed church of my vision, but more beautiful in every detail and in the harmony of its various parts than I could have dreamed possible. On the Sunday afternoon when the church was dedicated, the overflowing crowd of worshippers indicated the whole community's interest in its perfection. Promptly at the appointed hour the bishop knocked with his crozier at the closed outer door, begging permission to enter, according to the ancient ritual. By a brief prayer he dedicated the lynch gate and the garden, after which the long procession of choir, clergy of the diocese, members of the vestry and junior vestry, the architects, contractors, and some of the special craftsmen, stonemasons and painters, went slowly down the aisle and were seated in the chancel and sanctuary. The service of consecration was in itself of dignified beauty.

The miracle of the new church was complete.

Appendix C

Bishops, Rectors, and Senior Wardens

Bishops of the Episcopal Diocese of Indiana/Indianapolis[1]

The Rt. Rev. Jackson Kemper, first missionary bishop of Indiana and Missouri (1838–1849)

The Rt. Rev. George Upfold, second bishop of Indiana (1849–1872)

The Rt. Rev. Joseph Cruickshank Talbot, third bishop of Indiana (1872–1883)

The Rt. Rev. David Buel Knickerbacker, fourth bishop of Indiana (1883–1894)

The Rt. Rev. John Hazen White, fifth bishop of Indiana (1895–1899)[2]

The Rt. Rev. Joseph Marshall Francis, sixth bishop of Indiana, later of Indianapolis (1899–1939)[3]

The Rt. Rev. Richard Ainslie Kirchhoffer, seventh bishop of Indianapolis (1939–1959)

The Rt. Rev. John Pares Craine, eighth bishop of Indianapolis (1959–1977)

The Rt. Rev. Edward Witker Jones, ninth bishop of Indianapolis (1978–1997)

---

[1] In 1898, The Episcopal Church split the state-coterminous Diocese of Indiana into the northern Diocese of Michigan City and the southern Diocese of Indiana.

[2] In 1899, Bishop White, bishop of Indiana, was consecrated as bishop of Michigan City. In 1921, the Diocese of Michigan City changed its name to the Diocese of Northern Indiana, making Bishop White the bishop of Northern Indiana.

[3] In 1899, Bishop Francis was consecrated as bishop of Indiana. In 1902, the truncated Diocese of Indiana changed its name to the Diocese of Indianapolis, making Bishop Francis the bishop of Indianapolis.

The Rt. Rev. Catherine Maples Waynick, tenth bishop of Indianapolis (1997–2017)

The Rt. Rev. Jennifer Baskerville-Burrows, eleventh bishop of Indianapolis (2017–present)

Rectors of the Church of the Advent/
Trinity Episcopal Church, Indianapolis[4]

The Rev. Charles E. Bishop, first rector of the Church of the Advent (1919–1920)

The Rev. George H. Richardson, Ph.D., second rector of the Church of the Advent (1920–1922)

The Rev. Albert L. Longley, third rector of the Church of the Advent (1923)

The Rev. Clarence W. Bispham, S.T.M., fourth rector of the Church of the Advent (1924–1927)

The Rev. George S. Southworth, fifth rector of the Church of the Advent (1928–1942)

The Rev. Thomas R. Thrasher, sixth rector of the Church of the Advent (1942–1947)

The Rev. Laman H. Bruner, Jr., B.D., seventh rector of the Church of the Advent, later of Trinity Episcopal Church (1947–1953)

The Rev. G. Ernest Lynch, B.D., eighth rector of Trinity Episcopal Church (1953–1978)

The Rev. Roger J. White, ninth rector of Trinity Episcopal Church (1980–1984)

The Rev. Dr. James B. Lemler, tenth rector of Trinity Episcopal Church (1984–1998)

The Rev. Thomas Kryder-Reid, eleventh rector of Trinity Episcopal Church (2000–2014)

The Rev. Julia E. Whitworth, twelfth rector of Trinity Episcopal Church (2016–present)

---

[4]In 1951, the Church of the Advent, Indianapolis, changed its name to Trinity Episcopal Church.

Senior Wardens of the Church of the Advent/ Trinity Episcopal Church, Indianapolis[5]

Aquilla Q. Jones (1919–1926)
William W. Hammond (1926–1953)
Raymond F. Crom (1953–1954, 1958)
B. Lawrence Dorsey (1955–1956)
Eugene S. Pulliam (1957, 1960–1961, 1964–1965, 1978)
J. Edward Burns, Jr. (1959, 1962–1963, 1972, 1984, 1987)
Wendell C. Phillippi (1966, 1969–1970)
William J. Stout (1967)
John R. Fenstermaker (1968)
Stephen E. DeVoe (1971, 1975, 1985, 1989)
Blair E. Blage (1973)
William R. Ehrich (1974, 1982–1983, 1988)
James C. Wright (1976)
Phillip M. Morton (1977)
Thomas F. Whitten (1979–1980)
A. Douglas Ward (1981)
Warren L. Smith (1986, 1991, 1998, 2006)
Marie C. Robb (1990)
Jean M. Smith (1992)
Natalie J. Boehm (1993)
George M. Plews (1994, 2004)
Sally L. Morton (1995, 1999)
Daniel C. Marr (1996)
Gregory C. Lucas (1997)
Robert K. Bentley (2000)
Erick D. Ponader (2001–2002)
Mary A. Stewart (2003)
Jeannice Hight Owens (later Jeannice H. Shobe) (2005)
Michael A. Cuticchia (2007)

---

[5]The only two senior wardens of the parish while it was named the Church of the Advent were Aquilla Q. Jones and William W. Hammond, who served as senior wardens for a combined total of 34 years. Mr. Hammond continued serving as senior warden for a brief period after the parish's name was changed to Trinity Episcopal Church in 1951.

Ivan J. Jahns (2008–2009)
John B. Bridge (2010, 2016–2017)
Jody Danforth Root (2011)
Kathryn A. Watson (2012–2013)
Jeffrey A. Brinkmann (2014–2015)
Erik J. Hembre (2018)
Patricia Caress McMath (2019–2020)

Appendix D

Maps and Illustrations

Chapter 4: Advances During Peace and War: 1866–1918

Part Two: The Mission to the North: 1919–1949

Chapter 5: A Time of Good and Evil: 1919–1929

Chapter 6: Advent at 33rd and Meridian: 1919–1929

Chapter 7: The City and Advent in Crisis: 1930–1939

Chapter 8: The Last Decade of Advent: 1940–1949

Part Four: Change Is the Only Constant: 1968–1999

Chapter 12: The City Redux: 1968–1999

Chapter 13: Momentous Events: 1968–1983

Chapter 14: The End of a Millennium: 1984–1999

Part Five: The New Millennium: 2000–2019

Chapter 15: The City in the Twenty-First Century: 2000–2019

Chapter 16: Embracing the Neighborhood: 2000–2005

157, The Rev. Earl Wepley, first interim rector of Trinity.

158, The Rev. Thomas Kryder-Reid, eleventh rector of Trinity.

160, The Rev. Karen L. King, senior associate rector of Trinity.

163, Kevin DePrey, parish administrator of Trinity.

Chapter 17: Trinity in the Great Recession: 2006–2009

172, The Rev. Grace Burton-Edwards, Mother King, and Father Kryder-Reid leading worship.

174, Entrance to the Trinity Outreach Center, 3333 North Meridian Street, Indianapolis.

179, Trinity's choir singing at the dedication of the Trinity Outreach Center.

Chapter 18: The Strife Is O'er: 2010–2015

182, Mother Nancy Ferriani, senior associate rector of Trinity.

184, Trinity acolytes preparing for a procession.

187, The Rev. Gordon Chastain, one of Trinity's affiliated priests, leads a Sunday Adult Forum with Mother Burton-Edwards.

188, Sunday dinner team members ready to serve their guests at the Trinity Outreach Center.

190, Artwork for the Tree of Life Society.

191, Father Tom Kryder-Reid at the celebration of his time at Trinity.

192, The Rev. LaRae Rutenbar, second interim rector of Trinity.

194, Dr. Michael Messina, Trinity's director of music.

196, Cuisiniers Rob McMath and Jim Purucker with the Most Rev. Michael Bruce Curry, twenty-seventh presiding bishop of The Episcopal Church.

Chapter 19: Approaching 100 Years: 2016–2019

198, Bishop Waynick congratulating the Rev. Julia E. Whitworth, twelfth rector of Trinity, at her celebration of new ministry.

200, The Rt. Rev. Jennifer Baskerville-Burrows, eleventh bishop of Indianapolis, at her consecration with the Rt. Rev. Barbara Harris.

204, Welcoming worshippers at Trinity.

209, Mother Whitworth, the Rev. Dr. Benjamin J. Anthony, and the Rev. Erin Hougland ready to lead Sunday Worship.

210, Trinity's pilgrims to the Holy Land at St. George's Cathedral, Jerusalem.

211, Trinity's J2A pilgrims, including youth coordinator Missy Roetter, on the island of Iona, Scotland.

212, Trinity's choir and clergy in Ely Cathedral, England.

Acknowledgments and Special Thanks

My deepest and most heartfelt thanks to:

The clergy and vestry at Trinity, past and present, for their moral and spiritual support.

Mother Julia Whitworth for suggesting the title.

Tracey Lemon, Albie Marco, and Monica Beniste for their assistance with Trinity's archival material.

Father Ben Anthony for his help and guidance with the Episcopal Glossary.

Meghan McConnell for finding Edith Whitehill Clowes's *Miracles, Major and Minor.*

Christine Plews for reading and critiquing the very earliest manuscript.

Jim Lemler, Lee Little, John Craun, and David Amstutz for reading and critiquing other early manuscripts and providing valuable supplemental information.

Gary Potts for his artwork for the book cover and Kevin DePrey for obtaining Gary's permission to use it.

Jackie Means, Kyung-Won On, Jason Lavengood, Casey Cronin, Lindsay Haake, Chris Denny, and Kelly Kennedy Bentley for their photographs used in the book.

Leigh Anne Naas, Bill Coleman, Jeff Brinkmann, and Ivan Jahns for sharing their perspectives.

Amy Scott and Stephanie Moran for their help in preparing the appendices.

Renee Wilmeth, Jan Lynn, Claude Bell, Kelly Henthorne, and Laura Caddell for their editorial work.

Judy Cebula of Lilly Endowment, Inc., Yuri Rodriguez of Christ Church Cathedral, Indianapolis, John Beatty of the Episcopal Diocese of Northern Indiana, Jim Singletary of the Church of the Advent, Boston, Rebecca Wilson of Canticle Communications, Diane Hall of the Auburn Cord Duesenberg Automobile Museum, Donna Ferullo of Purdue University, Tom Britt of Towne Post Network Inc., and, especially, Nadia Kousari of the Indiana Historical Society, for their help in securing illustrations for the book.

Brock Brown, for his valuable help at the beginning and the end of this project.

The following works, which were among the more valuable secondary sources for me:

The Little Church on the Circle, Christ Church Parish, Indianapolis, 1837–1955, by Eli Lilly.

Trinity Episcopal Church 1919–1969, by Georgianne Strange.

A History of the Episcopal Diocese of Indianapolis 1838–1988, Sesquicentennial Edition, Joyce Marks Booth, Editor.

A Revised and Updated History of Trinity Episcopal Church, Diocese of Indianapolis, by William R. "Bill" Ehrich. Bill also was the principal photographer for Georgianne Strange's history, and a number of his photographs appear in this book, as well.

Index

(continues)

X–Y–Z

9 780692 037003